# The Europe[illegible]
# Annual R[illegible]

9600 Garsington Road, Oxford OX4 2DQ, UK
350 Main Street, Malden, MA 02148-5018, USA



First published 2003 by Blackwell Publishing Ltd

British Library Cataloguing-in-Publication Data applied for
ISBN 1405108770



For further information on
Blackwell Publishing, visit our website:
http://www.blackwellpublishing.com

# CONTENTS

JCMS 2003 Volume 41. Annual Review pp. 1–11

# Editorial: Moving Towards a 'Hub and Spokes Europe'?

LEE MILES
University of Hull

One of the key themes of the Danish EU Council Presidency in late 2002 was the building of a 'One Europe' – signifying that the European Union (EU) has entered yet another critical stage in its evolution (Royal Danish Ministry of Foreign Affairs, 2002). Yet, it would seem that there were at least three critical processes being undertaken by the Union in 2002 – each of which would have important repercussions for its future development. Indeed, every one of these three pathways may represent movement not to the creation of a single, more coherent, Union, but simultaneously towards different kinds of 'One Europe' reflecting the growing diversity and complexity of the EU as a supranational institution.

The first of the processes was, of course, the formal introduction of the notes and coins of the new single currency into public circulation and the replacement of 12 national currencies with the euro in 2002. To some extent then, the year corresponded to the physical implementation of a certain kind of 'One Europe' – namely the realization of a single euro area or economic and monetary union (EMU). It provides a formal division of the European Union into different forms of status with the 12 EMU 'insiders' now possessing a fresh institutional marker that each participating EU country can utilize to stake its place in the 'inner core' of the European Union.

As the disputes over the implementation of the Stability and Growth Pact (SGP) in 2002 illustrate, involvement in the euro area requires a much higher level of obligation on Member States and implies future movement not just on monetary policy, but on fiscal aspects as well. Increasingly, participation in the euro has become the fresh credential that a Member State must have if it wishes to be involved at the forefront of EU deepening. Yet, even this is not as simple as first seems. There are variations even as regards the size of the institutional marker bestowed upon the EMU insiders depending largely on their perceived importance to the key functioning of the new currency. Hence, even within our 'One EMU Europe' there are differences in the way specific Member States have been treated. Witness the stern hand that the more peripheral Portugal received when experiencing difficulties in meeting the budgetary requirements of the Pact, compared to the more tentative treatment handed out to the central players of France and Germany during the year when they also got into trouble in relation to the Pact.

The second process apparent in 2002 was, without doubt, the completion of the accession negotiations with ten candidate countries at the Copenhagen European Council summit in December 2002 (see Friis and also Smith in this *Annual Review*). The agreements at Copenhagen signified, once and for all, that further enlargement of the Union to become an EU-25 (provided all subsequent referenda in the candidate countries are positive in 2003) would become a reality in May 2004. On this basis, we can argue that a larger 'One Europe' will come into existence and that, ultimately, the expansion of membership will enable one of the key policies of the Union – the internal market – to be fully extended to cover most of central and eastern Europe. After 2004, we will certainly enjoy the possibilities of having a larger 'One Enlarged Europe' based, above all, on the concrete foundations of the internal market as the basic membership criteria. Indeed, full participation in the internal market provides one of the most potent glues holding the 25 Member States together and unites even EMU insiders and EMU outsiders on a key supranational policy platform. It also adds a key ingredient differentiating full EU members from non-EU countries in Europe and a persuasive rationale for other European countries considering an application to join the Union in the future.

The third process evident in 2002 was, as Dinan illustrates, the continuing deliberations of the Convention on the Future of Europe on a blueprint for a future EU Treaty scheduled for 2004. The aim of the Convention was not just to simplify and clarify the Union's procedures and decision-making structures, but also to elevate the new agreement to the form of a Constitutional Treaty. In other words, the Convention is attempting, either implicitly or explicitly, to construct a single constitution for Europe or in the language of this editorial, a 'One Constitutional Europe'.

The discussions in the Convention are of interest here precisely because they are not just focusing on trying to make the Union seem more relevant to its citizens. They are also helping to define the key characteristics that facilitate unity (or potential disunity) in the Union. Many political observers, for instance, have looked on the Convention's work with interest – not least because it has once and for all opened the EU debate to the language of constitution-building. They have also been interested since there were discussions in 2002 over whether involvement in a future 'One Constitutional Europe' may require not just a commitment to supranationalism. Several of the leading conventioneers argued that potential options, such as EU withdrawal, should be included for those who cannot accept the constitutional implications of the new treaty.

Have these three processes, whether implemented, completed or merely picking up speed in 2002 taken us any closer to the creation of a 'One Europe' in its entirety? Clearly the jury remains out on this one. Yet, early indications suggest that these three processes may be building different forms of a 'One Europe' that may be interlinked and far from mutually exclusive, but are ultimately based on participating Member States accepting a 'multi-speed Europe' involving ever more complex types of differentiation. The governments of Member States are not just being presented with incrementally more challenging thresholds of European integration. They are also being required to make choices as to which level or type of 'One Europe' they wish to reside in.

Furthermore, these three processes also show the continuing importance of the larger Member States and, indeed, the Franco–German axis to the development of the Union. As Pedersen in the keynote article to this *Annual Review* illustrates, the relationship between France and Germany is not without tension, yet agreement between these two powers was instrumental within each of our three processes in 2002.

We can briefly see this in three examples. First, as regards our 'One EMU Europe', it is by no means controversial to recognize that the French and Germans represent the core of the euro area and an integral part of its development. Moreover, when things go wrong there in economic terms, this is usually to the detriment of the prestige of the euro area as a whole. This was certainly the case in 2002, when fresh allegations about the weakness of the euro were reinforced by the fact that both France and Germany were in political difficulties in relation to meeting the obligations of staying within the parameters set by the SGP. Above all, the widespread criticisms of their poor governmental control of public finances, and budget deficits in particular, were a constant source of tension in 2002. Hence, just as participation in the euro can accelerate deeper integration, the relationship between the members of this inner EMU core can also set a slower pace if need be. Indeed, what is clear is that the difficulties of France and Germany in meeting the requirements of the Pact have provided the major catalyst for those advocating reform of the SGP to reflect a Member State's longer-term track record.

Turning to our second process of building a 'One Enlarged Europe', the Franco–German relationship was also instrumental. The most obvious example was the agreement between French President, Jacques Chirac and German Chancellor, Gerhard Schröder, just before the Brussels European Council summit in October 2002, that set out the budgetary expenditure limits of the common agricultural policy (CAP) post-2004. The agreement was presented as a 'done deal' by the two leaders later at the European Council meeting in Brussels; much to the consternation of other EU leaders like British Prime Minister, Tony Blair, who had little choice but accept it as a *fait accompli*.

Our third case relates to our 'One Constitutional Europe' and the work of the Convention on the Future of Europe. Here, the importance of the Franco–German axis in driving forward institutional reforms important to the inner core is reflected. Most notably, in their common approach towards reforming the leadership of the Union through the adoption of a dual Presidency of an elected European Commission President (advocated strongly by Germany) and the creation of a more permanent and elected President of the European Council (supported mostly by France).

Although we may thus be moving to a Europe with, in practice, many more speeds and nuances, there is still a key component within it that helps to shape the deepening of the Union and drive the organization along. Hence, within the Danish enunciated 'One Europe' ultimately exists an inner core that provides another type of cement that helps to set the overall direction of the Union and keep it together. To some extent, the continuing existence of this inner core may simply reflect the fact that the divisions (whether permanent or temporary) between the European countries that were roughly split into EMU insiders, EMU outsiders and non-member countries, have become even further internalized as the membership of the Union increases. Hence, the post-2004 EU will expand, not just to include a greater number of Member States, but also to incorporate wider divisions over policy and, above all, the overall direction that the evolving Union should take in the future. If a coherent strategy of deepening is to be furthered, it will become all the more important to have an inner core of states arising from within our 'One EMU Europe' to keep the Union's development moving forward.

Nevertheless, this is not to say that a widened EU represented in our 'One Enlarged Europe' should be automatically equated with implying a dilution of the goals of European integration. Rather, it may simply imply that, in a more diverse European Union, there may be a greater chance for ever more prominent pan-European concepts and priorities, as opposed to purely integrationist ideals, to come to the fore. Perhaps a good example of this may lie in the slight unease in the EU-15 during 2002 that the absorption of a further ten members may lead to a change in attitudes and in the relationship between the Union and some of its external partners, such as the United States. Throughout 2002 and with the crisis over Iraq beginning to unfold, many comments were made about the impact that the largely 'Atlanticist' candidate countries may have on the emerging foreign and security profiles of the Union, in the form of the common European security and defence policy (ESDP). They will certainly be keen to ensure that the primacy of the North Atlantic Treaty Organization (Nato) is assured and continues to be recognized within the emerging ESDP.

Thus, how can we reconcile these differing types and approaches to a 'One Europe'? Does a 'One Europe' consisting simultaneously of a 'One EMU Europe', a 'One Enlarged Europe' and bounded together by a 'One Constitutional Europe' need to be reshaped post-2004 into an efficiently working organization that maintains the loyalty of the Member State governments?

One thing does seem clear at least. Attention may once again need to turn to how the Union can utilize the principle of flexibility (formally introduced in the 1997 Amsterdam Treaty), as a tool to manage the Union's increasing complexity. The advantage of considering future uses of flexibility is largely that it constitutes a way of finding compromise and avoiding a log-jam (see Stubbs, 1997, p. 47). However, it does require Member State governments to face difficult questions about the future of the EU and what each state wants from it – be it in the form of a 'multi-speed Europe', 'concentric circles' or 'Europe *à la carte*' (see Warleigh, 2002). Given the latter, it will thus most likely be the case that a more flexible Europe emerges out of informal practice rather than out of concerted attempts at constitutional design.

A probable scenario will be that – in order to manage the growing diversity of the post-2004 European Union – we may see an even greater stress on the fact that the Union will consist of regional groupings of states sharing common goals within the EU. These groupings may facilitate competition for the expanded, yet limited resources presently on offer. Moreover, the relationship between the large and small states will also be a factor. On the one hand, it will be important to realize that the post-2004 Union of 25 Member States will be, more than ever, a Union of small states since the numerical majority of EU members will have a population below, say, 15 million people. Coalition-building between EU governments to produce majorities in favour of policy initiation, and that include a sizeable number of those drawn from the small EU members, will become the order of the day. On the other hand, the governments of the larger states – these being the 'Big Four' of France, Germany, Italy and the United Kingdom, plus the 'light heavyweights' of Spain and Poland – deem that they should have a greater role in steering the Union. After all, these six countries do represent the vast proportion of the Union's population.

Hence, one scenario may incorporate three important dimensions. First, there will an even greater emphasis as a means of managing the Union and enhancing influence within the Union's policy-making machinery on the larger countries utilizing strategies based on what Smith and Tsatsas (2002) have labelled the 'new bilateralism'. Here, the larger countries will seek to build bilateral agreements behind initiatives and present them as joint policy proposals within EU decision-making and at intergovernmental conferences (IGCs) in particular. Second, in order to build these common initiatives, and given the greater competition for scarce resources in the Union, we may see regional differences emerge between the larger six states and a greater focus on these states building partnerships with like-minded and/or neighbouring EU members. It is not impossible, for example, to see Spain and Poland colluding together within IGC processes to enhance the overall agenda of 'economic and social cohesion' within the Union. At the same time, it is also likely that Spain and Poland will see each other as competitors. They may also try to build 'Mediterranean' and 'central European' co-operation with their neighbouring fellow EU countries in order to enhance their regional voice when the allocation of the structural funds comes about.

So, post-2004 we are more likely to see a more diverse Union encompassing multiple approaches. However, we may also envisage the Union being more effectively managed through the creation of informal regional groups since the building of workable majorities or blocking minorities becomes even harder with the influx of such a larger number of countries. What perhaps will be unclear and, in any case, may prove to be an entirely academic exercise, may be to what extent our diverse EU constitutes simply a multi-speed Union, or one based on more permanent divisions synonymous with, say, a Europe *à la carte*. Yet, to some degree, this is to miss the point when trying to invoke strategies governing a more diverse Europe. Given the complex coalition-building behaviour endemic in the Union, it will depend ultimately on the policy issue in question and thus will, in practice, probably be an informal mixture of all of the above.

It may also be the case then that we are moving towards what can loosely be labelled a 'hub and spokes Europe'. Clearly, the central hub will be the euro area and our 'One EMU Europe' (and within that, perhaps, a smaller inner core). Certainly, the central hub will include a strong balance of larger countries – most notably, the Franco–German axis, plus Italy and Spain, as well as most of the Union's countries that are also members of the OECD. This (currently 12-member) hub will be critical in shaping the pace and form of deepening in the Union, since it will continue to represent the inner core Europe plus a few of the more important EU states. In 2002, there were already many indications that the 'Contact Group' of exclusively euro members would be used to a greater degree as a key institutional framework to agree policy proposals before being placed before the Union's European Council.

However, protruding from this central hub of a 'One EMU Europe' will be spokes leading to certain more peripheral larger EU countries that may, at various times, nominally lead either formally or informally regional groups within the Union. In the post-2004 enlarged EU-25, two such spokes can be readily identified. One leads north-westerly from the hub of 'One EMU Europe' to the UK. Britain will most probably coalesce – as it does already – with other traditional EMU outsiders, such as Denmark and perhaps Sweden (if the September 2003 public referendum produces a negative result) to form a *de facto* 'northern European grouping of euro-reluctance'. Common attitudes towards the euro area will, most probably, be the driving force behind this collusion. The second identifiable spoke will lead out towards Poland, who, once a full member, will most likely try to act as the spokesman for central and eastern Europe on questions relating to economic and social cohesion, and perhaps even reform of the CAP.

Although the strength of these spokes may vary over time, and they are not permanent features of the Union and may alter according to the respective policy issue under consultation, they may provide useful supports, balances or voices of caution to the activities proposed by the hub of 'One EMU Europe'.

Moreover, on certain issues such as, say, attitudes towards the emerging ESDP, then co-operation between these two spokes in pushing the cause of Atlanticism may be a useful counter to those in the Union's hub pushing for a more European-centric attitude towards European defence co-operation. In addition, these two spokes may be joined by another after 2007, if the road to accession is finally laid open for Turkey with a positive report by the Commission on meeting the political aspects of the Copenhagen accession criteria. If (or when) Turkey were to join, its size and political influence may quickly lead to the creation of a new spoke leading out from our central hub of 'One EMU Europe' in a south-easterly direction. Given that, under existing post-Nice rules, Turkey would join the ranks of the Big Four (to make a Big Five) then it is not hard to envisage that Turkey would soon also become a major advocate of an even greater profile for economic and social cohesion and for perhaps a differing external relations policy towards the Middle East on the part of the Union. The Turks would certainly become a major spokesman and competitor for EU structural aid to the eastern Mediterranean, at the very least, and an additional counter to the voices within the Union's hub.

Without doubt, we are certainly in for exciting times. The Union will continue to be an 'unsettled Europe' for several more years to come (Laffan *et al.,* 2000, pp. 3–10). However, the Union does not follow textbook forms of either the political or economic order and its trajectory is difficult to plot. On this basis, I would agree with the assertions of Laffan *et al.* (2000, p. 193) that it might be better to abandon the notion that the Union is 'something' and consider in what ways it is in the 'process of becoming'. Indeed, the notion of a hub and spokes Europe may provide a tentative method to explain the strategies used within this 'process of becoming'.

Perhaps the burning question for academics then will be how this hub and spokes Europe corresponds to more traditional models of flexibility, such as a 'multi-speed Europe', 'concentric circles' or closer to a 'multi-tier' version of 'Europe à la carte' (see Warleigh 2002, 2003). However, since the stress within our hub and spokes Europe is on a recognition that the Union is a complex system where coalition-building is an integral norm, then the decision on whether the leadership of the spoke state is utilized and leads a regional group will be partly dependent on the issue under debate. On some questions, the hub and spokes Europe may be temporary or multi-speed (say in some cases, on attitudes towards joining the single currency or euro area) and in others, say in the sphere of defence co-operation (for EU non-aligned states), it may be more permanent or multi-tier. Hence, a mixed approach reflecting the practical realities of EU coalition behaviour is part of the hub and spokes dimension of our diverse post-2004 Europe.

This also allows us to return to a further reflection on the notion of a hub and spokes EU, that is, its potential implications for the building of a coherent vision of a future Europe. Redmond and I (1996, p. 304) argued some years ago that each successive enlargement has progressively eroded the federalist voice in the Union and that 'in a European Union of twenty-plus, the federalists will be in the minority'. The events of 2002 and, especially, the comparatively superficial reforms being debated in the Convention on the Future of Europe (see Dinan in this *Annual Review)* only seem to reinforce these assertions. Moreover, several impressive studies such as that by Warleigh (2003), also seem to suggest that the Union may not necessarily have a federal future stamped on it, or at least that this may not be an evolution extended to all of its Member States. Although it should be recognized that the Member States do not fundamentally dominate the EU system nor that the important roles of other EU actors such as the supranational institutions should be ignored, the former do nonetheless matter in shaping the Union's future (see Wessels *et al.*, 2003).

Given this line of thinking, it may be the case that our hub and spokes Europe provides a way of understanding how one can envisage simultaneous deepening and widening, as well as the creation of a federal 'inner core' and its erosion at the pan-European level at one and the same time. Certainly, the further implementation of the 'One EMU Europe' (and the inner core even within that) makes it more than likely that the states in this grouping will continue to push the boundaries of integration, not least through fiscal harmonization and security and defence co-operation. For some of these Member States, the attraction of a potential merger into a 'Federal core Europe' may be very strong.

In contrast, for those on the periphery, not part of the 'One EMU Europe', yet active in the 'One Enlarged Europe' (based on the glue of the internal market), and bound together through the supranational ties of a 'One Constitutional Europe', the attraction of constructing a Constitutional Treaty based on openly federalist principles may not be strong enough. Hence, the best forecast in 2002 – based on the processes continued or completed in this year – is that if a federal Europe develops at all, it will be as a merged Member State (of countries probably drawn from the inner core) rather than the Union transforming itself *en bloc* into a European federation. This new merged Member State would in all likelihood arise out of our 'One EMU Europe', be a leading player in our 'One Enlarged Europe' and accommodated within the 'One Constitutional Europe' embodied perhaps in a future Constitutional Treaty.

In essence then, the hub of the Union may one day become a newly emerged 'European federation', yet the spokes will continue to lead to a host of Member States that may choose a supranational Europe, yet prefer to remain outside a federation. Those associated with the spokes will continue to favour supranational solutions governed through a new post-2004 EU constitution that provides the framework for a multi-speed, yet partially integrated Union still involved in a unsettled 'process of becoming'.

However, clearly such a rejection of the option of a 'Federal core Europe' should not be translated into meaning simply a preference for an intergovernmental one by the rest. There is room within the 'One Enlarged Europe' to have greater degrees of supranationalism or fusion without resorting to an explicitly federal structure for Europe (see, e.g., Wessels *et al.*, 2003).

Nevertheless, such a movement, be it to a clearer strategy of hub and spokes or to a more distinct enunciation of a multi-speed Europe, may be too much for those still debating in the 'Convention on the Future of Europe' (at the time of writing). It will require politicians, practitioners and scholars to accept that the Union will remain 'an unfinished system, subject to internal differentiation, almost shy of its ultimate condition' (Bellamy and Warleigh, 2001, p. 7). It may also force them to advocate – as the events in 2002 illustrate – that an unfinished supranational system may be the best that can be hoped for if the Union is to continue to meet all its ambitious policy agendas, accruing from simultaneous deepening and widening and maintain the semblance of constructing some kind of 'One Europe'.

## Acknowledgements

This acknowledgement section of the editorial, my first as the new editor of the *Annual Review,* begins, as it should, by welcoming readers once again. It also provides an opportunity for me to extend a vote of thanks to the previous editors, Geoffrey Edwards and Georg Wiessala, who have provided invaluable advice at various times over the last year.

The new editor is fortunate enough to be taking over in a year when the European Union has made some important leaps forward – not least concerning European monetary integration and further EU enlargement. Partly in order to reflect the fact that the *Review* should cover events affecting the development of the Union pertaining in the applicant countries as well as the existing Member States, I have undertaken a minor reform of the structure. Two new chapters, one examining political developments and the other economic trends in the applicant countries have been commissioned so that the *Annual Review* will provide coverage of the main key issues affecting a much larger European Union. In future years, these two chapters will be renamed to reflect the fact that their coverage will focus on the 'new Member States' after the 2004 enlargement. Furthermore, we are extremely fortunate in having Karen Henderson and Debra Johnson join the ranks of the existing long-term contributors as the first authors to write these two valuable new additions to the *Annual Review*. Thanks should also be extended to Michael Bruter for agreeing to take over the 'Developments in the Member States' chapter, vacated by my appointment as the new editor.

Unfortunately, there is always a cost to making change. I regret that, due to issues of space, the commissioning of the new chapters has come at the cost of decommissioning the sections examining EU documentation and books on European integration. This was a hard decision to take, and certainly not based on any negative assessment of the value of these chapters. Rather, I feel that they can most easily be replaced by sources outside the *Annual Review*, and not just by internet and web sources for EU documentation. In addition, the most recent books on European integration are already easily accessed and adequately serviced by the Book Reviews section of the *JCMS*. Moreover, I am confident that these changes will continue to ensure that the *Annual Review* remains a vital and easily accessible resource for those interested in the European Union. So please enjoy!

## References

Bellamy, R. and Warleigh, A. (eds) (2001) *Citizenship and Governance in the European Union* (London: Continuum).

Chryssochoou, C. (2001) *Theorizing European Integration* (London: Sage).
Laffan, B., O'Donnell, R. and Smith, M. (2000) *Europe's Experimental Union: Rethinking Integration* (London/New York: Routledge).
Miles, L. and Redmond, J. (1996) 'Enlarging the European Union: The Erosion of Federalism?'. *Cooperation and Conflict,* Vol. 31, No. 2, pp. 285–309.
Royal Danish Ministry of Foreign Affairs (2002) *One Europe – Programme of the Danish Presidency of the EU, July to December 2002* (Copenhagen: Royal Danish Ministry of Foreign Affairs).
Smith, J. and Tsatsas, M. (2002) *The New Bilateralism: The UK's Relations Within the EU* (London: Royal Institute of International Affairs).
Stubbs, A. (1997) 'The 1996 IGC and the Management of Flexible Integration'. *Journal of European Public Policy,* Vol. 6, No. 4, pp. 579–97.
Warleigh, A. (2002) *Flexible Integration: Which Model for the European Union?* (London: Continuum).
Warleigh, A. (2003) *Democracy in the European Union* (London: Sage).
Wessels, W., Maurer, A. and Mittag, J. (eds) (2003) *Fifteen into One? The European Union and its Member States* (Manchester: Manchester University Press).

JCMS 2003 Volume 41. Annual Review pp. 13–25

# Keynote Article: Recent Trends in the Franco–German Relationship

THOMAS PEDERSEN
University of Aarhus

'I thought he was a … man of promise.
But it appears he is a … man of promises'.
*Arthur Balfour on the young Churchill (quoted in Bonham Carter, 1965, p. 47)*

## Introduction

Balfour obviously got it wrong. Yet, perhaps the phrase is an apt characterization of the Franco–German relationship at the start of the new millennium? It is certainly true that often rhetoric has been a substitute for substance in Franco–German relations. In fact, this was the case right from the start. The Elysée Treaty was signed only a few years after France had, under Charles de Gaulle, tried (in vain) to set up a global *directoire* with the United States (US) and the United Kingdom (UK) – and without Germany. It was also soon after de Gaulle had attempted unsuccessfully to impose a confederal model on the European Economic Community (EEC).

There is a sense in which history has come full circle, with France once again confronting a wider Europe that threatens to curtail its traditional power. However, unlike the 1950s, the wider Europe is seen today from Paris as a threatening reality. Patterns of European coalition-building are becoming more fluid. Indeed, former German Chancellor Helmut Schmidt even believes that 'the Franco–German motor no longer exists' (*Le Monde*, 23 January 2003). More interestingly, he does not lament the fact. He stresses the continuing need for Germany to act in concert with France, yet recognizes that the former now has new alternative options in the east – and a freedom of action that allows it to place greater emphasis on its own internal affairs. Recent years have also seen examples of British leadership brought about largely through the use of shifting bilateral alliances (for instance, with Spain on labour market policy, see Smith and Tsatsas, 2002). The Franco–German relationship has always been ambiguous, with tensions swept under the carpet for many years. The acrimonious clashes between France and Germany at the Nice European Council summit in December 2001, for example, indicate just how fragile the official power 'parity' between these two large powers is nowadays. It is somewhat ironic perhaps, yet also rather symbolic that the leaders of these two countries signed a renewed Elysée accord actually in the 'chamber of wars' (*Salle de Bataille*) at Versailles (see below).

Nevertheless, the obituary of Franco–German collaboration has often been written prematurely. Time and again, French and German leaders have overcome misperceptions and misunderstandings, and instead stressed the benefits that accrue to them when operating from a common policy platform, especially when dealing with external powers like the US, as well as with their EU partners. Germany has proved adept at sharing power and reassuring France. It largely pre-empted, for instance, any Franco–British 'balancing' after 1989 in ways that fly in the face of traditional neo-realist propositions (Pedersen, 2002). Nor can one entirely overlook the degree to which Franco–German relations have become institutionalized with advisers and civil servants trying to ensure that politicians keep their promises (Mazzucelli, 1997). Mazzucelli, for example, refers to the 'politicisation of bureaucrats and the bureaucratisation of politicians' in European politics. On more than one occasion, the former French President François Mitterrand is known to have leaned on the brake when learning how far consultation between French and German civil servants had gone on behind his back (see Pedersen, 1998).

## I. The Shadow of Nice

2002 was a year of elections and Franco–German tension. Yet, it was also a period of renewal. French President Jacques Chirac and German Chancellor Gerhard Schröder have long been suspected of placing their primary emphasis on domestic politics. It was therefore logical that any reactivation of Franco–German collaboration should have had to await a reinforcement of the domestic political position of Chirac. After the spring 2002 parliamentary elections that gave Chirac a comfortable parliamentary majority from which to work, the French President could act more freely. Evidently Chirac has been the driving force behind the recent renewal of the partnership.

An editorial in *Le Monde* in January 2003 carried the evocative heading: 'France–Germany, the Age of Reason'. It argued that the days of 'conviction politics' within Franco–German relations may indeed be over, especially given that there exists a younger generation (especially on the German side) showing signs of impatience with historical lessons and with revisionist historians, such as Jörg Friedrich, painting Germany's recent history in lighter colours. As Alexander Wendt (1999) tells us, interaction may transform identity. Indeed, some perceive contemporary Franco–German relations as an anarchical culture of a Kantian nature, that is, based not on enmity but on friendship. Yet, the ambivalence of the relationship was illustrated by the clashes at Nice suggesting that Lockean rivalry is more pronounced than Kantian friendship. However, rivalry, of course, is not the same as enmity. Enmity between France and Germany seems over time to have been replaced by a regulated rivalry interspersed with elements of friendship and driven not so much by interaction as by strategic learning on the part of their national elites.

In any case it would be wrong always to interpret activity as a sign of health. The Nice summit in December 2001 saw clashes between the two countries and yet, during the summit, it was decided to strengthen Franco–German co-operation by introducing more intimate, informal meetings on a monthly basis. The arrangement was initiated in Blaesheim in January 2002 (*Le Monde,* 5 February 2002). This meeting was devoted mainly to preparing for the Convention on the Future of Europe and for discussions on the Middle East, and it featured discussions on the candidacy for President of the European Central Bank (ECB) and the replacement of Wim Duisenberg before the expiry of his formal mandate.

The spring of 2002 was dominated by the French parliamentary elections. Doubts were also raised about France and Germany's willingness to abide by the rules of economic and monetary union (EMU) and the related Stability and Growth Pact (SGP). In particular, France seemed to want to water down the SGP with the French Finance Minister, for instance, being quoted as saying that the Pact 'is not written in stone' (euobserver.com, 7 June 2002). France and Germany thus suddenly formed a community of complicity.

At the Seville summit in June disagreements, most notably over the future of the Union's common agricultural policy (CAP), resulted in public clashes. At a later July meeting in Schwerin in the former DDR, Chirac and Schröder tried to repair and reignite the relationship by setting up several working groups. Of the four working groups, none dealt directly with the main bone of contention, namely agriculture. Instead, agricultural issues were to be dealt with under the auspices of the working group on enlargement. Two other groups addressed institutional reform, and foreign and security policy. In defence discussions, agreement was reached on Germany taking part in Helios-2, the French military observation satellite programme. The goal was to achieve a 'federalization' of two programmes since Germany also runs its own, rather modest, military reconnaissance programme called SAR-Lupe. It is doubtful, however, whether such a 'federalization' should be read as a sign of deeper understanding. It is more likely to be shorthand for a failure to agree in practice in the short term. Italy, Spain and Belgium have also joined Helios-2. A final working group was given the task of devising ways of relaunching the Elysée Treaty. An effort was to be made to keep perceived disagreements outside the EU setting and to solve any bilateral problems blocking eastern EU enlargement (*Le Monde,* 30 July 2002).

At the Schwerin meeting, the two governments also decided to relaunch the partnership in association with the 40th anniversary of the 'axis' in January 2003, and made further preparations for the summits in Brussels and Copenhagen (scheduled for late 2002). A number of ministers took part, although not the ministers for agriculture, suggesting that in this policy field the gap between the two countries' positions was considerable (*Financial Times,* 29 July 2002). Moreover, the meeting focused on the special theme of the role of the media in shaping European public opinion. Finally, it endorsed the proposal of the Belgian Prime Minister, Guy Verhofstadt, aimed at creating a common European defence (Euobserver.com, 31 July 2002).

Political interconnectedness between France and Germany is considerable, with each side trying to influence the domestic politics of the other. Several examples spring to mind, such as François Mitterrand's speech to the German Bundestag on INF-missile deployment some 20 years ago or, perhaps, Helmut Kohl's risky appearance on French television to support Mitterrand in the run-up to the referendum on the Maastricht Treaty. Prior to the German elections (September 2002), the French President similarly intervened in the German campaign by extending an invitation to the CSDU/CSU leader Edmund Stoiber, to come to Paris. The fact that Stoiber was not only well received in Paris but also had the red carpet rolled out for him, including the award of the medal of the *légion d'honneur,* was bound to annoy Schröder. However, it failed to poison general Franco–German relations – a reflection of the degree to which the partnership is governed by interests rather than personal links.

Following his re-election in September 2002, Schröder embarked on new efforts to solve the differences on EU agricultural policy that threatened to damage the Franco–German relationship (*Financial Times,* 2 October 2002). At the end of October, Chirac and Schröder duly reached an accord on the subject prior to the Brussels summit and the main lines of the Franco–German deal were subsequently endorsed by the EU-15 (*Le Monde*, 25 October 2002). The new eastern European members will receive their subsidies progressively, with the level of support being reduced modestly from 2007. Thus support will only grow at the rate of inflation. CAP reform should be decided in 2004, although it will not be implemented until 2006 (*Financial Times*, 4 November 2002).

This deal may be acceptable to France, yet it remains far removed from the more ambitious plans of the German Minister of Agriculture, who advocated a shift of funds towards 'rural development' (*Financial Times*, 26 February 2002). It should not be forgotten that Chirac had previously put a spoke in the wheel of the German cart during the latter's European Council Presidency in 1999, when he blocked German attempts to overhaul the CAP. Nevertheless, Germany avoided a major clash with France on the issue in 2002. Chancellor Schröder chose to adopt a somewhat softer line on the issue for reasons of 'grand strategy'. With the confrontation with the US over Iraq becoming entrenched, Schröder calculated that he could not afford a conflict with his main European ally, especially since he could lean on Chirac for support during the Iraqi crisis.

## II. New Bilateral Initiatives

The autumn of 2002 also saw joint calls from Berlin and Paris for a more flexible EU approach towards the Stability and Growth Pact so that it should take more account of inflation and employment indicators. This was obviously a concerted attempt to deflect attention from the failure of the two countries to stay within the Pact's criteria on budget deficits (3 per cent of GDP). In yet another attempt to move the goal posts during the match, European Commission President Romano Prodi called the Pact 'stupid', principally on the grounds of the rigidity of its criteria and much to the consternation of the smaller EU countries that had abided by it (*Financial Times*, 4 November 2002). The serious side to all this was the accompanying need not to lose face with the financial markets that influence the exchange rate of the euro. As is often the case in EU negotiations, successful crisis management can inspire new initiatives. Hence, in November 2002, France and Germany launched a joint proposal on defence and security that included the creation of a European armaments agency. The initiative looked good on paper, yet glossed over some rather deep differences between the two governments, such as over Germany's unwillingness to buy the A400M Airbus military aircraft. In particular, the joint paper proposed to:

- introduce a passage on 'solidarity and common security' in the new 2004 EU Treaty and to annex a political declaration with the same title to the Treaty. The declaration should identify common security risks, including terrorism;
- facilitate greater flexibility in the decision-making process by ensuring that reinforced co-operation is easier to apply by, for example, lowering the threshold for the number of participants;
- allow explicitly for recourse to reinforced co-operation in the field of the common foreign and security policy (CFSP);

- develop a common European armaments policy, including the creation of a European armaments market and a European armaments agency.

Yet there are other instances of recent concerted Franco–German initiatives aimed at structuring further European integration. First, a separate paper tabled at the Convention on the Future of Europe proposes closer judicial collaboration within the EU. It includes, amongst other things, the creation of a sort of European public prosecutor, the right of Europol to conduct enquiries, and the extension of its other activities, as well as the right of the European Commission to propose initiatives in the field of police co-operation (see European Convention paper CONV 435/02, Contrib. 156).

Secondly, the two countries also pushed for greater European tax harmonization that represented a challenge to the UK's position that taxation must remain subject to a national veto. The proposal is aimed mainly at neutralizing the effect of the very low rates of taxation in some EU countries, such as Ireland (*Financial Times,* 1 December 2002).

A final area where Franco–German co-operation paved the way for subsequent EU agreement was on the Union's position in 2002 on future Turkish EU accession. Schröder appeared to have misgivings about Turkish accession for a long time, yet was supposedly converted to Ankara's cause by late 2002. On the other hand, the CDU/CSU opposition remained vehemently against Turkish membership, with former CDU chairman Schäuble, calling the Franco–German deal on the issue 'a grave error'. Schäuble instead preferred the alternative of a 'neighbour-agreement' with Turkey.

Interestingly, the Franco–German agreement on Turkey reached at a meeting in Storkow in early December 2002 stipulated that, provided the Commission reaches a favourable verdict on Turkish membership, it should be decided by unanimity whether to open accession negotiations. If the decision is favourable, negotiations will start on 1 July 2005. This date was changed to 1 December 2004 at the Copenhagen European Council summit following pressure from the British, in particular. The significant preparatory role of Franco–German co-operation is illustrated by the fact that Javier Solana was simply 'informed' of the joint French and German conclusion that 'was to be adopted in Copenhagen' (*Die Welt*, 6 December 2002). Furthermore, although Chirac kept a rather low profile at the Copenhagen summit, the German Chancellor was at the centre of key discussions, especially in ensuring that Poland obtained favourable accession terms.

The need to placate a belligerent domestic audience often leads to public clashes that do not always reflect the real sentiments of national elites. The UK, for example, is not as isolated from its continental partners as often first appears to be the case. Sometimes it is domestic political fog that makes it difficult to see eye to eye. Thus, trilateral agreements between France, Germany and the UK were rare but not entirely absent. In early 2003, these three major EU powers took an initiative on labour market policy after a period of five months in which Blair had largely been kept out in the cold by Paris and Berlin (*Financial Times*, 5 February 2003). The initiative was essentially 'tactical' in inspiration – representing an attempt to offset a 'cooling' of both French and German relations with the UK in the defence area. In June 2002 the three Member States, together with Ireland and Poland, also submitted a supposedly 'secret' paper to the Convention. The paper proposed that any conflicts regarding EU competencies should be solved by a new political committee (referred to by critics as an 'over-parliament') consisting either of national parliamentarians or appointees of the EU leaders.

For several years, the British Prime Minister, Tony Blair, had been (partly) filling the leadership 'vacuum' left by the limited collaboration of Chirac and Schröder. Through a strategy of 'new' or 'multi-bilateralism', Blair had succeeded in setting the pace on a number of specific EU issues. With the assistance of the Spanish Prime Minister, José-Maria Aznar, Blair launched and refined the agenda on economic liberalization. As regards the Convention on the Future of Europe, the British had until recently also been the key player in the discussions. As late as the end of 2002, Pascal Lamy stated that the UK was 'leading the dance' (*Financial Times*, 2 December 2002). Moreover, the additional British success in recruiting eastern Europe to its cause over approaches to European security caused not just irritation, but also alarm in Paris.

However, the fact that Chirac and Schröder wished to handle the Iraqi situation in 2002 in a similar way served as a catalyst for a closer partnership. For Schröder, the growing tensions with Washington over Iraq incurred costs, not least because Berlin can no longer play off Paris against Washington. By implication, France's power within the bilateral relationship has been enhanced in the short term. Yet, in the longer term, the picture is less clear. There are signs that Germany – at least under a Red-Green government – would like to revert to a moderate version of Bismarck's '*Schaukel-politik*', namely a strategy of two competing coalitions: a western grouping encompassing France and other allies, and an eastern one, including central and eastern Europe (witness Schröder's adamant support for Poland at Copenhagen in December 2002) and/or – less likely – Russia. There is certainly a feeling in Paris that time may be running out for Franco–German cameraderie and that German politicians are finding it harder to concentrate when listening to French overtures.

## III. The 40th Anniversary of Franco–German Collaboration

A specific situational logic pertaining to the Iraqi crisis and the unilateralism of US President, George W. Bush has, however, given the Franco–German partnership what looks like a new lease of life. The 40th anniversary of the Elysée Treaty was duly celebrated on a high note – though with more circumstance than pomp. The entire membership of the Bundestag was flown to Paris, where it met its counterpart at Versailles. As many as 1200 parliamentarians from the two countries gathered for the first time to celebrate the bilateral partnership. The comprehensiveness of this bilateral relationship is quite unheard of. President Chirac also visited Berlin as part of the anniversary.

As part of the relaunch of the partnership, it was decided that all ministers from the two sides should from now on meet twice yearly. In addition, two general secretaries (one on each side) will be given the task of ensuring better preparation for these meetings. The general secretaries will each have an assistant from the partner country. Every bilateral pair of ministers is to negotiate a schedule for the coming six months in order to aid continuity and co-ordination. Interestingly, *Die Welt* (22 January 2003) conducted an opinion poll on the celebrations: 86 per cent of Germans regard the relationship with France as 'friendly' and 85 per cent of Germans also view the French as 'likeable'. However, only 51 per cent regard the French as 'reliable'.

The growing institutionalization of Franco–German relations could be a sign of a strengthening of collaboration. Caution is, of course, needed here. Not all relations characterized by high levels of trust are propped up by common institutions. Nordic collaboration and Anglo-American relations are cases in point. On the other hand, the varying philosophical approaches must be taken into account, since France and Germany share a tradition of 'formalism' that naturally influences their choice of the type of collaboration. Nonetheless, there has to be more to Franco–German co-operation than mere common traditions. 'Formalist' states, such as Italy and Germany, have managed to collaborate rather well together, yet neither has felt it necessary to establish bilateral institutional arrangements as is the case with Franco–German relations.

France is the *demandeur* within the relationship. In this connection it is worth revisiting the fate of the original Elysée Treaty: when German Chancellor Konrad Adenauer failed to deliver on his promise of closer relations, the Bundestag duly voted down the Treaty and de Gaulle consequently neglected the relationship with Germany (McCarthy, 1993, p. 11). There is a risk that once again a Franco–German pact may be buried by the German side – this time not because of a dependence on the United States but rather because alternative options, including better relations with central and eastern Europe, exist for the Germans.

## IV. The Dual Presidency Proposal

However, the most important joint Franco–German initiative during 2002 was the proposal for a new 'dual leadership' in the EU (see *Die Welt*, 22 January 2003). The proposal envisaged the election of a President of the European Council balanced by the election of the European Commission President by the European Parliament (EP). At the same time, it was also suggested that the Union should have a genuine 'EU foreign minister' with a seat on both the Council and the Commission (see the press communiqué of 14 January 2003 on the Franco–German agreement).

Outside reactions to this Franco–German initiative were mixed. Whereas the 'dual Presidency' model attracted widespread criticism (though not from the UK), the idea of creating an 'EU foreign minister' enjoys general support. In particular, a number of small states have criticized the 'dual Presidency' proposal. Jacques Santer, the former Commission President, argued, for instance, that the proposal would 'change the balance in the EU in favour of the governments'. The Dutch government was equally critical.

What the precise division of labour between the two Presidencies would be is as yet unclear. Nevertheless, two analogies suggest themselves – one historical, the other contemporary. The historical analogy of the Holy Roman Empire comes to mind. The Empire had a 'dual leadership', namely that of the German Emperor and the Pope in Rome. As originally conceived, the idea was that the Emperor would govern in worldly affairs and the Pope led on spiritual matters. In practice, the dividing line between their two roles was hard to delineate, and a conflict emerged over the investiture of bishops that resulted in total humiliation for the Emperor. To seek forgiveness from the Pope, he was forced to walk to the castle of Canossa where he stood barefoot in the snow with his wife and child for two days whilst awaiting a pardon.

Our contemporary analogy is more encouraging. From French politics, *cohabitation* indicates how a President with a primarily external role can co-exist quite harmoniously with a Prime Minister whose responsibilities are mainly domestically oriented. The arrangement may actually have inspired the French contribution to the Franco–German proposal, although the joint plan advocates that the Council President will have both external and internal tasks. These roles essentially represent a strengthening of implementation duties. Such a blurred overlapping of competencies – including the obscure relationship between the envisaged European Council President and the 'EU foreign minister' – may make political sense, but it is also likely to be unstable.

Some leading personalities, including the German Foreign Minister, appear to think in terms of a personal union between the two Presidencies – at least in the longer term (*Die Welt*, 22 January 2003). Although some political observers understandably view such developments as a return to a Europe of the 'Kaiser', history may serve us once again as a guide for interpretation. The German Empire of 1871, for instance, also had a single yet 'double-hatted' leadership, with the Prussian ruler acting as both King of Prussia and Emperor of the German Federation. Clearly, the envisaged EU post of European Council President would be filled by a senior politician capable of making Member State governments deliver on their promises (see Grant, 2003). In addition, having the European Parliament elect the President of the European Commission should further enhance the legitimacy and prestige of the Commission. It would also probably pave the way for a more party-political Commission, since a stronger President of the Commission may intervene in decisions relating to the appointment of other Commissioners. It would also become difficult for Member States to refuse the next 'logical step' – namely, the election of the entire Commission by the dominant party group or majority in European Parliament.

## V. A More Polycentric Europe

How, then, are we to interpret the renewal of the Franco–German axis? It should be recalled that France had envisaged a more wide-ranging initiative, principally in the form of a new foundational pact with Germany. However, this was later abandoned by the French government on the grounds that any such pact would have required extensive fresh negotiations that would probably have exposed latent Franco–German divergences. Instead, the two sides decided on more modest talks revolving around the completion of the original aims of the 1963 Treaty.

In particular, Schröder seemed to want to downplay the role of the Franco–German axis, stating that the 'Franco–German friendship is no longer a goal in itself. It must all the time be redefined and also prove itself [valid]. We shall in the future be as much inspirators as motors' (*Le Monde*, 24 January 2003). The Chancellor's statement seemed also to signal to his French counterpart that the marriage between the two countries is based on reason, and that Germany has other options than simply a *pas de deux* with Paris. This view is also echoed by London, where there is a tendency to interpret most Franco–German initiatives as a '*fuite an avant*' – a flight forward – whilst at the same time building counter coalitions on the continent.

Even in France it is recognized that 'the European system has become more multilateral' and that as former Foreign Minister Hubert Vedrine puts it, 'the Franco–German motor is but one motor – amongst others' (*Le Monde*, 17 January 2003). Other large EU countries, such as the UK, Italy and Spain, also increasingly play the role of entrepreneurial leader, whilst even small states are able to act as effective managers during their term as European Council President, witness the way Denmark succeeded in overstepping its mandate during the enlargement negotiations in the autumn of 2002 (see Friis in this Review).

Yet, as a negotiating platform, the Franco–German axis remains useful for the simple reason that each of the two is able to speak for a sizeable section of opinion within the European Council. Moreover, when confronted with an influx of new Member States with traditions that may be often alien to French *mores*, the French government needs co-operation with Germany more strongly than it usually dares to say in public. President Chirac, for example, has skilfully used the Iraq crisis to steer Germany away from closer co-operation with the UK, despite broad common ground being shared by the British and Germans in the 'new Europe'.

While important, Franco–German collaboration is essentially elite-driven and appears to be very much a tip without the proverbial iceberg. In Franco–German business circles problems abound. The German side often knows French society better than *vice versa*. Working habits differ (*Le Monde* 25 January 2003). The French, for instance, often complain that Germans 'start early without taking long breaks at midday, but on Fridays there is nobody at the office at 3 pm'. In contrast, the Germans criticize the French for 'often arriv[ing] late and [being] badly prepared at meetings'. The French typically reiterate that many Germans hate to improvise and love deciding things collectively. In the new enlarged Europe, Germany will have plenty of opportunities for deciding things collectively – and France will find it more difficult to improvise.

## Conclusion

Developmental trends in 2002 in Europe's informal leadership are contradictory. On the one hand, France and Germany seem to have overcome the crisis in their relationship and, in early 2003, used the 40th anniversary of the Elysée Treaty as an opportunity to reinforce and further institutionalize their collaboration. On the other hand, further EU enlargement to include central and eastern Europe has put France on the defensive, whilst offering new leadership opportunities for the UK. Hubert Vedrine's point thus seems valid: France –Germany is only one motor amongst others in the new EU. The attraction of the Franco–German core is limited by Germany's economic troubles, by the existence of alternative options for German governments emanating from central and eastern Europe, and by the fact that, in the area of defence policy, the two have little to offer the rest of Europe.

As William Riker (1964) has suggested, large states can only lead within integration processes if they are able to offer protection to smaller countries. Insofar as international politics is becoming more militarized, France and Germany are likely to lose 'political clout'. Conversely such European militarization carries a political bonus for the UK in particular. Whether the loss in regional attractiveness will be compensated by greater bilateral cohesion through a higher degree of Franco–German institutionalization remains to be seen. As Cole (2001) points out, a number of the Franco–German institutions, such as the Defence and Security Council, are largely symbolic, and part of the rationale behind the relationship remains domestic political priorities.

Overall then, grand Franco–German plans perhaps cut a considerable amount of ice with voters, though less so than in the past (Cole, 2001, p. 51). Whilst recent voices have been heard proposing a Franco–German federation – a kind of new 'Carolingean Europe' – it remains doubtful if these views have much influence. From a wider systemic perspective it appears unwise to accelerate Franco–German integration. After all, ambitious interaction may also be a source of friction, and limited interaction could actually be a source of stability (see Waltz, 1979).

On balance, the new Franco–German promises appear rather empty. True, American unilateralism will continue to serve as a force for solidarity. Yet, not only is the continental EU core too small to exert effective leadership within an enlarged and more Atlantic Europe, it also lacks the internal stability that is the essential prerequisite for credibility. The recent revival of Franco–German co-operation is likely to be short term in nature and may well prove to be, as it were, old Europe's 'Indian summer'. It is indeed more a relationship of promises than of promise.

## References

Bonham Carter, V. (1965) *Winston Churchill as I Knew Him* (London: Reprint Society).

Cole, A. (2001) *Franco–German Relations* (London: Pearson Education).

Grant C. (2003) *The Twin Peaks of European Leadership* (London: Centre for European Reform).

Haig S. (1985) *The Privileged Partnership. Franco–German Relations in the European Community 1969–1984* (Oxford: Oxford University Press).

McCarthy, P. (1993) *France-Germany 1983-1993. The Struggle to Cooperate.* (London: Macmillan).

Mazzucelli C. (1997) *France and Germany at Maastricht* (London: Garland Publishing).

Pedersen, T. (1998) *Germany, France and the Integration of Europe* (London: Continuum).

Pedersen, T. (2002) 'Co-operative Hegemony: Power, Ideas and Institutions in Regional Integration'. *Review of International Studies*, Vol. 28.

Riker, W. (1964) *Federalism. Origin. Operation. Significance* (Boston: Little, Brown).

Smith, J. and Tsatsas, M. (2002) *The New Bilateralism: The UK's Relations Within the EU* (London: Royal Institute of International Affairs).

Waltz, K. (1979) *Theory of International Politics* (Boston: Addison-Wesley).

Wendt, A. (1999) *Social Theory of International Politics* (Cambridge: Cambridge University Press).

JCMS 2003 Volume 41. Annual Review pp. 27–43

# Governance and Institutions: Anticipating the Impact of Enlargement

DESMOND DINAN
George Mason University

## Introduction

The conclusion in 2002 of the accession negotiations with the countries of central and eastern Europe, plus Cyprus and Malta, complemented the launch earlier in the year of the Convention on the Future of Europe. Just as the accession negotiations took many years to complete, the EU took a long time to come to terms with the likely institutional impact of the current round of enlargement. Having failed in the Intergovernmental Conferences of 1996–97 and 2000 to prepare the EU institutionally for enlargement, the Member States took a new tack and established the Convention in Brussels to pave the way for widespread institutional reform. Consisting of representatives of national governments, the Commission, the European Parliament (EP), and national parliaments (with equal representation in a non-decision-making capacity for representatives of the candidate countries), and soliciting input from other institutions, academia and non-governmental organizations, the Convention gathered momentum throughout the year and quickly became of paramount political importance.

The Convention was a unique political animal. Despite having being created by the European Council, it was not a creature of the national governments. The Nice Treaty, the widely reviled outcome of the 2000 Intergovernmental Conference, represented the end of the road for the traditional method of treaty reform. Hitherto, national governments had dominated the reform process through a series of intergovernmental negotiations; following the Nice debacle, national governments agreed to open the process to other institutional actors, while hoping to retain ultimate control. Whether national governments would establish mastery of the new reform process raised important practical and theoretical questions about the future of European integration. Regardless of the eventual outcome, however, it was obvious by the end of the year that, although intended only to prepare the next Intergovernmental Conference, the Convention had in effect become the forum for negotiating treaty reform.

The varied composition of the Convention assured a key role not only for the Commission, but also for national parliaments and the European Parliament, actors hitherto marginalized in the process of treaty reform. Precisely because of its varied composition, the Convention's greatest challenge was to avoid fragmentation and forge consensus, hence the decisive role of the Convention's chairman and governing præsidium. The slow start of the Convention's work served to socialize the conventioneers, inculcate a sense of historical importance, and build political momentum. By the year's end, members of the Convention appreciated the necessity of drafting a single text, with as few dissensions as possible, in order to have the greatest possible impact on the reform process.

The work of the Convention overshadowed important institutional developments within the Council, Commission and Parliament, and in the institutions' relations with each other. The Council underwent significant internal reform in 2002 in areas not requiring treaty change, notably the composition and working methods of Council formations. The Commission continued with the reform programme begun in the wake of the resignation crisis in 1999, focusing on unglamorous but essential issues like recruitment, staff mobility and financial control. The Commission also addressed the personnel and internal procedural implications of enlargement.

The European Parliament (EP) experienced a minor political upheaval when Pat Cox, leader of the small Liberal and Democratic Group, was elected President in January 2002. Cox's election, the consummation of a pact made after the last direct elections by the Liberals and the European People's Party (Christian Democrats), the largest group in the Parliament, ended an era of collaboration between the Christian Democrats and the Party of European Socialists, the next largest group, on the election of the President and management of parliamentary business. Cox's presidential style and goals also represented a new departure. Eager to enhance his institution's public image and political importance, Cox unsuccessfully urged the Parliament to be less confrontational with the Council on procedural matters, and to compromise on the contested question of a statute for its members. Nevertheless relations between the institutions were noteworthy in 2002 for efforts to work more closely together on legislative and work programming, an essential step for more efficient policy-making in an EU of ten additional Member States.

## I. The Convention

The Convention held its inaugural plenary session on 28 February. During the previous two months, since the European Council's decision to convene the Convention, the relevant institutional actors were busy selecting their representatives. The European Council had appointed only three members of the Convention (the chairman and two vice-chairmen); national leaders, national parliaments, the Commission and the European Parliament were to choose the rest, according to the following formula: national leaders – one each; national parliaments – two each; Commission – two representatives; European Parliament – 16 representatives.

A row immediately broke out over the right of national leaders to appoint one representative each. The European Council had agreed that Valéry Giscard d'Estaing, the Convention Chairman, would not represent the French Head of State, thereby allowing President Jacques Chirac to nominate a separate representative (indeed, Chirac insisted on Giscard being appointed chairman in order to 'denationalize' and thereby neutralize him on the French political scene). Despite an implicit understanding that neither the Belgian nor Italian leaders would appoint a representative because the two vice-chairmen were Belgian and Italian, Silvio Berlusconi, Italy's Prime Minister, insisted on appointing his own representative. Berlusconi eventually got his way, and the national governments also authorized the Belgian Prime Minister to appoint a representative. The row was symptomatic of the bad blood between Berlusconi and other national politicians, which was evident in meetings of the European Council and the General Affairs Council (Berlusconi acted as Foreign Minister as well as Prime Minister between January and November 2002). Resolution of the dispute with Berlusconi brought the size of the Convention, including representatives from the candidate countries, to 105 members.

National parliaments generally selected their representatives from among the two largest parties or groups of parties in the respective legislature, or selected a representative from the upper and lower houses of parliament. The European Parliament allocated its representation in proportion to the size of party groups in the assembly. The choice of individual representatives was nonetheless delicate politically, involving minor battles in each institution. As for their views on European integration, members of the European Parliament's delegation ran the gamut from strongly Eurofederal to vehemently Eurosceptical. Overall, the majority of the conventioneers had a pragmatic approach to European integration, appreciating the need for greater efficiency, accountability and legitimacy in the EU.

Apart from the representatives of the Commission and European Parliament, other delegations included a number of former Commissioners and

European Parliamentarians, the most notable being former Commission President and European Parliamentarian Jacques Santer, representing the Prime Minister of Luxembourg. Some of the national parliamentary representatives were former senior ministers, such as former Irish Prime Minister John Bruton. The national leaders' personal representatives ranged from senior government ministers (such as Belgian Foreign Minister Louis Michel), to prominent officials, to a member of the European Parliament (representing the Spanish Prime Minister). Giscard himself was both a former President of France and a former member of the European Parliament. Thus the variety of institutional experience and perspectives was greater than appeared from a casual glance at the Convention's composition.

The vast majority of the conventioneers were politicians belonging to national parties that were members of European umbrella parties, such as the Christian Democrats or the Party of European Socialists. The European parties discussed the Convention throughout 2002. Indeed, the Christian Democrats submitted a general draft constitution in October. Yet, the heterogeneity of the European parties made it difficult for them to reach agreement on specific proposals or take precise initiatives in the Convention.

Formal and informal networks proliferated among the conventioneers. Those from the same Member State, whether representing national governments, national parliaments, the Commission or the European Parliament, met occasionally to exchange information and ideas. A Friends of the Community Group included representatives of most small Member States. National parliamentarians formed a caucus, as did the representatives of the national governments. A Like-Minded Group brought together representatives from Ireland, Britain, Sweden, Denmark, Finland, the Netherlands and Portugal (its members cannot have been like-minded on every issue). Representatives of neutral Member States collaborated on security and defence issues. The European Parliament's delegation to the Convention met on the margins of monthly plenary sessions of the Parliament in Strasbourg. The European Parliament itself adopted positions on the Convention by means of deliberations in the EP's Constitutional Affairs Committee and debates in plenary sessions. Despite the diversity of opinion within the European Parliament and its delegation in the Convention, the Parliament's main objectives were reasonably clear-cut: namely to hold the Commission more accountable, extend co-decision to all legislative areas, win full budgetary authority, and replace the 'pillar' structure with a unitary EU.

The Commission set up a task force to assist its two representatives in the Convention. The College of Commissioners followed the work of the Convention at its regular meetings and held special sessions to prepare the Commission's two submissions to the Convention (in May and December). The

Commission's preferences for the outcome of the reform process were hardly a surprise. They included defending the Commission's traditional right of initiative and extending it into security and defence policy; increasing the President's and the College's legitimacy and influence; strengthening the Commission's role in policy implementation; and supporting the European Parliament's supranational aspirations.

Nevertheless the Commission did not present a united front. Chris Patten, the Commissioner for External Relations, objected to the Commission's call in May for the incorporation of the High Representative for the Common Foreign and Security Policy (a Council position) into the Commission, arguing that it was unrealistic and could provoke a Council backlash. Much more embarrassing was Commission President Romano Prodi's failure to win the Commission's endorsement of a draft treaty that he had asked a group of legal experts to prepare for submission to the Convention, without consulting his fellow Commissioners about it until the last moment. Yet the debacle over the Commission's draft treaty may have been more indicative of poor presidential leadership than disarray in the Commission's approach to the Convention.

As for leadership in the Convention, the European Council's choice of Giscard to chair the proceedings generated considerable criticism because of his age, aristocratic demeanour, authoritarianism and institutional preferences. A septuagenarian, Giscard seemed an unlikely personification of Europe's future. Yet he quickly dispelled concerns about his vitality, showing considerable energy before and after the launch of the Convention by visiting national capitals, receiving countless delegations and holding innumerable meetings. A short-lived dispute over allowances and expenses fanned rumours about Giscard's extravagant lifestyle and risked becoming a public relations disaster. Whereas it was difficult to get serious press coverage of the Convention, the media eagerly seized on the story of Giscard's reimbursements, thereby casting the Convention in a bad light and reinforcing a negative stereotype of the EU.

Giscard's alleged authoritarianism may have been his strongest asset. Managing a Convention consisting of politicians with strong egos and different preferences was like 'herding cats'. Giscard drew on his vast managerial experience and considerable leadership skills to move the Convention along. The Convention that drew up the Charter of Fundamental Rights in 2000, on which the Convention on the Future of Europe was based, offered some guidance. Yet, because of its scope and potential impact, the Convention on the Future of Europe was largely *sui generis*.

The Convention's chairman, his two vice-chairmen and the other members of the præsidium wrote the rules on a clean slate. Their tasks included establishing a secretariat, agreeing on the role and working methods of the præsidium and plenary sessions, setting the agenda, making seating arrangements, choosing a language regime (an issue with political and financial implications), approving the subject matter and the composition of working groups (while preventing their proliferation), and dissuading members from digging themselves into entrenched positions by voting on issues. Despite criticism from some conventioneers that Giscard was high-handed and domineering, his chairmanship generally won praise and respect, both inside and outside the Convention.

Giscard's political baggage, in particular his record as President of France and founder of the European Council in the 1970s, was a more serious cause of concern to many in the Convention. Giscard was notorious at the time for his disdain of the Commission and dismissal of small countries' interests. Since the 2000 Intergovernmental Conference, where the large Member States had succeeded in tipping the institutional balance in their favour, small EU countries were on the defensive. Finland's (then) Prime Minister, Paavo Lipponen, echoed the concerns of many small Member States when he accused Giscard shortly after the beginning of the Convention of working hand-in-glove with the large Member States to skew the EU's institutional balance.

Concerns about institutional balance focused on the Member States' representation and voting weights, as well as on the role and influence of the institutions themselves. As the father of the European Council and a senior French statesman, Giscard was, as he told the European Parliament early in the Convention's existence, a 'Council man'. He favoured institutional reforms that would strengthen the role and influence of the Council and European Council, implicitly at the expense of the Commission and the Parliament. Giscard's selection of John Kerr, a former British Permanent Representative and, like Giscard, an intergovernmentalist, to head the Convention's secretariat, and the latter's location within the Council secretariat, fuelled supranationalists' suspicions.

Giscard's views on institutional issues were no secret. Nor was it a surprise that the European Council had appointed someone with such a bias to chair the Convention. Although the European Council included leaders whose countries strongly supported supranationalism, it also included leaders of large Member States that traditionally advocated greater intergovernmentalism. Chirac, the key decision-maker in the selection of the Convention chairman, insisted on Giscard getting the job not only for domestic political reasons but also because of Giscard's institutional preferences. Giscard revelled throughout the year in reporting on the Convention at meetings of the European Council, a setting in which he felt completely at home.

Giscard demonstrated his inclination toward greater intergovernmentalism and sympathy for the large Member States by supporting a call, emanating from Spanish Prime Minister José Maria Aznar, British Prime Minister Tony Blair, and Chirac (the so-called ABC proposal), to elect the President of the European Council from among its current or former members, for a period of up to five years. Giscard liked the proposal partly because he could imagine himself, in earlier days, holding such a position (Aznar and Blair made the proposal partly because they could imagine themselves, in days to come, holding such a position). Representatives of small EU countries (who feared that a new European Council Presidency would become the preserve of the large Member States), and supporters of greater supranationalism (who worried that it would undermine the authority of the Commission President), reacted strongly to the proposal. It was testimony to Giscard's political skill that he kept the proposal alive in the Convention in the face of widespread hostility towards it.

The possibility of a 'permanent' Presidency of the European Council was one of the most radical ideas to emerge in and around the Convention, a point that shows how conservative the work of the Convention really was. Although likely to bring about important institutional innovations, the Convention was unlikely to propose a radical overhaul of the Union's institutional architecture or political system. There were no serious proposals to turn the EU into a fully-fledged federation, perhaps by strengthening the power of the European Parliament, transforming the Council of Ministers into the upper house of parliament, and recasting the Commission as the executive branch of government appointed by, and politically accountable to, the European Parliament. On the contrary, and understandably, most proposals sought to tweak the EU's institutional architecture without altering it fundamentally.

The French government and Giscard were almost alone in championing a structural alteration to the institutional edifice: a new 'Congress of the Peoples of Europe'. The Congress would include representatives of the European Parliament and national parliaments and would vet high-level appointments and legislative proposals (applying the principle of subsidiarity). Even Giscard's political skills could not keep that proposal alive in the Convention in the face of widespread apathy toward it. While eager to involve national parliaments more closely in EU decision-making, most of the conventioneers did not want to have to explain to their constituencies the emergence of yet another European-level institution.

The use of the word 'constitution' in relation to the Convention and its possible outcome was one of the most politically important parts of the proceedings. Giscard used the word unabashedly from the outset, yet faced little serious opposition. Even the British, devoid of a written constitution and wary of the political symbolism of formally constitutionalizing the EU treaties, went along with it. Rather than proclaiming a constitution for the EU, however, the Convention was careful to call for a 'Constitutional Treaty', thereby emphasizing the EU's unique political and legal nature. The constitutional aspects of the proposed new Treaty would not be entirely novel, but would draw from the existing treaties, EC case law and the Charter on Fundamental Rights. Given that the Court of Justice had already interpreted the treaties as constitutional texts, the significance of calling the outcome of the Convention a Constitutional Treaty had greater political than legal salience.

The Convention began with a listening phase that lasted until the end of the summer. Giscard was in no hurry. Hoping to build political momentum, he wanted the shortest possible gap between the end of the Convention and the beginning of the Intergovernmental Conference, scheduled for 2004. In its declaration setting up the Convention, the European Council called for the Convention to end in March 2003. Fearing that the delay between the end of the Convention and the start of the Intergovernmental Conference would be too long, Giscard tried to drag out the proceedings. Member States eventually agreed that the Convention could continue until June 2003, and also that the Intergovernmental Conference would start shortly thereafter. By the end of 2002 it seemed highly likely that, far from taking place in 2004, the Intergovernmental Conference would end at a summit in Rome in December 2003.

Apart from the timing of the Convention and the Intergovernmental Conference, and aside also from the desirability of letting the conventioneers settle slowly into their roles, Giscard wanted the political dust to settle in France and Germany, where presidential and general elections were scheduled later in 2002, before moving the proceedings into high gear. During its first few months, therefore, the Convention dealt mostly with procedural problems and, in accordance with a mandate from the European Council, established a forum, a 'structured network of organizations', to provide input from civil society. The forum met in Brussels in June; otherwise it existed virtually, on the internet.

The Convention moved into a deliberative phase in the autumn, especially after the German elections in September (the French elections took place in May and June). By that time the working groups established early in the Convention began to submit their reports, providing meat for the Convention's deliberations. But the Convention still had to proceed cautiously until after the second referendum in Ireland on the Nice Treaty (on 20 October). Although the Convention existed largely because of dissatisfaction with the conduct of the previous Intergovernmental Conference and content of the Nice Treaty, for political reasons the EU desperately wanted the Treaty to be ratified. Undue emphasis in the run-up to the referendum on the work of the

Convention, the purpose of which was to rectify the Nice Treaty's obvious inadequacies, would have undermined the exaggerated claims of the pro-Nice lobby in Ireland that ratification of the Treaty was essential for the survival of the EU.

Success in the second Irish referendum avoided another black eye for the EU and allowed the Convention to accelerate its work. A week after the referendum, the præsidium unveiled a draft Constitutional Treaty. Earlier, following the German elections, Foreign Minister Joschka Fischer announced that he would become the Chancellor's representative at the Convention. The following month, French Foreign Minister Dominique de Villepin announced that he would replace the President's representative at the Convention, a hold over from the former government. The arrival of the French and German foreign ministers demonstrated the growing political importance of the Convention and heralded the beginning of the final negotiating stage in early 2003. It was also a harbinger of a major Franco–German initiative at the Convention, building on a decision at the Franco–German summit in July 2002 to establish bilateral working groups on key Convention agenda items.

Based on the monthly plenary sessions, regular meetings of the præsidium, the deliberations of the working groups, and the draft Constitutional Treaty drawn up by the præsidium in October, it was possible by the end of the year to identify the Convention's main sticking points, likes and dislikes, preferences and possible proposals. Apart from what to call the new Treaty and whether to change the Presidency of the European Council (discussed above), these can be listed as follows (in no particular order):

- *Council Presidency*: reform the rotating Presidency in order to provide greater continuity in the policy-making process and strengthen the EU's external representation while keeping a rota of some sort, at least for some Council formations, as a means of expressing the principle of equality among Member States;
- *Commission Presidency*: election of the Commission President by the European Parliament, with approval of the winner by the European Council, thereby enhancing the legitimacy and possibly also the political authority of the office;
- *role of national parliaments*: give national parliaments a role (or the appearance of a role) in EU decision-making and allow them to apply the principle of subsidiarity to legislative proposals without establishing a new institution or a potential legislative roadblock. This could possibly be done by reforming the conference of representatives of the European Parliament and European affairs committees of national parliaments (known by its French acronym, COSAC);

- *right of initiative*: protect the Commission's exclusive right of initiative in social-economic affairs and extend the Commission's right of initiative in political-security affairs;
- *general decision-making*: reduce the number and complexity of decision-making procedures;
- *voting in the Council*: make greater use of qualified majority voting in legislative decision-making (notably where the Council and European Parliament co-decide), but on a case-by-case basis, and not in the highly sensitive area of taxation. Possibly change the criteria for majority voting to a majority of Member States and a majority of the EU's population (although this would involve a radical revision of the contentious Nice package);
- *co-decision*: extend the applicability of legislative co-decision between the Council and European Parliament to additional policy areas, notably agriculture;
- *budgetary authority*: abolish the distinction between 'compulsory' and 'non-compulsory' expenditure and simplify budgetary procedures;
- *legal personality*: give the EU legal personality (currently only the European Community, subsumed into the EU under the Maastricht Treaty, has legal personality), thereby clarifying the EU's international status and representation;
- *simplification of the treaties*: do away with separate treaties for the European Community and the European Union; abolish the pillar structure that distinguishes between social-economic policy, police and judicial co-operation, and foreign and defence policy, while maintaining separate decision-making procedures in each area; and write a comprehensible Constitutional Treaty;
- *structure of the Constitutional Treaty*: organize the Constitutional Treaty into a first part (containing provisions that are obviously constitutional in nature); a second part (incorporating detailed provisions on legal bases, institutions and decision-making procedures); and a third part (including entry into force and amendment provisions);
- *external representation*: combine the positions of High Representative for the Common Foreign and Security Policy and Commissioner for External Relations in a new position (Foreign Secretary of the EU?). This should be done without weakening national control over a sensitive policy area or undermining the Commission's authority over economic aspects of external relations (this was one of the most tricky issues on the Convention's agenda);
- *ratification and treaty change*: at present, the Constitutional Treaty would probably have to be ratified in the usual way (by every Mem-

ber State according to national constitutional provisions). However, future treaty change could take place without necessitating ratification in each Member State and therefore risking another embarrassment (for the EU) like Ireland's first rejection of the Nice Treaty (in 2001);

- *Charter of Fundamental Rights*: incorporate the Charter into the Constitutional Treaty, possibly following modification of some of the Charter's provision.

## II. Institutional Developments

Apart from the conduct of the Convention, there were important developments in 2002 within the main institutions and in their relations with each other. Both the European Council and the Council of Ministers undertook procedural reforms of a kind not requiring treaty change. Clearly overwhelmed in his role as Secretary General of the Council Secretariat as well as High Representative for the Common Foreign and Security Policy, Javier Solana tried to lighten the load by improving the way that the Council operates, while at the same time promoting greater transparency of the legislative process. Solana, a former Spanish Foreign Minister, worked closely with the Spanish Presidency in the first part of 2002 to bring about such changes. Based on a report from Solana on Council reform, the European Council, meeting in Barcelona (March), instructed the Presidency to consult with all interested parties and prepare a report for the next summit, in Seville (June), with specific reform proposals.

Over the years, especially with the onset of the common foreign and security policy, the General Affairs Council (GAC) had become sclerotic. Foreign ministers were unable to devote adequate time to preparing meetings of the European Council, co-ordinating the work of the other Council formations, and managing the EU's external relations. Solana and the Spanish Presidency recommended breaking up the GAC into a European Affairs Council, made up of European affairs ministers or deputy prime ministers, and an External Relations Council, consisting of foreign ministers and dealing exclusively with external affairs. The other Member States were divided on the issue. A number of them opposed forming a new European Affairs Council because of the domestic political difficulty, in countries with coalition governments, of designating a European affairs or deputy prime minister equal or greater in rank to the foreign minister. Nor did the Member States agree that splitting the GAC would alleviate the problem of the Council's excessive workload.

The solution agreed by the European Council in June was a typical EU compromise. The General Affairs Council became the General Affairs and External Relations Council, authorized to hold separate meetings for its two areas of activity, including separate agendas and conclusions. The new General Affairs and External Relations Council met for the first time on 22 July. Thereafter its monthly meetings took place on succeeding days, with a discussion of external relations one day and general affairs the next. Inevitably, the foreign ministers of the large Member States turned up for sessions dedicated to external relations, yet rarely stayed the next day for the general affairs session, where their countries were represented instead by junior foreign ministers or permanent representatives. As a result, the old GAC in effect was split into two, with its external relations component gaining precedence over the Council's other work. Although creation of the General Affairs and External Relations Council amounted to creating two council formations within one, Solana and the Spanish Presidency succeeded in reducing the overall number of Council formations to nine.

This reform, implemented by the incoming Danish Presidency (July–December 2002), reduced the number of Council meetings but not the number of national ministers attending those meetings, as several ministers could participate as full members in the same Council. Moreover, in a new development in 2002, defence ministers began to attend the external relations sessions of the General Affairs and External Relations Council. Defence ministers also held an informal Council meeting, despite efforts by the national governments to reduce the number of informal Council configurations.

The European Council also decided in June to open Council meetings to the public when the Council acted as a legislature, using the co-decision procedure. This emanated in part from a call in February by Tony Blair and German Chancellor Gerhard Schröder to make the Council's legislative proceedings more transparent. Blair and Schröder called as well for an improvement in the functioning of the European Council. Having already decided to centralize summit meetings in Brussels (thereby making it impossible in future to distinguish between summit meetings by their location), the European Council agreed in June 2002 to limit the meetings to one day only, preceded by dinner the evening before; to limit the size of each delegation to 20 people; to permit each delegation only two seats in the meeting room; and to tighten up the preparation and conduct of the meetings themselves.

These procedural changes, driven by the need for greater efficiency, especially in view of impending enlargement, alarmed some members of the Convention, who thought that the Council should subsume all reform initiatives into the Convention. Many of the conventioneers were particularly concerned about discussions in the Council on reform of the rotating Presidency, something largely subject to treaty change and therefore falling within the realm of the Convention. The European Council agreed minor changes relating to the Presidency in June 2002. These included, amongst others, an improvement in the continuity of certain policy areas by allowing a Member State due to hold the next Presidency to chair meetings of committees (other than the Committee of Permanent Representatives) and working groups during the current Presidency, and extending the number of working parties that members of the Council's Secretariat-General could chair.

Earlier in the year, based on a unanimous decision (as provided for in the Treaty), the General Affairs Council allowed Germany and Finland to switch presidential places in the second half of 2006 and first half of 2007, in order to avoid disruption due to scheduled general elections in each country. The GAC discussed the principle and practice of the rotating Presidency in November, without reaching agreement on possible reforms. Most Member States acknowledged the constraints of the current system, but not all of them wanted to do away entirely with the six-month rota. Although the Danish Presidency submitted a report on the rotating Presidency to the European Council in December, far-reaching reform would have to await the outcome of the Convention and ensuing Intergovernmental Conference.

In an effort to improve the Council's effectiveness in the light of an increasing workload and imminent enlargement, the European Council also agreed in June 2002 to strengthen the process of strategic programming. Thus the European Council gave the General Affairs Council the task of recommending to it a three-year strategic programme (the first one to be adopted in December 2003). As part of the new process, the European Council asked the next two Presidencies in line to propose, in December of each year (beginning in 2002), an annual operating programme of Council activities. The growing emphasis on strategic programming reflected an effort, regardless of the future of the rotating Presidency, to make the work of the Council more predictable and less idiosyncratic.

### *The Commission*

The Commission continued in 2002 to implement wide-ranging administrative reform, and took a number of practical steps to flesh out the White Paper on Governance (adopted in July 2001). These reforms and initiatives assumed added importance because of imminent enlargement. Having failed to win authorization from the Council early in the year to hire 500 new officials in 2003 (part of the 3,900 new posts requested by the Commission between then and 2008 in order to cope with enlargement), the Commission put renewed emphasis on early retirement in order to free up new positions. As the Court of Auditors observed, that put the Commission at odds with EU policy on the retention of older workers, part of the Lisbon strategy for economic modernization.

In an effort to encourage staff mobility at the highest level, the Commission aimed by the end of July 2002 to ensure that no Director-General or Deputy Director-General had been in the same post for seven years. That triggered a game of musical chairs as Member States, acting mostly through the Committee of Permanent Representatives, sought to ensure positions for their nationals at the top of the Commission bureaucracy. Earlier in the year, the Court of First Instance invalidated the appointment of an Italian official as a Deputy Director-General because he lacked sufficient knowledge of the common agricultural policy (CAP), a prerequisite for the job. As the official had been appointed because he was Italian, the case highlighted the sensitive issue of national quotas in the Commission.

Clearly the civil service of an international organization, especially one as politically important as the Commission, needs to enhance its legitimacy by recruiting members from all EU countries. Yet Member States seemed more determined than ever, in the run-up to enlargement, to ensure within the Commission 'respect for geographical balances' (code words for the politically incorrect and legally unacceptable term of 'national quotas'). A number of ministers pressed the Commission, at a meeting of the GAC in April, to respect geographical balances. A Commission communication on recruitment and enlargement, issued later in the month, proposed a system that, regardless of the criteria used, would guarantee Germany a minimum of 12.5 per cent of administrative positions in the post-enlargement Commission.

The Member States' determination to maximize their representation in the Commission mirrored the growing intrusion of national governments into the Commission's work and increasing criticism of the Commission's actions. Schröder tried to make domestic political capital by publicly taking the Commission to task for a number of unpopular decisions affecting Germany, especially in the area of competition policy. Prodi raised this with Schröder at the Barcelona summit in March and offered to visit Berlin for further discussions. Other Commissioners, wary of giving the impression of Commission weakness, urged Prodi not to go. Instead, Prodi and Schröder met in Brussels in late April.

Sensing that Schröder was on weak ground, Edmund Stoiber, Schröder's Christian Democratic rival and a persistent critic of the Commission, took the opposite tack. He defended the Commission before the election. Yet had he won, Stoiber could have caused considerable embarrassment in Brussels by insisting on replacing one of Germany's Commissioners with a member of his own party. Such a step would have smacked of overt Member State interference in the Commission's affairs. As it was, the Commission faced a frontal assault on its members' supposed independence of national governments early in 2002 when a Spanish Commissioner intervened in the formulation of fisheries policy to push a position strongly advocated by her government.

The Commission continued in 2002 to undertake administrative reform. As part of a more integrated and coherent policy planning process, a key objective of its administrative reform programme, the Commission adopted an annual policy strategy in February 2002, setting out the main political priorities for 2003 (enlargement, security and stability, and a sustainable and inclusive economy). For the first time, a 'structured dialogue' on the annual policy strategy followed with the Council and the Parliament. Based on these, the Commission (in October 2002) adopted its legislative and work programme for 2003, highlighting the practical steps necessary to achieve its political priorities.

The internal reform process in 2002 included the implementation of a new system of activity-based management, covering the complete cycle from policy planning to execution. The Commission examined the first in a series of annual activity reports by Directors-General and heads of services, which showed continuing problems with financial control and the challenge of adapting for enlargement. The Commission pressed ahead with the simplification of working procedures and documents, and the decentralization of human resources management and budgetary control. The Commission also presented a set of proposals to the Council on staff reforms in all the institutions, covering such politically-sensitive issues as remuneration, pensions, language requirements and expatriate allowances (surely an anachronistic perk in today's EU). The Council's initial reaction concerned the cost of the reforms and the growing gap between pay for national and EU civil servants.

In June 2002 the Commission adopted a first set of initiatives to flesh out the previous year's White Paper on Governance. The so-called 'better regulation' package, which the European Council endorsed at the Seville summit, included a new mechanism to assess the economic, social and environmental impact of major legislative proposals. In a second communication on better regulation, adopted in December, the Commission outlined steps to improve consultation on legislative proposals. These initiatives followed extensive input from all interested parties. Whatever their effectiveness, they represented a genuine effort on the Commission's part to make EU decision-making more efficient and transparent.

### *The European Parliament*

In January 2002, Pat Cox, a Liberal, was elected President of the European Parliament. The Liberals were the third largest political group in Parliament, but, with 52 members, were far behind the Socialists (181 members) and the Christian Democrats (232 members). Cox owed his election to a pact with the

Christian Democrats. For more than two decades, the Socialists and the Christian Democrats alternated the EP Presidency between them (every two-and-a-half years). In 1999, after the last direct elections, the Christian Democrats decided to end its cosy condominium with the Socialists in the management of parliamentary affairs and made a deal with the Liberals instead. Given the size of the Socialist and Christian Democratic groups, it was better for them, and for Parliament's sake, to oppose each other than to collaborate in the allocation of leadership positions.

Cox's election represented a change not only in relations among the largest groups, but also in terms of presidential style and ambition. Cox was neither a figurehead nor an aggressive defender of entrenched parliamentary interests. He was a pragmatist who wanted to enhance his institution's image and authority by co-operating with the Council rather than confronting it head-on. One of his first decisions as President was not to challenge before the Court of Justice the legal basis of the Council's adoption of the European Company Statute, contrary to the advice of the Parliament's legal service. He also accepted the Lamfalussy Report on integrating financial markets, despite pressure from many parliamentarians to oppose it because it supposedly weakened Parliament's legislative authority.

The approach of Cox seemed to have paid off when he received a warm welcome from national leaders at the Barcelona summit in March 2002. Far from being a perfunctory exchange of views, the traditional meeting between the President of the Parliament and members of the European Council turned into a substantive session. A sentence in the first paragraph of the summit's conclusions suggested a breath of fresh air in relations between national governments and the European Parliament: 'The European Council welcomes the [European Parliament] President's initiative for political dialogue and pragmatic change'. Three months later, in the conclusions of the Seville summit, the European Council welcomed 'the considerable momentum that has been given to the dialogue between the Parliament, the Council, and the Commission … and gave a favourable reception to the setting up of the High-Level Technical Group for Interinstitutional Cooperation'. In other words, co-operation between the institutions on programming and legislative planning seemed to be well on track, thanks partly to Cox's new approach.

Despite such a propitious beginning, however, the momentum toward closer inter-institutional co-operation faltered later in the year. The incoming Danish Presidency wanted to develop better ties with the Parliament and Commission, not least because the Danish government sought to change the country's image as a bastion of Euroscepticism. Yet, the European Parliament seemed less interested in raising inter-institutional relations to a new level than in maintaining the *status quo* and fighting old battles. One of the most bitter of these, which took the wind out of Cox's sails, concerned the ongoing saga of a statute for members of the European Parliament dealing with, among other things, pay and expenses.

The relevant parliamentary committee adopted an amended report on the statute (the Rothley Report) in April. Like the original version, the amended report took a position on the vexed question of parliamentarians' expenses that many members of the Council, which would have to approve the statute unanimously, strongly opposed. Whereas the Rothley Report insisted that parliamentarians should be allowed to receive a flat-rate reimbursement for expenses, many national governments were equally adamant that parliamentarians should be reimbursed only for expenses actually incurred. For many parliamentarians the issue was one of institutional rights: the European Parliament alone should settle the question, even if the case for flat-rate reimbursement was inherently weak.

The issue was embarrassing for Cox, who wanted to remove an irritant in Council–Parliament relations by enacting the statute as quickly and quietly as possible. Cox urged his colleagues early in the year to allow him to negotiate an agreement directly with the Council. Frustrated by lack of progress and deeming Cox too conciliatory, Parliament voted in a plenary session in December to adopt the Rothley Report as the basis of its dealings with the Council, despite a statement in the plenary session by a Danish minister that the Council would reject the Parliament's demands. Far from celebrating a departure in inter-institutional relations, Council and Parliament became locked at the end of the year in a bitter dispute over parliamentarians' expenses, with Cox's authority correspondingly weakened.

The European Parliament's dogged defence of flat-rate reimbursement in the face of determined Council opposition demonstrated a strong streak of institutional righteousness and insensitivity to public concerns about extravagance in Brussels and Strasbourg. Having taken the ethical high ground during the Commission resignation crisis of 1999, the European Parliament appeared in late 2002 to take a morally questionable position on the reimbursement of members' expenses. Whereas allegations of corruption in the Commission received widespread publicity, however, the story of the parliamentarians' statute was not generally reported. Looking beyond the dispute itself, the fact that the parliamentarians' statute remained unresolved at the end of 2002 was worrying in one important respect. It showed that, despite Parliament's growing awareness of the impact of enlargement and appreciation of the need for reform, old habits impairing the effectiveness of EU governance would persist well into the future.

JCMS 2003 Volume 41. Annual Review pp. 45–8

# The Spanish Presidency: Catalysing a New Axis in the EU?

ESTHER BARBÉ
Universitat Autònoma de Barcelona

## Introduction

The beginning of the Spanish EU Presidency coincided with the launch of the euro in January 2002, and taking charge of its launch was one of the six priorities included in the Spanish programme for the Presidency (entitled 'More Europe'). The other five were the fight against terrorism, the promotion of the 'Lisbon process', the enlargement of the Union, the reinforcement of the role of the EU in the world and activating the debate on the Future of Europe. Hence, the Spanish Presidency programme had a broad agenda encompassing two basic dimensions. First, Spain assumed responsibility for the management of policies adopted earlier by the Union, such as the launch of the euro, eastern enlargement and the Convention on the Future of Europe. Second, the Spanish government promoted in particular the struggle against terrorism, economic liberalization and the development of European foreign policy (mostly relating to the Mediterranean region) as motors of the European integration process. Moreover, due to domestic pressures, the Spanish Prime Minister, José-Maria Aznar, prepared an action programme on illegal immigration to be discussed at the Seville Council.

## I. Leading the Lisbon Programme

The 'Lisbon process', launched by Tony Blair and José-Maria Aznar in 2000, was the main topic of discussion at the spring 2002 European Council. At the Barcelona Council summit (16–17 March), Aznar, along with Blair and the Italian premier Silvio Berlusconi, hoped to encourage the liberalization of the EU energy sector and labour market. However, French reluctance meant that the Spanish government achieved less than it would have wished. This was especially true of liberalization in the energy sector: electricity supply will be liberalized in 2004, but only for businesses. On labour market policies, the Barcelona Council maintained its objective of full employment by the year 2010, although it specified no tangible mechanisms to enable this target to be reached. The results of Barcelona thus revived the 'Lisbon process', although they did not live up to Spanish ambitions on economic liberalization.

The Spanish Presidency enjoyed other minor successes at the Barcelona meeting, however. It achieved EU agreement on the Galileo project and the creation of a health insurance card available to all EU citizens in 2003. Spanish interests and concerns were also addressed, for example, on increasing Spanish electrical connections with the rest of the EU, and on securing the support of all Member States for the British–Spanish decision to reach an agreement on Gibraltar based on shared sovereignty.

## II. A Window of Opportunity in the Fight Against Terrorism

The Spanish government benefited from the international context that followed the events of 11 September 2001. Even before the beginning of its Presidency, Spain succeeded in winning one of its traditional objectives at the European level: namely the application of an order allowing almost automatic extradition within the Union. The events of 11 September created a window of opportunity for the Spanish agenda on terrorism in the EU. Indeed, by February 2002, seven Member States, including Spain, expressed their willingness to start applying the order from January 2003, one year ahead of schedule.

In an atmosphere which encouraged the fight against terrorism, the Spanish Presidency also took the opportunity to promote new objectives. As a result, the Seville Council concluded that the CFSP/ESDP will incorporate the fight against terrorism within its tasks, and the EU began negotiations with the United States on judicial collaboration, including the delicate issue of extradition. Aznar had to press other members to begin those talks. As part of this emerging 'mono thematic' relationship, Aznar and US President George W. Bush focused on the struggle against terrorism during the EU–US summit in May 2002. As a result, other (more) problematic issues in the EU–US relationship, such as the Kyoto agreement on climate change, the International Criminal Court and trade, were swept under the carpet during the Spanish Presidency.

Although illegal immigration had not initially been among the primary concerns of the Spanish Presidency Aznar, with the support of Blair and Berlusconi, presented a proposal in Seville to control it. The proposal would have introduced a policy with penalties such as a reduction in development aid for third countries not taking back illegal immigrants expelled from the

EU. But Spain failed in its intentions, clashing primarily with France and Sweden. So the Fifteen once again showed their differences over migration issues, for instance on the control of external frontiers and integration policies.

## III. South and East

In external relations, the work of the Spanish Presidency had a clear Mediterranean focus. Besides trying to manage a Middle East conflict, the Presidency's aspiration was to provide a review of progress on the Euro–Mediterranean Partnership at the Valencia EU meeting (April 2002). The success of the Presidency was in the fact that the meeting took place at all, since it gathered together Israel and most of the Arab countries in the middle of yet another Middle East crisis. The main aim of the Presidency (the creation of a Euro-Mediterranean Bank), was diminished by a specific financial line being set up within the European Investment Bank (EIB). Apart from this primary issue, Spain presented an action plan with tangible initiatives, such as the creation of a Euro–Med Parliamentary Assembly, new lines of financing for the partner states, a Euro–Mediterranean Foundation and the opening of the Tempus programme to the Mediterranean Partners. The results of Valencia, however, were mixed. Whereas approval of the action plan and the EIB finance line for the Mediterranean were undoubtedly positive outcomes, the Middle East conflict and the uneasy relationship between Spain and Morocco cast a shadow over the meeting.

On enlargement negotiations, the Spanish hope of closing the agricultural and budgetary chapters with the candidate countries during its Presidency proved too ambitious. It was impossible to achieve given the paralysing atmosphere created by the electoral process in Germany. It was also obvious that Spanish willingness to promote the enlargement negotiations clashed with the attempt by Germany and other EU net contributors to link the enlargement process to reform of the common agricultural policy (CAP). The clash between Germany and Spain (plus France) over the CAP would therefore be delayed and would take place during the Danish Presidency (see Friis in this *Review*).

## IV. A New Axis?

Success or failure? The main success of the Spanish Presidency relates to one of the main domestic concerns of Aznar's government: namely the struggle against terrorism. The Presidency also enjoyed two half successes, by implementing the 'Lisbon process', and in facilitating steps forward in the Euro–

Mediterranean Partnership. During the Spanish Presidency two subjects dominated the European agenda: further EU enlargement and the Convention on the Future of Europe. In the first, Spain was unable to manage the agenda due to the deadlock created by the German elections. In the second, Spain was simply absent from the European debate, giving the impression that the Convention was irrelevant to the Spanish government. The most relevant factor during the Spanish Presidency was doubtless the way Prime Minister Aznar managed sensitive EU issues (such as the 'Lisbon process', immigration and transatlantic relations). This facilitated the idea that a new axis was being created in the Union, formed by Aznar, Blair and Berlusconi, as an alternative to the traditional Franco–German axis (see Pedersen in this *Review*).

JCMS 2003 Volume 41. Annual Review pp. 49–51

# The Danish Presidency: 'Wonderful Copenhagen'

LYKKE FRIIS
Confederation of Danish Industries

## I. From Villain to Superhero

Denmark received a chilly welcome when it took over the Presidency in July 2002. How could a country that had recently (in November 2001) chosen a new liberal-conservative government (which was seen by many as closing Denmark to immigrants) possibly open the EU's door to candidates largely from central and eastern Europe? And how could a country, which had been 'specially allowed to "opt out" of several of the EU's biggest ventures [the euro, defence, justice and home affairs and citizenship] … tell others what to do'? (*Economist,* 28 January 2002).

By December 2002 the potential villain, headed by Prime Minister Anders Fogh Rasmussen, had suddenly been transformed into the EU's 'superhero' (*Financial Times,* 16 December 2002) and 'Wonderful Copenhagen' seemed like the obvious theme song. According to the Heads of State and Government the Copenhagen European Council (December 2002) was indeed 'an unprecedented and historic milestone' (European Council Conclusions).

## II. All the Money on One Horse

Although there were other items on the Presidency's agenda, Denmark in reality put all its money on one horse, namely enlargement. After all, Denmark had been a fierce supporter of enlargement since 1989. Agreement in Copenhagen also had the additional symbolic advantage of allowing Denmark to close the circle 'from Copenhagen to Copenhagen'. Way back in 1993 the then European Communities extended the membership perspective to central and eastern Europe in Copenhagen and now, in 2002, it would conclude the negotiations in the very same city. The Copenhagen deadline was by no means a Danish invention, since it had been agreed at the European

Council in Göteborg (June 2001). And since Denmark – due to its substantial opt-outs – had great difficulties in getting on national hobby horses, it acted as a Presidency *par excellence*, refraining from pushing specific domestic concerns.

The Danish spell in the chair was very brief. Although six months on paper, the going could not get tough before the German elections (22 September) were over. Hence, up until that date, Denmark concentrated on closing most of the technical negotiation chapters with the candidate countries. In the run-up to the informal Brussels European Council summit (22–23 October), the European Commission launched its final progress reports. The Czech Republic, Estonia, Hungary, Latvia, Lithuania, Poland, Slovenia, Slovakia, Malta and Cyprus were all judged ready to close negotiations.

At the Brussels European Council, the existing Member States agreed on how much money (i.e. structural funds and agricultural aid) the EU should offer the candidates. To the great frustration of the candidates, the EU-15 insisted on keeping some of the money, which in *Agenda 2000* had been allocated for enlargement, in their national coffers. Instead of the original €42.6 billion the EU offered €39.3 billion for the period 2004–06.

At the Copenhagen European Council (12–13 December), the Union closed accession negotiations with ten candidates. Poland proved to be an especially hard nut to crack. However, after a last-minute concession from the EU (an additional €430 million for the candidates), it also accepted the deal. Secondly, the Member States agreed new steps regarding Turkey. After vigorous Turkish pressure, the EU settled on offering Turkey a date when it would take another look at its application (December 2004). If Turkey (at this time) were able to fulfil the criteria, the EU would open negotiations 'without delay'.

Finally, the European Council also strengthened the membership perspective of the two countries that had not finalized negotiations in Copenhagen. Bulgaria and Romania were thus offered 2007 as a target date for membership.

## III. 'Success has Many Fathers; Failure is an Orphan'

Had the Danish Presidency failed to close accession negotiations, it would have struggled hard to avoid taking most of the blame. In contrast, after success, everyone is eager to share the limelight. Looking back at the six months, it seems safe to argue that France and Germany played a crucial role. In practice, the budget deal in Brussels (October 2002) was not 'made in Denmark', but by France and Germany. Just as important – and beyond presidential control – was the second referendum on the Treaty of Nice in Ireland. Had the

Irish public once again voted 'No', it would have been difficult to close accession negotiations.

That said, two presidential moves did play an important role. The first was the decision to frame the Copenhagen summit as a now or never for enlargement. If enlargement negotiations were not closed by then, foot dragging states would have to live with the fact that they were the ones that postponed enlargement – possibly right up to 2007. This statement was repeated over and over by Prime Minister Rasmussen and he exerted heavy pressure on the governments of other Member States (*Uniting Europe,* 3 June 2002).

The second Danish move was to go beyond the Brussels compromise (of October 2002) and offer candidates slightly more financial support. More specifically, the Presidency added €1.3 billion to the Brussels compromise. This was a risky ploy, since the Brussels deal was already too generous for many Member States. At the end of the day the gamble paid off, and Denmark influenced the 'win sets' of both sides. After the candidates had accepted these Danish sweeteners, it became difficult for other existing Member States to have them reversed. Hence, notably Germany accepted an agreement that was more generous than its original 'win set'. The candidates, having at least succeeded in increasing the EU's offer, climbed down and accepted the deal, which was less profitable than they had demanded. In total, the EU set aside €40.8 billion for enlargement.

## IV. When the Party is Over

Just like any other celebration, the enlargement party in Copenhagen will be followed by a thorough clean-up. The candidate countries will carry out referenda on accession and concentrate on, for instance, implementing the environmental *acquis*. The Member States will be preoccupied by two central issues: how can the Union's institutions function within an EU-25? And how can the common agricultural policy (CAP) be adapted within an enlarged Union? In particular, this has not exactly been made any easier by the EU (and the Danish Presidency's) decision to postpone CAP reform until after enlargement. The clean-up is further complicated by the fact that new candidate countries are already lining up for the next enlargement round. In that respect Copenhagen was actually not the beginning of the end, but the end of the beginning of the enlargement process.

JCMS 2003 Volume 41. Annual Review pp. 53–73

# Internal Policy Developments

HUSSEIN KASSIM
University of London

## Introduction

The single most significant development during 2002 was the introduction of euro notes and coins on 1 January. The Lisbon process continued to structure action in several policy areas, though progress towards the goals specified in March 2000 was slower than hoped. Policy adjustment in the EU and preparation for the accession of the candidate countries proceeded in advance of enlargement. Reviews of industrial policy, the common fisheries policy (CFP) and the common agricultural policy (CAP) took place, and the reform of competition policy continued to move forward. Two-thousand-and-two was also the year when the sixth environmental action programme (EAP), the sixth framework programme for research and technological development (RTD), and an action programme in public health were launched.

## I. Economic and Related Policies

### *The Lisbon Process: Competitiveness, Growth and Employment*

The Barcelona European Council – the second annual spring meeting – met to consider progress made during the first two years of the Lisbon strategy. Despite some important successes, the Heads of State and Government (HOSG) expressed disappointment that progress had been slow in some areas, and called, in particular, for a clear commitment to economic reform aimed at increasing EU growth and employment.

Specific measures were outlined to advance the four Lisbon goals. First was the greater harmonization of statistics and indicators, an analysis of the relevant policy mixes, and the strengthening of fiscal co-ordination mechanisms in order to improve the co-ordination of economic policies. Second, more effort was to be expended on the better take-up of environmental technologies, infrastructure charging in transport, the inclusion of a sustainability dimension in relation to the better regulation initiative, the adoption of an energy tax directive, and greater progress towards energy efficiency in the interests of sustainable development. This latter goal was added by the Stockholm European Council (March 2001).

The third measure was quicker and full implementation of the Charter for Small Enterprises as well as all internal market legislation, the updating of Community competition rules, a reduction in and the better targeting of state aid, progress on public procurement, and simplification of regulation to alleviate the burdens on small and medium-sized enterprises (SMEs) in order to create a more favourable environment for entrepreneurship and competitiveness. Fourth was the attempt by the social partners to increase the involvement of workers in areas of related interest, to reduce the number of people at risk from poverty and social exclusion, and reform of the pensions systems in order to ensure their financial sustainability and compatibility with the goals of reinforcing social cohesion. Three areas were singled out:

- *Creating more and better jobs*: the HOSG called for the reform of employment and labour market policies and asked social partners to develop appropriate strategies. At the Community level, the Luxembourg Employment Strategy (synthesizing the Cologne, Luxembourg and Cardiff processes) was to be simplified and aligned with the 2010 Lisbon deadline. At the national level, the Member States were asked to prioritize the needs of low earners as regards cutting taxation, ensuring that tax and benefit systems make working pay, and linking wage developments with labour market conditions. They were also exhorted to review national rules relating to contracts, to remove disincentives to female participation in the labour force, and to reduce early retirement incentives. The HOSG welcomed the Commission action plan to remove labour market barriers by 2005;
- *Connecting European economies*: the HOSG called for progress across European financial markets, in integrating energy, transport and communication networks, as well as in assuring the quality of public services;
- *Creating the e-economy*: the European Council looked to implementation of the work programme for 2010 on education and training systems, for more action on ensuring the transparency of diplomas and qualifications, on improving levels of basic skills, and in promoting a 'European dimension' within education. There were also calls to close the gap with EU competitors in the key fields of research and development (R&D) and innovation.

Looking beyond Barcelona, the European Council asked the Council and Commission to streamline relevant processes and to focus on implementation rather than the annual elaboration of guidelines.

*Employment*

In its review of the European employment strategy in July, the Commission observed that the improved performance of the European Union's labour market was structural, that employment strategies had converged towards the priorities of the guidelines and that the Luxembourg process had proved effective. In February, it adopted an action plan for skills and mobility. The plan (endorsed by the Council in June) called for the removal of legal and administrative barriers to geographical movement, and cross-border recognition of qualifications to improve occupational mobility. The Council also supported the creation of a 'one-stop' information web site on employment and training opportunities across the Union, as well as a European health insurance card. The problems of migrant workers and their families were highlighted in a Commission communication in December.

The employment guidelines for 2002, including recommendations on national employment policies, were adopted by the Council in February (they had previously been endorsed at the Laeken European Council in December 2001). This completed the fifth annual cycle of the European employment strategy. The sixth began in November with the Commission's adoption of the draft Joint Employment Report for 2002. The Commission called on Member States to step up labour market reform even though employment had improved in 2001 despite the economic slowdown.

*Enterprise*

In May, the Commission presented a review of labour productivity in the EU, in which it argued that greater efforts would be necessary if the Lisbon goals were to be met. In November, it proposed applying the 'open method of co-ordination' to enterprise policy, to enable businesses to learn from each other. The Commission also published a pilot study assessing the impact of regulation on business as part of its campaign to simplify the regulatory environment. The continued implementation of the multi-annual programme for enterprise and entrepreneurship (2001–2005) was marked by the launch of numerous 'Best' projects that apply the open method of co-ordination to encourage the exchange of information on enterprise policy between the Member States.

The Commission's Second Annual Report on the Implementation of the European Charter for Small Business was presented in February, and the 'innovation scoreboard' in December. The contracts of the innovation relay centres (to promote the transfer of technologies across Europe) were extended until March 2004. Arrangements were also made to establish closer collaboration with Eureka and the European Space Agency. The intellectual property rights desk opened on 1 January, and a new Cordis service began, aimed at the beneficiaries of the sixth framework research programme. The Euro Info Centres assumed an additional function during the year: they will now relay SME feedback on EU policy to the Commission.

*A Knowledge-Based Economy*

The Commission took stock of the 'e-Europe 2002' programme, and concluded that important disparities remained. In May, it presented a new action plan ('e-Europe 2005'), designed to promote an environment favourable to private investment, job creation, improving public services, and broadening access to the internet (as highlighted by the 2001 Stockholm European Council). Particular attention was paid to online public services, general high-speed internet access and computer network security. The plan was endorsed by the Seville European Council. The Parliament and Council also passed a regulation relating to the top-level internet domain, '.eu'. The Commission produced an action plan on the safer use of the internet, and communications on moving to the EU Ipv6 internet protocol. It also examined the issue of third generation (3G) licences in mobile telecommunications. The regulatory framework for telecommunications was overhauled in March with the introduction of four directives aimed at promoting greater harmonization, defining access rights, and ensuring universal service provision.

*Research*

The sixth framework programme for RTD came into operation in November. With a budget of €16.27 billion covering 2002–06, it aims to strengthen the European research area (ERA), mostly through the creation of networks and infrastructures. Activities are concentrated in priority areas where Community action can add the greatest value, and the candidate countries are fully eligible. The Member States agreed at Barcelona to increase investment in research and technology from 1.9 per cent of GDP in 2002 to 3 per cent in 2010.

The Commission submitted recommendations arising from the benchmarking of national research policies in March. It began to implement the action plan, adopted in December 2001, aimed at strengthening links between citizens, scientists and policy-makers. In October, the Commission presented its review of the first 30 months of the European research area (ERA) and called for greater Member State involvement in research activities. The promotion of innovation and SME participation continued, while the joint research centre focused on sustainable development and health hazards.

*Economic and Monetary Union (EMU)*

Euro notes and coins were introduced in the 12 participating Member States of the euro area (population 300 million) on 1 January. By the beginning of February, the euro was used in over 95 per cent of cash transactions and the dual-circulation period ended in March. A regulation to create a single payment zone in the euro area came into force in July. Fees for cash withdrawals will be the same, irrespective of whether the cash dispenser is located in the same country as the user's bank account or elsewhere in the Union. Uniform charges for domestic and cross-border euro transactions will apply to payments made by charge cards and credit transfers.

After a modest recovery in early 2002, the EU economy began to slow, prompting the Commission to revise its growth forecasts down from 1.5 to 1 per cent (0.8 per cent in the euro area). Unemployment began to rise. The ECB cut interest rates, as it sought to maintain price stability. Budget deficits rose slightly above the 2 per cent GDP benchmark in the euro area.

The Commission's 'EU Economy 2001 Review' provided the basis for the 2002 Broad Economic Policy Guidelines (BEPG). In its assessment (as part of the multilateral surveillance procedure of the implementation of the BEPG in 2001), the Commission argued that macroeconomic policy was on the right track, but that further structural change was necessary. The 2002 BEPG (adopted by the Council in June) focused on strengthening the macroeconomic framework, increasing employment and combating unemployment, as well as promoting the conditions necessary for high productivity growth and sustainable development.

The Council reaffirmed its commitment to the Stability and Growth Pact and to keeping national public finances under control. The Commission presented its third report on public finances in May. The Council's draft recommendation was approved by the Seville European Council in June. It also adopted conclusions on how output gaps might be assessed the following month. Based on the Commission's recommendations, the Council approved opinions on the stability programmes for the euro area countries.

In February, the Council ratified statements on the budgetary situations of Germany and Portugal. The Commission opened the first stage of the excessive deficit procedure in relation to Portugal, following official confirmation that the Portuguese general government deficit in 2001 stood at 4.1 per cent of GDP (higher than the permitted 3 per cent ceiling). The Council asked the Portuguese government to remedy the situation. The Commission issued a further report on Germany in November. An early warning was also sent to

France, where an excessive deficit looked likely. The Council adopted opinions on the convergence programmes of those Member States not participating in the euro. The Commission's report on Sweden argued that the country was not ready to participate in the single currency since it did not meet the exchange rate criterion.

A number of initiatives were launched with a view to improving the operation of EMU. First, Ecofin agreed that the annual economic and employment policy co-ordination cycles would be streamlined and synchronized. The Commission also sought greater co-ordination of budgetary policies in order to improve the operation of both the Stability and Growth Pact and the conduct of national budgetary policies. In further communications, it called for better statistics for the European Union and the euro, and for a quarterly report on economic developments in the euro area.

The ECB continued to demonstrate its commitment to transparency, and to promote co-operation among national authorities on prudential supervision and financial stability. It was involved in meetings of international multilateral institutions, and worked within the framework of the 'Europe agreements' to strengthen its relations with the central banks of the candidate countries. Accession negotiations in relation to EMU and capital liberalization were also concluded, and pre-accession surveillance continued. The Commission published a report on macroeconomic and financial stability in the candidate countries in March.

The Commission presented its report on financial assistance to third countries in 2001. It reviewed existing operations and recommended that there should be greater emphasis on the economic and structural conditions attached to aid. During the year, the Union committed additional assistance to the western Balkans, Moldova, Ukraine and Romania. The European Investment Bank (EIB), meanwhile, granted loans totalling €39.6 billion (compared to €36.8 billion in 2001) in support of EU objectives. €33.4 billion were granted to recipients in the EU-15, and €3.6 billion in the candidate countries, as well as €2.5 billion in partner countries.

### *Internal Market Developments*

The Commission presented its proposals for the third update of the internal market strategy in April. Despite a number of successes in 2001, the Commission reported that overall progress had not been satisfactory and warned that if the 'delivery gap' could not be closed, the credibility of the Lisbon strategy would be called into question. While recognizing its own shortcomings, it noted that most delays occurred in the European Parliament and the Council. The Council agreed that the strategy's main objectives be kept, but that the number of 'target actions' should be reduced. However, by the end of the year, only six out of 16 initiatives targeted in April had been completed (IP/03/40).

With the approach of the tenth anniversary of the internal market, concern about implementation increased. At Barcelona, the HOSG noted that only seven Member States had achieved the transposition target of 98.5 per cent (set in the previous year at Stockholm). They extended this deadline until March 2003 and called for the total transposition of all directives whose implementation was two years or more overdue. The Commission reported in November that the 'implementation deficit' (the percentage of internal market legislation not yet transposed into national law) had risen from 1.8 per cent in May to 2.1 per cent in November, reversing a decade of continuous improvement. Only five Member States – Sweden (0.4 per cent), Finland (0.6), Denmark (0.7), the Netherlands (1.3), and the UK (1.4) – were below the 1.5 per cent ceiling, while France, Greece and Portugal had deficits of more than double the target. The position of latter group, together with Germany, Ireland and Austria, had deteriorated even since May. The internal market remained fragmented, with 9 per cent of all legislation not implemented in all 15 Member States.

The number of infringements – 1500 open cases – remained high. France and Italy faced the highest number – 216 and 190 respectively – and accounted for nearly 30 per cent of total cases. Only Denmark reduced the number of infringements relating to the misapplication of secondary legislation by 10 per cent or more.

A Commission-sponsored survey of business and citizen opinion on ten years of the internal market reported that 70 per cent of citizens welcomed the increased competition. Eighty per cent believed that the internal market has broadened the range of available products, 67 per cent saw an effect on product quality and 41 per cent on prices. Seventy-six per cent of those exporting to six or more Member States were positive about the impact of the internal market on their business, while 46 per cent of all EU businesses reported a beneficial impact. In contrast, only 11 per cent said that the impact had been negative. More than 80 per cent believed that improving the operation of the internal market should be a key EU priority, along with further measures to ensure fair competition and closer tax alignment. These averages conceal, of course, considerable cross-national variation.

Significant developments took place in three areas. First, with respect to financial services, the Heads of State and Government reaffirmed (at Barcelona and Seville) their commitment to the Commission's 1999 action plan, and looked forward to the integration of the securities and risk capital markets by 2003 and the financial services market by 2005. New directives were adopted on undertakings for collective investment in transferable securities

(UCITS), financial collateral arrangements, insider dealing, solvency in insurance, and the supervision of credit institutions, insurance undertakings and investment firms in financial conglomerates. The Commission reported progress in implementing the action plan; yet noted that a similar pace would have to be maintained if the target dates were to be realized. Parliament sounded a more cautious note, however, with the EP describing as 'premature' the Council's decision to extend the 'Lamfalussy process'.[1]

Second, the Council agreed on measures to simplify and modernize public procurement. A common position was adopted on co-ordinating procedures for the awarding of public works, supply and service contracts, and on procurement procedures in water, energy and transport sectors. A regulation on a common procurement vocabulary and standard forms for publishing public procurement notices was agreed.

With respect to taxation – the third area – the Parliament and Council adopted a new programme, 'Fiscalis 2007', that promises to make co-operation between national administrations more effective. The Council noted the progress made by the Code of Conduct Group as regards company taxation, and cited negotiations (begun in 2001) with numerous third countries on measures equivalent to the proposed directive on the taxation of savings income.

Other notable initiatives and developments included:

- a Council decision to extend 'Customs 2002', as part of the 2001 customs union strategy;
- the creation of a 'citizens' signpost' service to direct queries to the relevant authorities and services and the 'Solvit' network to deal with problems arising from internal market rules misapplied by government departments;
- a Commission proposal to merge existing directives on regulated professions;
- the biennial Commission report on the application of the principle of mutual recognition in the internal market;
- a report by the Commission as part of first phase of the internal market strategy for services;
- the directive extending the liberalization of postal services;
- Commission communications on a methodology for evaluating services of general economic interest. From 2003, the Member States will

[1] This process refers to the high-level group created at Ecofin's instruction in July 2000 to review wholesale market securities regulation in the EU and to make proposals as to how it might be improved. Its final report, presented in February 2001, proposed greater flexibility in the law-making process governing financial supervision, and was approved by the Stockholm European Council. A compromise was reached between Council and Parliament under the co-decision procedure in February 2002. Ecofin decided in April to extend the approach to other areas of banking.

produce annual assessments of their services in transport, electricity, gas, post services and telecommunications sectors;

- a directive harmonizing the structure and rates of excise duty on tobacco (with the aim of combating fraud and smuggling);
- an initiative on the taxation of passenger cars in order to improve the operation of the internal market and contribute towards Kyoto commitments on reducing greenhouse gases;
- proposals on the introduction of international accounting standards and the independence of the statutory auditor.

*Competition and Industrial Policies*

The overhaul of Community competition rules continued. In December, the Council adopted the Commission's proposal for recasting Regulation No. 17 implementing Articles 81 and 82 of the EC Treaty. In the most far-reaching reform of anti-trust norms for 40 years, Community competition rules can now be applied by national competition authorities, acting in co-operation with the Commission, and are directly applicable by national courts. Agreements need no longer be notified to the Commission.

As regards anti-trust legislation, the Commission adopted (in April) a notice under which it can grant 'conditional immunity from fines' to the first firm that contributes to the identification or banning of a cartel. Following consultation arising from its 2001 Green Paper, the Commission presented its proposal for amending the merger regulation. As well as advocating greater flexibility in terms of the time necessary to investigate complex cases and strengthening the Commission's investigative powers, the proposal seeks to clarify the regulation's application in situations where there is an oligopoly. It also abolishes the rigid rules requiring the notification of mergers, and simplifies the rules for referring cases between the Commission and national competition authorities. Internal organizational changes are also planned. In state aid, the Commission launched a reform aimed at simplifying procedures for cases that do not raise major legal concerns. These changes will enable the Commission to concentrate on the most serious cases and will also reduce the legal costs for business.

Further important decisions were taken by the Commission during 2002. The 'block exemption' for the International Air Traffic Association's tariff conferences was renewed (until 30 June 2005). Complaints against FIFA's rules on players' agents and against UEFA concerning the rules stipulating that two or more clubs may not be controlled by the same entity were rejected. The Commission granted conditional exemptions to a co-operation agreement between Austrian Airlines and Lufthansa, and a multilateral interchange fee for cross-border payments by Visa card. It also exempted the International Federation of the Phonographic Industry, allowing a 'one stop shop' for issuing licences to broadcast music on the internet, and to the Transatlantic Conference (TACA), a grouping of shipping companies that provide container transport between northern Europe and the US.

Fines were imposed on eight Austrian banks, two producers of methionine, seven Dutch industrial and medical gas companies and the Japanese video games manufacturer, Nintendo. The world's two leading fine arts auction houses, Christie's and Sotheby's, and four plasterboard manufacturers were also penalized for infringements of Community's rules on restrictive practices.

In the cases of Tetra Laval/Sidel and Schneider Electric/Legrand (where the Commission took decisions prohibiting these mergers, but the operations had in any case gone ahead), the Commission issued decisions requiring the companies to 'demerge'. In both cases, the companies concerned successfully appealed against the initial prohibitive decisions and the order requiring the 'demerger'. Using the accelerated procedure for the first time, the Court annulled all the Commission's prior decisions.

The Commission presented its 'state aid scoreboard' in May. Germany granted the highest number of state aids, followed by France and then Italy. It indicated an overall trend towards a reduction in state aid levels, something also noted in the Commission's (October) progress report on the reduction and reorientation of state aid. In February, the Commission revised the rules on regional support for large investment projects. Reports were presented on aid to the steel and coal industries, as well as on the guidelines for state aid relating to services of general interest. Temporary measures were introduced to assist the Community's shipbuilding industry. The Commission also exempted from the obligation to notify any aid aimed at reintegrating disadvantaged or disabled workers into the labour market.

The Commission reported on the competition agreements with Canada and the US (in January and September respectively), and highlighted 'best practice' in terms of bilateral co-operation with US authorities in merger cases. It signed an accord with the Japanese competition authority in May.

Following the expiry of the ECSC Paris Treaty, the sectors previously covered (coal and steel), as well as the related procedural rules and secondary legislation, became subject to the EC Treaty. In June, the Commission indicated how it would treat competition cases resulting from the changeover. The following month, it issued a regulation amending previous arrangements relating to motor vehicle distribution, that aims to increase competition and consumer benefits, in particular as regards multi-brand dealerships. It also introduced a new initiative on takeover bids, following the Parliament's rejection of its original proposal in 2001. The Council approved an action plan on corporate governance, seeking to improve the regulatory framework of company law.

*Other Developments*

The 2001 White Paper on Transport Policy guided developments during the year. Initiatives aimed at improving security and safety, especially in air and sea transport, and making transport, especially multi-modal transport, more efficient. The Galileo project was launched, five proposals on railways adopted, and several measures taken in the area of maritime transport, including the creation of a European Maritime Safety Agency. In a judgment that may have significant consequences, the European Court of Justice confirmed the Community's external competence in air transport.

Following its 2000 Green Paper, the Commission sought to enhance the security of the Union's energy supply, while at the same time making the industry more competitive and environmentally friendly. It proposed revised Community mechanisms for oil and gas stock rises, an 'intelligent energy for Europe' programme, and improvements in energy efficiency, including in renewable energy sources. In November, the Council reached agreement on opening the internal market for gas and electricity.

In September, the Parliament and Council adopted a public health action programme (2003–08). With a budget of €312 million, the programme should increase information and knowledge and the capacity to further and react appropriately to health issues.

*Structural Funds and Regional Policy*

Consolidating the quality of structural funds programmes (for 2002–06) was the main concern in 2002. The management of the funds was examined by the Parliament, the Commission and the Council (the latter discussing two special documents by the Court of Auditors). The Commission also presented a progress report, following up its second cohesion report (of 2001), and considered the future of cohesion policy in the light of enlargement.

In commitments made during the year, Spain, Greece, Italy, Portugal and Germany were the main beneficiaries under objective 1 (regions where level of development is below 75 per cent of the EU average). France, the UK and Germany also benefited under objective 2 (regions undergoing structural change), and objective 3 (modernization of education, training and employment systems), and Germany, Spain, Italy and the UK under the four Community initiatives (Leader, Interreg, Equal and Urban). Allocations from the cohesion fund were split roughly evenly between environment and transport. A solidarity fund, proposed by the Commission and agreed by the Council in

November, was created to assist the regions in Germany, Austria and a number of candidate countries affected by the severe summer floods.

## II. Social Policies

The Commission directed its energies to implementing the social agenda, launched by the Nice European Council in December 2001 – the multi-annual framework that gives practical effect to the social policy provisions of the Amsterdam Treaty and to the reform agenda agreed in March 2000 at Lisbon aimed at modernizing the European social model.

A new community action programme was launched in January to encourage co-operation between the Member States in combating social exclusion. The hope is that the programme, which runs until 2006, will aid the understanding of poverty and social exclusion by comparing experiences, presenting national action plans, and increase the capacity for dealing with these problems through networking at the Community level and between the social partners.

Ageing also remained a concern. The use of the open method of co-ordination was extended to pensions. The Commission also presented the Union's response to ageing at a world assembly in March, began consulting European social partners on supplementary pension rights, and published its analysis of the first national strategy report on pensions in December. The Commission submitted its sixth annual report (2001) on equal opportunities, and looked ahead to examining the reconciliation of work and family life in 2002. The Council called on the Commission to integrate gender into its policy initiatives and requested future Presidencies to continue gender mainstreaming in all Council formations.

A directive was adopted (in March) setting out a general framework for informing and consulting employees in undertakings or establishments employing at least 50 or 20 employees respectively, while Directive 80/987/EEC was amended to ensure equal treatment of men and women in cases of insolvency. The Commission set out guidelines for the development and promotion of employee financial participation. In June, the Commission reviewed the operation of the 'social dialogue' since the Amsterdam Treaty came into force, and suggested how it might be enhanced in an enlarged Union. It also canvassed the idea of holding of a tripartite social summit in advance of the spring European Council. The social partners presented their multi-annual work programme (covering 2003–03), at the ninth social dialogue summit in November.

The Commission continued to receive responses to its 2001 Green Paper on corporate social responsibility and issued a communication (in July) outlining a European strategy to promote the paper and its compatibility with sustainable development. The Council called on the Commission to take account of all views in developing its strategy and on Member States to further the debate.

In March, the Commission set out a Community strategy (2002–06) for health and safety at work (endorsed by the Council in June), based on a comprehensive approach to 'well-being' and aimed at creating a culture of risk prevention. Directives on working conditions for temporary workers and the organization of working time were also introduced. With respect to freedom of movement, the Commission proposed extending social security coverage to nationals of third countries not presently covered on grounds of their nationality. The Council called for better cross-border co-operation on access to high-quality health services.

## III. Finances

The reform of financial management, control and audit continued. The 2002 budget year was the first in which the Union's 'strategic planning and programming cycle' (the system introduced as part of administrative reform in order to ensure better management of resources) came into operation. The preliminary draft of the 2003 budget was the third to be presented using both traditional and the activity-based budgeting nomenclature. The new financial regulation, adopted by the Council in June, clarifies budgetary principles and incorporates a new structure corresponding to activity-based budgeting, an emphasis on output and performance, and modern accounting rules. Implementing rules have been placed in a separate regulation.

Rules governing Community bodies set up to carry out activities, as well as executive agencies operating EC programmes, were introduced. On the control side, the implementation of the control concept defined in 2001 continued. With respect to auditing, the Commission's internal auditor carried out assessments in high-risk areas, especially the way in which the Commission's departments produce annual activity reports and declarations of assurance (presented for the first time in 2001). A programme of internal audits began in September with the aim of covering all the services before the end of 2003. Debate continued on the Commission's 2001 Green Paper on the protection of financial interests of the Community and the creation of a European prosecutor. The Convention of the European Communities' Financial Interests, signed in 1995, came into force after being ratified by the remaining Member States.

The preliminary draft budget was approved by the Commission in April. Small increases were proposed across all categories (agriculture, structural operations, internal policies, external relations, pre-accession and administration). Commitment appropriations were up by 1.4 per cent and payments by 2.7 per cent compared with 2002. The Council proposed numerous reductions in the draft budget (adopted in July), with the categories of agriculture and administration the most deeply affected.

At its first reading, the Parliament restored most of the cuts. Negotiations in conciliation in advance of the second Council reading focused on the funding method for restructuring the Spanish and Portuguese fishing fleets, external relations (especially the common foreign and security policy) and administrative expenditure. The Council agreed to €99.454 billion for commitments and €96.896 billion for payments. The 2003 budget was agreed in December, following the Parliament's second reading (see Table 1). The budget totals €99.686 billion in appropriations for commitments and €97.503 billion in appropriations for payments – 0.3 and 1.9 per cent higher than the 2002 budget respectively. The payment appropriations amount to 1.02 per cent of EU-15 gross national income (the ceiling is 1.24 per cent).

The Parliament agreed a resolution on the implementation of the 2002 budget in July. The implementation of appropriations for commitments at 31 December is shown in Table 1. On the revenue side, own resources totalled €94,331.7 million (or 1.02 per cent of gross national income). The sources of revenue are shown in Table 2. Following a Council recommendation in March, the EP gave the Commission discharge of the 2000 budget.

In preparation for enlargement, the Copenhagen European Council agreed expenditure requirements, subject to the enlargement-related spending limits for 2004–06 as set out at Berlin in April 1999 (see Table 3).

In accordance with the own resources decision of 29 September 2000, the new Member States will contribute fully to the financing from the first day of accession.

## IV. Agriculture and Fisheries

### *Agriculture*

The agricultural agenda was dominated by ongoing preparation for enlargement in accordance with the framework set by *Agenda 2000*. In its mid-term review of the CAP (*COM* (2002) 394), the Commission outlined several aims: namely of stabilizing markets and improving common market organizations (CMOs), introducing simpler and more sustainable direct support, achieving a better balance between agricultural support and environmental considerations, and strengthening rural development.

The review called for direct aid to be 'uncoupled' from production. It proposed that payments be made conditional on compliance with environmental,

Table 1: 2003 Budget

| *Heading* | *2003 Budget* | *2002 Budget* | *Financial Perspective 2003* | *% Diff. 2003 over 2002* |
|---|---|---|---|---|
| 1. AGRICULTURE | | | | |
| Agricultural exp. (excl. rural dev't) | 40 082 450 000 | 39 660 080 000 | | 1.1 |
| Rural dev't and accompanying measures | 4 698 000 000 | 4 595 000 000 | | 2.2 |
| Total | 44 780 450 000 | 44 255 080 000 | 47 378 000 000 | 1.2 |
| Margin | 2 597 550 000 | 2 331 920 000 | | |
| 2. STRUCTURAL OPERATIONS | | | | |
| Objective 1 | 21 577 061 305 | 21 329 627 745 | | 1.2 |
| Objective 2 | 3 651 793 231 | 3 729 793 231 | | 2.1 |
| Objective 3 | 3 718 927 200 | 3 646 007 301 | | 2.0 |
| Other structural measures (except Obj. 1) | 171 900 000 | 168 900 000 | | 1.8 |
| Community initiatives | 1 866 017 000 | 1 860 322 000 | | 0.3 |
| Innovative measures and techn. assistance | 143 301 264 | 144 349 723 | | 0.7 |
| Other specific structural measures | 12 008 240 | 170 000 000 | | 92.9 |
| Cohesion Fund | 2 839 000 000 | 2 789 000 000 | | 1.8 |
| Total | 33 980 008 240 | 33 838 000 000 | 33 968 000 000 | 0.4 |
| Margin | 12 008 240 | 200 000 000 | | |
| 3. INTERNAL POLICIES | | | | |
| Research and tech. development | 4 055 000 000 | 4 055 000 000 | | 0.0 |
| Other agricultural operations | 44 597 000 | 55 320 000 | | 19.4 |
| Other regional operations | 15 000 000 | 15 000 000 | | 0.0 |
| Transport | 54 000 000 | 29 000 000 | | 86.2 |
| Other measures – fisheries and sea | 70 420 000 | 65 130 000 | | 8.1 |
| Education, vocational training and youth | 562 682 000 | 523 350 000 | | 7.5 |
| Culture and audiovisual sector | 117 500 000 | 116 700 000 | | 0.7 |
| Information and communication | 116 847 000 | 113 705 600 | | 2.8 |
| Social dimension and employment | 180 775 000 | 157 955 000 | | 14.4 |
| Contributions to European parties | 7 000 000 | 7 000 000 | | 0.0 |
| Energy | 48 000 000 | 33 000 000 | | 45.5 |
| Euratom nuclear safeguards | 18 800 000 | 17 700 000 | | 6.2 |
| Environment | 237 300 000 | 196 030 000 | | 21.1 |
| Consumer policy & health protection | 22 572 500 | 22 500 000 | | 0.3 |
| Aid for reconstruction | 611 000 | 898 000 | | 32.0 |
| Internal market | 200 256 500 | 184 805 000 | | 8.4 |
| Industry | p.m. | | | |
| Labour market and tech. innovation | 122 500 000 | 104 600 000 | | 17.1 |
| Statistical information | 35 400 000 | 34 000 000 | | 4.1 |
| Trans-European networks | 725 057 000 | 677 000 000 | | 7.1 |
| Freedom, security and justice | 153 635 600 | 143 020 000 | | 7.4 |
| Fraud | 7 200 000 | 6 100 000 | | 18.0 |
| EU Solidarity Fund | p.m. | 599 000 000 | | 100.0 |
| Reserve for administrative exp. | 647 400 | | | |
| Total | 6 795 801 000 | 7 156 813 600 | 6 796 000 000 | 5.0 |
| Margin | 199 000 | 598 813 600 | | |
| 4. EXTERNAL ACTIONS | | | | |
| European Development Fund | p.m. | p.m. | | |
| Food aid and support measures | 425 637 000 | 455 000 000 | | 6.5 |
| Humanitarian aid | 441 690 000 | 441 845 000 | | 0.0 |

Table 1: 2003 Budget (Contd)

| *Heading* | *2003 Budget* | *2002 Budget* | *Financial Perspective 2003* | *% Diff. 2003 over 2002* |
|---|---|---|---|---|
| Co-operation – Asia | 562 500 000 | 558 000 000 | | 0.8 |
| Co-operation – Latin America | 337 000 000 | 346 671 500 | | 2.8 |
| Co-operation – southern Africa & S. Africa | 127 000 000 | 124 790 000 | | 1.8 |
| Co-operation – third countries in the Mediterranean and the Middle East | 753 870 000 | 861 320 000 | | 12.5 |
| EBRD Community sub. to the capital | p.m. | p.m. | | |
| Assistance – E. Europe and C. Asia | 507 370 000 | 473 900 000 | | 7.1 |
| Other Community financing –E. Europe, Central Asia and western Balkans | | | | |
| Co-operation – western Balkans | 684 560 000 | 765 000 000 | | 10.5 |
| Other co-operation measures | 505 470 000 | 419 578 500 | | 20.5 |
| European initiatives for democracy and human rights | 106 000 000 | 104 000 000 | | 1.9 |
| International fisheries agreements | 192 500 000 | 193 193 000 | | 0.4 |
| Ext. aspects of certain Community policies | 79 862 000 | 78 702 000 | | 1.5 |
| Common foreign and security policy | 47 500 000 | 30 000 000 | | 58.3 |
| Pre-accession strategy – Med countries | 174 000 000 | 21 000 000 | | 728.6 |
| Reserve for administrative expenditure | 4 403 000 | | | |
| Total | 4 949 362 000 | 4 873 000 000 | 4 972 000 000 | 1.6 |
| Margin | 22 638 000 | 0 | | |
| 5. ADMINISTRATION | | | | |
| Part A (excluding pensions) | 2 758 100 371 | 2 739 182 929 | | 0.7 |
| Other institutions (excluding pensions) | 1 870 598 727 | 1 753 659 209 | | 6.7 |
| Pensions (all institutions) | 731 372 000 | 685 619 000 | | 6.7 |
| Total | 5 360 071 098 | 5 178 461 138 | 5 381 000 000 | 3.5 |
| Margin | 20 928 902 | 538 862 | | |
| 6. RESERVES | | | | |
| Monetary reserve | 250 000 000 | | 100.0 | |
| Guarantee reserve | 217 000 000 | 213 000 000 | | 1.9 |
| Emergency aid reserve | 217 000 000 | 213 000 000 | | 1.9 |
| Total | 434 000 000 | 676 000 000 | 434 000 000 | 35.8 |
| Margin | 0 | 0 | | |
| 7. PRE-ACCESSION AID | | | | |
| Agriculture | 564 000 000 | 555 000 000 | | 1.6 |
| Instrument for Structural Policies for Pre-Accession (ISPA) | 1 129 000 000 | 1 109 000 000 | | 1.8 |
| Phare pre-accession instrument | 1 693 000 000 | 1 664 000 000 | | 1.7 |
| EU Solidarity Fund | p.m. | 129 000 000 | | 100.0 |
| Total | 3 386 000 000 | 3 457 000 000 | 3 386 000 000 | 2.1 |
| Margin | 0 | 129 000 000 | | |
| Total commitments | 99 685 692 338 | 99 434 354 738 | 102 315 000 000 | 0.3 |
| Margin | 2 629 307 662 | 1 404 645 262 | | |
| Payment appropriations | | | | |
| Total payment appropriations | 97 502 937 098 | 95 656 387 238 | 102 938 000 000 | 1.9 |
| Margin | 5 435 062 902 | 4 588 612 762 | | |
| Payment appropriations as % of GNP | 1.02 | 1.05 | 1.07 | |

*Source:* Bulletin EU 12-2002.

Table 2: Budget Revenue

| | *2002 (€ million)* | *2003 (€ million)* |
|---|---|---|
| Agricultural duties | 1 180.2 | 1 173.1 |
| Sugar and isoglucose levies | 864.8 | 728.8 |
| Customs duties | 12 918.9 | 14 285.2 |
| Own resources collection costs[a] | –3 725.7 | –4 046.8 |
| Regularization of collection costs for 2001[b] | –2 023.0 | – |
| VAT own resources | 22 687.4 | 24 121.2 |
| Gross national income (GNI)-based own resources | 45 850.6 | 59 404.0 |
| Balance of VAT and GNI own resources from prev. years | –53.5 | p.m. |
| Surplus available from previous year | 15 375.0 | 1 000.0 |
| Other revenue | 1 257.0 | 837.4 |
| Total | 94 331.7 | 97 502.9 |
| Maximum own resources which may be assigned to the budget (% of GNI) | 1.24 | 1.24 |
| Own resources actually assigned to the budget (% of GNI) | 1.02 | 1.00 |

*Source:* Commission (2003) *General Report on the Activities of the European Union* (Luxembourg: OOPEC).
*Notes:* [a] The new financial regulation applicable does not allow negative revenue to be shown in the budget.
[b] This refers to the amount repaid to member states as a consequence of the retroactive effects of the new own resources decision on collection costs they incurred between March and December 2001.

Table 3: Maximum Enlargement-related Commitments (€ m at 1999 prices) 2004–06 for Ten New Member States

| | *2004* | *2005* | *2006* |
|---|---|---|---|
| Heading 1 Agriculture: | 1,897 | 3,747 | 4,147 |
| – 1a CAP | 327 | 2,032 | 2,322 |
| – 1b Rural development | 1,570 | 1,715 | 1,825 |
| Heading 2 Structural actions: | 6,095 | 6,940 | 8,8812 |
| – Structural fund | 3,478 | 4,788 | 5,990 |
| – Cohesion fund | 2,617 | 2,152 | 2,822 |
| Heading 3 Internal policies and additional transitional expenditure: | 1,421<br>1,376 | 1,351 | |
| – Existing policies | 882 | 917 | 952 |
| – Transitional nuclear safety measures | 125 | 125 | 1256 |
| – Transitional institution-building measures | 200 | 120 | 60 |
| – Transitional Schengen measures | 286 | 286 | 286 |
| Heading 5 Administration | 501 | 558 | 612 |
| Total | 9,952 | 12,657 | 14,958 |

*Source:* Presidency Conclusions, Copenhagen European Council, 12–13 December 2002, Annex 1, p. 11.

food safety, animal welfare and occupational safety standards, and the introduction of a new farm auditing system and rural development measures improving production quality, food safety and animal welfare (the latter to cover the costs of the farm audit). The Parliament endorsed these objectives, but emphasized the importance of multi-functionality, adjusting to new social requirements, and the interests of poorer countries. The Commission produced an 'issues paper' on enlargement (in January) that ruled out the possibility of a 'two-speed' approach.

The Commission amended the rules covering the import of bananas into the Community (as part of the second of three stages for the management of tariff quotas agreed with the US and Ecuador in April 2001). Arrangements affecting the cereals market were altered in line with the agreements between the Community and Canada and the US. In line with the World Trade Organization's Doha agenda, the Community drew up proposals for a more market-oriented trading system.

*Fisheries*

The Commission continued work on reform of the common fisheries policy (CFP). In the wake of its March 2001 Green Paper – criticized by the European Parliament for its recommendations on fishing fleets and the consistency of the CFP with the Community's co-operation and development policy – the Commission presented its action programme and timetable in May. The underlying aim is to create a framework that ensures the sustainable development and economic viability of the sector, whilst also guaranteeing that individuals dependent on fishing enjoy a reasonable standard of living.

After lengthy and difficult discussions, the Council agreed a reform package (in December). The deal included the abolition of state aid for fleet renewal after 2004, recovery and management plans for key fish stocks, safe biological life, and increased premiums for the scrapping of vessels (in exchange for reductions in fishing effort). At the same meeting, the Council approved a Commission communication detailing future strategy for managing fisheries in the Mediterranean. On external aspects, the Commission presented a new partnership strategy for enhancing fisheries agreements with third countries based on concerns for sustainable fishing in the waters of partner countries (rather than merely access).

As regards conservation, the Commission drew up an action plan envisaging the integration of environmental considerations. The plan utilizes the precautionary principle and the 'polluter pays' principle, and establishes a system to monitor the integration of environmental concerns. In December, the Council passed a new framework governing the conservation and sustainable exploitation of fish stocks, based on the first of these principles. In September, the Commission presented a communication on the sustainable development of European aquaculture. The same month, the Council approved measures relating to deep-water fish. Earlier in the year, the Council had introduced mechanisms protecting the spawning grounds of cod stock in the Irish Sea, while in December the Commission proposed measures to replenish cod and hake, and to protect juvenile sea organisms in December.

Irregular fishing remained a concern. In May, the Commission advocated new measures implementing the plan endorsed by the UN Food and Agriculture Organization Council. The Commission observed that there had been an increase in the number of reported breaches, called on Member States to hasten the pursuit of such breaches and monitored compliance with total allowable catches (TACs). Twenty-four fisheries were closed and over-fishing infringements investigated. The Commission recommended measures to strengthen the system for monitoring fishing activities, including the use of satellite, and the establishment of uniform penalties. It also envisaged a new fishing effort scheme for the Atlantic.

The Council twice amended Regulation (EC) No. 2555/2001 to adjust certain TACs in the light of new scientific evaluations and extended Decision 97/413/EC on the restructuring of the Community fisheries sector until 31 December. The Community's fishing effort declined during the year and, in November, the Commission presented an action plan on the consequences of restructuring. Assistance measures were taken linking withdrawal with the introduction of new capacity, limiting public aid, and encouraging fishermen to retrain. In December, the Council made it possible for Member States to offer extra funds to owners for the break-up of vessels.

## V. Environmental Policy

The sixth environment action programme (EAP), adopted in July, established a ten-year framework for promoting sustainable development. The EAP incorporated a new approach to meeting environmental targets, drawing on the experience of previous programmes. Although the same objectives are retained (climate change, nature and biodiversity, environment and health, and natural resources and waste) fuller application is envisaged. In October, the Council stressed the importance of reinforcing the 'Cardiff strategy' and the promotion of sustainable development. It invited the Commission to conduct an annual review of the Cardiff process. In December, the Council adopted a report on the integration of environmental protection and sustainable development in the internal market's competition policy. The proposals on CFP reform and the mid-term review of the CAP were high points in the integration of environmental protection priorities into other Community policies. Environmental considerations were also incorporated in the BEPG.

On the international front, the Council approved the Kyoto protocol to the UN Framework on Climate Change (in April), committing the Community and Member States to reducing greenhouse gas emissions. It expressed regret at the refusal of the United States to sign the protocol and disappointment at Australia's non-ratification.

In December, the Commission reported that emissions in 2000 were 3.5 per cent lower than in 1990, although much progress still had to be made. There was a third report on the effectiveness of the Community's strategy for reducing carbon dioxide emissions from cars. The EU took a leading role in the World Summit on Sustainable Development, and signed up to its targets of reducing biodiversity loss by 2010, raising fish stocks to sustainable levels by 2005, and minimizing harmful effects arising from the production and use of chemicals by 2020. The Union further agreed to launch a ten-year work programme on sustainable consumption and production, and started two strategic partnerships for managing water and energy. It also announced the formation of a 'coalition of the willing' that would act together to increase the use of renewable energy sources, based on ambitious time frames and clear targets.

The EU also participated in the Sixth Conference of Parties to the Convention on Biological Diversity (in April), which agreed to reduce biodiversity loss by 2010, and the Seventh Conference of Parties to the Bonn Convention on the Conservation of Migratory Species of Wild Animal (in September). Other initiatives or measures included:

- a Commission communication explaining the simplification and improvement of environmental regulation;
- directives restricting the use of hazardous substances in electrical and electronic equipment and avoiding waste from these products;
- recommendations on integrated coastal zone management in Europe;
- a Commission report on the protection of waters from pollution by nitrates;
- proposals for the revision of the Bathing Water Directive;
- Commission communications outlining a strategy to conserve the marine environment and a plan for soil protection;
- the amending of forest protection regulations against pollution and fire;
- a Council resolution aiding the creation of networks between training centres active in civil protection;
- a joint programme on the prevention and limitation of risks from terrorism;

- a regulation incorporating the Rotterdam Convention on international trade in hazardous chemicals into EC rules;
- further proposals on the sustainable use of pesticides;
- the suggested inclusion of the Cartagena protocol on genetically modified organism (GMO) notification into EC legislation, followed by three decisions on GMOs by the Council;
- a directive on ozone in ambient air and the Commission's report assessing directives on air quality between 1997 and 1999;
- a directive reducing the emissions of gaseous pollutants by two or three wheeled vehicles;
- a common approach to avoiding and/or reducing the harmful effects of exposure to environmental noise;
- further preventative measures and the suggested introduction of a liability scheme covering damage caused to the environment.

## References

Commission of the European Communities (2003a) *General Report on the Activities of the European Union* (Luxembourg: OOPEC).

Commission of the European Communities (2003b) *Bulletin of the European Union 12-2002* (Luxembourg: OOPEC).

Presidency Conclusions, Copenhagen European Council, 12–13 December 2002

- a regulation incorporating the Rotterdam Convention on international trade in hazardous chemicals into EC rules;
- further proposals on the sustainable use of pesticides;
- the successful inclusion into the Cartagena protocol of genetically modified organisms (GMO) applications into EC legislation, followed by three decisions on GMOs by the Council;
- a directive on access to public information and the Commission's report assessing directives on air quality between 1997 and 1999;
- a directive to reduce the emissions of gaseous pollutants by two- or three-wheeled vehicles;
- a common approach to avoiding and/or reducing the harmful effects of exposure to environmental noise;
- further preventative measures and the suggested introduction of a liability scheme covering damage caused to the environment.

## References

Commission of the European Communities (2003) *General Report on the Activities of the European Union* (Luxembourg: OOPEC).
Commission of the European Communities (2003) *Bulletin of the European Union* 12-2002 (Luxembourg: OOPEC).
Presidency Conclusions, Copenhagen European Council, 12–13 December 2002.

JCMS 2003 Volume 41. Annual Review pp. 75–8

# The European Central Bank in 2002: Waiting for Recovery

MASSIMO BEBER
University of Cambridge

## Introduction

The year began for the European Central Bank (ECB) with the smooth introduction of the actual euro notes and coins; an operation as complex logistically, and as important symbolically, as it was marginal in substantive terms. After all, bank deposits (which make up 95 per cent of the euro area's money supply) had been converted some three years earlier.

There was no change in interest rates until early December, when half a percentage point cut brought the interest rate back to its 1999 low of 2.75 per cent. Figure 1 illustrates the ECB's policy stance: notwithstanding monetary

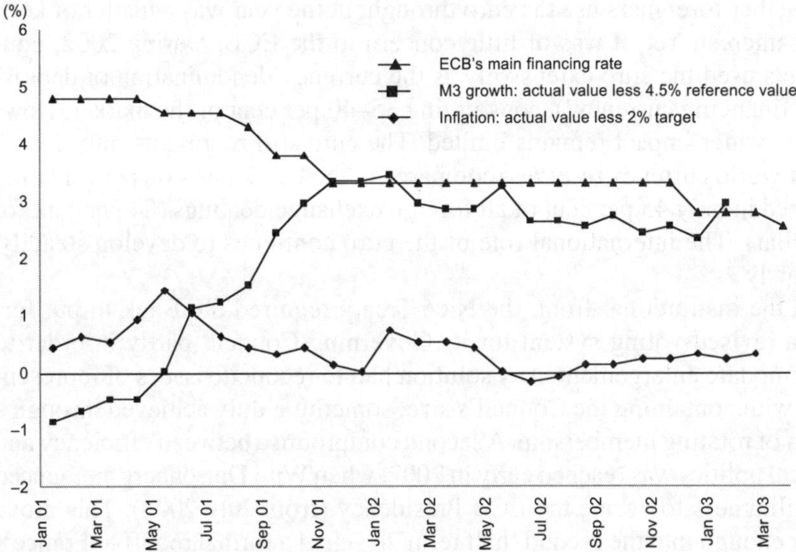


Figure 1: Interpreting Monetary Signals
*Source:* Author's calculations from ECB Monthly Bulletin, various issues.

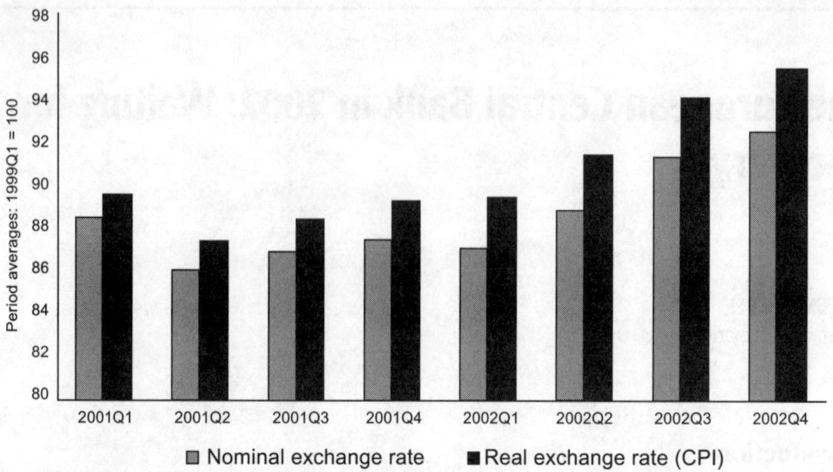


Figure 2: The Euro's Nominal and Real Exchange Rate
*Source: ECB Monthly Bulletin,* successive issues, Table 10.

growth being above its reference value (by as much as 50 per cent), inflation has stayed relatively close to target.

At the same time, the euro's exchange rate strengthened throughout 2002. The single currency's value at the end of 2002 was comparable to the stability of the European Currency Unit (ECU) in 1997–98. According to the Bank's own assessment, this was in line with established fundamentals (see Figure 2).

Whether foreigners use the euro throughout the year was a matter of keen public interest. Yet, it was of little concern to the ECB. During 2002, non-residents used the euro extensively as the currency denomination of debt issues ('financing currency'), constituting 35–40 per cent of the market. However, its wider impact remains limited. The euro still represents only 13 per cent of world currency reserves (compared to the US dollar's 68 per cent) and was used in only 43 per cent of all foreign exchange dealings (84 per cent for the dollar). The international role of the euro continues to develop steadily, but slowly.

On the institutional front, the Nice Treaty required the Bank to put forward a revised voting system for its Governing Council, partly in order to accommodate enlargement. Any solution had to reconcile issues of representation with containing the Council's size, something duly achieved through a system of rotating membership. A second compromise between efficiency and practical politics was reached early in 2002, when Wim Duisenberg announced his willingness to vacate the ECB Presidency (from July 2003). This move fell far enough into the second 'half term' to signal a formal rebuff to France's political designs for the Presidency, while still allowing the likely (French) successor a good run in the chair.

## I. Monetary Policy

Monetary policy aims at keeping total expenditure in step with changes in the economy's ability to produce goods and services, eschewing inflation ('too much money chasing too few goods') for price stability, which the ECB has translated into an inflation target of below 2 per cent. The main *direct* instrument at the Central Bank's disposal is now the interest rate (and interest rate policy) that provides liquidity to the commercial banks. However, the effectiveness of interest rate policy depends crucially on how the Bank's actions affect market expectations.

From the outset, the aim of the ECB has been to establish the credibility that will facilitate the smooth implementation of policy, where much of the work is done by the market's adjustment through the 'term structure of interest rates'. Such credibility rests on two pillars: first, the analysis of monetary aggregates which, from the beginning of the ECB's operation, has been equated with a reference value of 4.5 per cent for the yearly growth of 'broad money'; second, attention to everything else that is believed to matter (such as the state of bond, equity and housing markets, and productivity and wage trends, as well as the exchange rate). As Figure 1 indicates, the complementary nature of the two strands of analysis during 2002 continued to result in an acceptance of monetary overshooting, interpreted by the Bank primarily as investors' preference for liquidity in response to continuing political uncertainty and falling asset prices.

The ECB works on three assumptions: in the first place, its policy should be *exclusively* aimed at (and assessed against) inflation *over the medium term*; second, price stability is the sole, albeit rather crucial, contribution that a successful monetary policy can make to economic performance. Article 2 of the EU Treaty requires the Bank to support the Union's ultimate objectives of full employment, growth and equitable income distribution, yet, this is an aspect the ECB chooses not to preach about (unlike the Stability and Growth Pact). Third, deliberate deficits usually fail to stimulate the economy, and fiscal policy should therefore focus on reducing both taxes (to restore economic incentives) and deficits in order to 'make room' for the fiscal consequences of ageing national populations.

Nevertheless, the natural economic recovery expected by the Bank at the start of 2002 proved elusive. Independent output forecasts for 2003 and 2004 were repeatedly lowered. The job of a central banker was once compared to 'taking the punch bowl away just when the party is getting going'. Given this, the main policy issue for 2002 was deciding what the host should do when the party-goers do not come forward spontaneously to have their glasses filled – especially since there was also no co-host (in the form of last resort fiscal borrowing), or indeed a gate-crasher (such as greater demand for exports) to lead by example.

As Figure 3 shows, the 'music' of inflation may have been in tune. Yet, the euro area's economic party was a rather miserable affair in 2002. This prompted challenges to the Bank's rather conservative definition of price stability (lower than the Bank of England's), the scope of its formal remit (currently limited to price stability alone), as well as the nature of its links to Ecofin and to the Stability and Growth Pact. Indeed, the European Parliament developing (credible) discretion as regards demand management (see Fitoussi and Creel, 2002; Begg *et al.,* 2003; European Central Bank 2002a, b) will certainly be the main issue influencing the relationship between the Bank and other EU economic institutions, and ultimately between the ECB and the public it serves.

## References

Begg, I., Hodson D. and Maher I. (2003) 'Economic Policy Co-ordination in the European Union'. *National Institute Economic Review*, No. 183, pp. 66–77.

European Central Bank (2002a) *Testimony before the Committee on Economic and Financial Affairs of the European Parliament* (17 February).

European Central Bank (2002b) *The International Role of the Euro* (various issues).

Fitoussi, J.-P. and Creel, J. (2002) *How to Reform the European Central Bank* (London: Centre for European Reform).

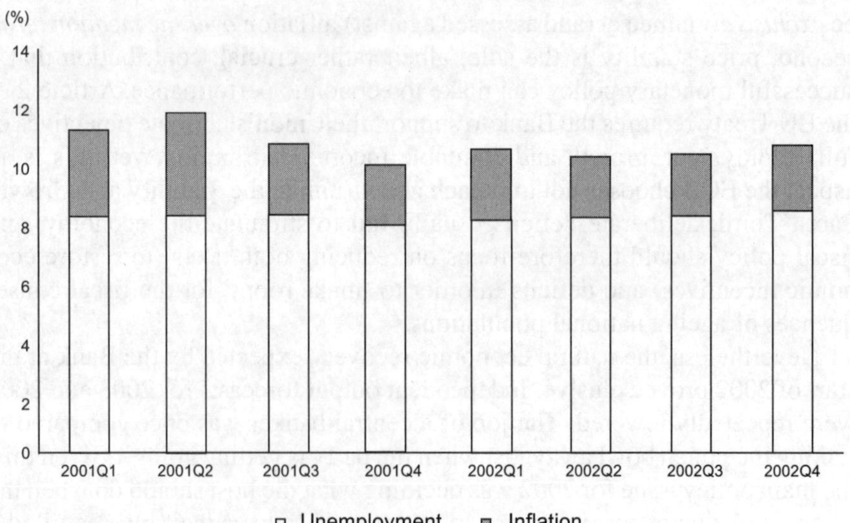


Figure 3: The Euro Area's Misery Index

*Source:* Calculated from ECB's *Monthly Bulletin*, various issues.

JCMS 2003 Volume 41. Annual Review. pp. 79–95

# Legal Developments

JO HUNT
Cardiff Law School, University of Wales

## Introduction

On 4 December 2002, key figures from political and judicial institutions from across Europe and beyond gathered in Luxembourg for a formal, ceremonial sitting of the European Court of Justice (ECJ). Those present at the ceremony, who included their Royal Highnesses the Grand-Duke and Grand-Duchess of Luxembourg, the Presidents of the European Community institutions, senior judges from international courts from across the world, and judges from the constitutional and supreme courts of the current and prospective Member States, had come together to mark the 50th anniversary of the European Court of Justice. The ECJ was established in 1952 as the Court of the European Coal and Steel Community, becoming the Court for the European (Economic) Community with the coming into force of the 1957 Treaty of Rome.

According to the now familiar, yet remarkable story, over the course of its 50-year history, the ECJ has played a vital role in the process of European integration. That story is one of how the ECJ was involved in fundamentally transforming the nature of the bargain struck between the Member States: from an interstate organization founded on the basis of an international treaty, to a supranational legal order constructed upon a *constitutional* framework.[1] As the current President of the ECJ reflected in his address on the occasion of the ECJ's anniversary, the language of 'constitutionalism' was adopted by the Court during its very earliest incarnation when, in 1956, it described its review of the legality of ECSC secondary legislation, as a 'review of constitu-

[1] Explanations for the Court's motivations, and for the response of other actors in the process of course differ greatly, not only between, but also within disciplines. For a recent review (in the context of a theory of judicial politics which, from a 'legal' perspective, underestimates the force and power of the rule of law) see Carrubba, C.J. (2003) 'The European Court of Justice, Democracy and Enlargement'. *European Union Politics,* Vol. 4, p. 75.

tionality'.[2] The process of the 'constitutionalization' of the EEC Treaty order meanwhile progressed through the development of doctrines that created a *de facto* federal legal order. This order began with the Court's early, crucial findings of the supreme and directly effective nature of Community law, enabling it thereby to 'trump' conflicting national law, and create rights which could (under certain circumstances) be relied on directly before national courts, in the face of national intransigence or incompetence in legal transposition of Community law measures.

In turn, the Court was to identify a set of overarching general principles, including fundamental human rights, which could operate as legally enforceable constraints on exercise of power by the EU institutions, and by Member States in the context of their application of EC law. Added to this has been the Court's role in determining the extent of the EU's internal and external competencies, as well as its creation of further mechanisms to ensure that Member States honour their commitments under EC law, such as the construction of a right to damages for individuals in the event of sufficient serious breaches of EC law by the Member States; in short, one might suggest, its self-positioning as a supreme constitutional court for Europe.[3]

In 2002, 16 years after the Court first openly referred to the EC Treaty as the 'basic constitutional charter' of the Community,[4] the Convention on the Future of Europe began working towards a document which will formally carry the title of the 'Constitution'. The process of constitutionalization is providing a critical opportunity for both pro and anti-integrationists (and those somewhere in between) to present their model for the future of Europe. It is also necessarily involving attempts to formalize and concretize certain constitutional doctrines which formerly existed in the Court's jurisprudence (and 'received' by the national courts), and which had never, as such, been held up to a binary accept/reject determination on the part of Member State governments.

The Court is not itself directly represented in the Convention framework, though it has provided assistance to the working groups which met, listened and reported over the course of 2002, and certain of its members have been involved in presenting evidence (in a personal capacity) to the groups.[5] None

[2] G.C. Rodriguez Iglesias, President of the Court of Justice of the European Communities, Speech of 4 December 2002, available via the ECJ's home page at «http://www.curia.eu.int». All judgments cited in this review are also available via the curia site, as is the ECJ's own *Annual Report* for 2002.

[3] The standard works in this area include: Mancini, G.F. (1989) 'The Making of a Constitution for Europe'. *Common Market Law Review,* Vol. 26, p. 595; Weiler, J.H.H. (1991) 'The Transformation of Europe'. *Yale Law Journal*. Vol. 100, p. 2403; Dehousse, R. (1998) *The European Court of Justice: The Politics of Judicial Integration* (Basingstoke: Macmillan); and Slaughter, A-M., Stone Sweet, A. and Weiler, J.H.H. (eds) (1998) *The European Courts and National Courts: Doctrine and Jurisprudence* (Oxford: Hart).

[4] Case 294/83, *Parti Ecologiste 'Les Verts'* v. *Parliament* [1986] ECR 1339, at 1365.

[5] See, e.g., the submission by Advocate General Jacobs to the Working Group on the Charter, below at n. 20.

of these groups has been devoted exclusively to considering the future role of the Court, though issues relating to the Court and the legal order were on the agendas of a number of groups. The simplification of legislative instruments and procedures has been proposed, and (conditional) support for the inclusion in the Constitution of the increasingly prevalent, extra-legal technique of the open method of co-ordination (OMC) has been proposed.[6] Perhaps one would have expected to see more comprehensive consideration of the future role of the ECJ in the *EU* legal order, and possibly of whether its limited role outside the Community pillar will be developed particularly if, as is proposed, the formal, separate pillar structure is to be replaced by a more integrated single pillar approach.[7]

Whilst the Court may not have been centre stage in the Convention process in 2002, many of the crucial issues being addressed by the working groups over the year were at the same time 'live' before the European Court of Justice. Not least, among these were questions about the proper limits of the competencies of the EU, both internally and on the international stage; and about the place of human rights in the EU order, and the legal force of the EU Charter of Fundamental Rights.

This review of legal developments in 2002 will concentrate on the work of the ECJ, and of its junior partner institution, the Court of First Instance (CFI), highlighting a range of cases selected for their legal and political significance, with a concentration on constitutional legal issues. Where relevant, linkages are made with the rather more high-profile constitutional debates occurring away from the Courts.

## I. Fundamental Rights and General Principles

The issue of whether the EU Charter of Fundamental Rights should be inserted into a formal constitutional document was under consideration by one of the 11 Convention working groups in 2002. By a clear majority, the group recommended both the Charter's insertion, and its recognition as legally binding on EU institutions and Member States when implementing EU law. At present, the Charter, solemnly proclaimed in December 2000 is, in itself, without binding legal force, though certain elements of its provisions (but by no

[6] Working Group IX, Simplification, Final Report CONV424/02, 29 November 2002. See further on the relationship between 'law' and governance techniques such as the OMC, Scott, J. and Trubek, D. (2002) 'Mind the Gap: Law and New Approaches to Governance in the EU'. *European Law Journal,* Vol. 8, p. 1.

[7] In this respect, the absorption of the second, CFSP, pillar clearly lags behind the juridification of the third pillar. The role of law in the latter was discussed by the Working Group IX, Simplification, Final Report CONV424/02, 29 November 2002. The CFSP was not considered in 2002. Rather belatedly, a 'discussion circle' on the Court was established in February 2003, CONV 543/03, 7 February 2003. Whilst the ECJ's role in the area of CFSP was not formally placed on its agenda, the circle is reported as having turned its attention to this issue.

means all) have previously been recognized and enforced by the ECJ as part of an overarching set of general principles of law. Almost immediately following its proclamation, litigants and Advocates General began pleading the terms of the Charter before the Courts.

Eventually, in January 2002, a response came from the CFI. It referred to Articles 41(1) and 47 of the Charter (the right to have affairs handled impartially, fairly and within a reasonable time, and the right to an effective remedy before a tribunal where rights are infringed) in the context of an action brought by a mobile telecommunications firm, challenging the Commission's alleged inaction as regards the company's competition law complaint against the Austrian government.[8] The Commission challenged both the admissibility and the substance of the action. Referring to the Charter rights (which are also, it said, recognized in the state's constitutional traditions), the CFI found that action *could* be brought by individuals (the relevant article, 86(3) having been silent on this point), though found against the applicant on the merits of the case. Over the course of the year, two further references to the Charter were made by the CFI, in *Jégo-Quéré*[9] and in *Tideland*.[10]

Before the ECJ, meanwhile, the persistent references to the Charter being made in the submissions of Advocates General[11] were apparently having a more limited impact. In December, however, something of a minor breakthrough occurred in the Court's judgment regarding British American Tobacco's challenge to the legality of the Tobacco Control Directive.[12] The judgment, handed down by the Full Court almost exactly two years since the Charter's proclamation, marks the first reference to the Charter in a judgment of the ECJ. This reference is, however, found in the part of the judgment dealing with the observations of the parties,[13] rather than in the part where the ECJ presents its own findings. The ECJ reports the applicant's submission that his right to property is a fundamental human right, protected by Article 17 EU Charter. In the ECJ's own findings, this right is instead described, without reference to the Charter, as one of the general principles of EU law.[14] The ECJ's continued aversion to using the Charter may continue until such a time that the Charter is formally granted legally binding status in a new Constitu-

[8] T-54/99 *max.mobil Telekommunikation Service* v. *Commission* [2002] ECR II-313.

[9] Case T-177/01 *Jégo-Quéré et Cie SA* v. *Commission* [2002] ECR II-2365.

[10] Case T–211/02 *Tideland Signal Ltd* v. Commission [2002] ECR II-378. This case also saw the use of the CFI's accelerated procedure, which was used for the first time in Joined Cases T-195/01 and T-207/01 *Gibraltar* v. *Commission* [2002] ECR II-2309. The procedure enabled the Tideland case to be dealt with in only 11 weeks, whilst the average length of proceedings is around 20 months.

[11] Of the eight Advocates General, at least five of them (Jacobs, Geelhoed, Ruiz-Jarabo Colomer, Alber and Stix-Hackl) made reference to the Charter in their opinions in the course of 2002.

[12] Case C-491/01, *The Queen* v. *Secretary of State for Health, ex parte British American Tobacco Investments) Ltd and Imperial Tobacco Ltd*, considered further below.

[13] At para. 144.

[14] At para 149, where the ECJ further states that the right is qualified by its 'social function'.

tion. That said, the ECJ may come to use the Charter without waiting for the 'assent' of the Member State governments, and its *BAT* judgment may be one early step in an incremental process of drawing the Charter more fully into its tool kit.

Whilst references to the EU Charter have thus been few and far between, much greater use was being made of the European Convention of Human Rights (ECHR), to which all Member States (but not the Community itself) are, independently, contracting parties. The ECHR, which operates under the auspices of the Council of Europe (and which is not a creature of the European Union) was drawn upon in a number of notable decisions, particularly in the area of free movement of persons and citizenship, to be considered below. The issue of accession by the Community/Union[15] to the ECHR, previously ruled out by the ECJ in its 1996 opinion on the grounds of lack of Community competence,[16] was re-opened by the Convention on the Future of Europe. Although the ECJ routinely refers to the rights contained in the Convention in its judgments, considering them to constitute general principles of law by which the EU is bound, accession by the Union to the ECHR would open up the possibility of the review of the actions of the EU institutions by a body outside the EU framework, the European Court of Human Rights.

This, for some, has presented a stumbling block to accepting the idea of accession. However, the relevant working group[17] declared its support for the inclusion of an enabling legal basis in the new Constitution which would grant the Union competence to accede. According to the working group, accession is considered necessary for the Union's credibility. Acceptance of the jurisdiction of the ECHR would also counter the potential for the emergence of two different, possibly conflicting sets of 'European' Courts' human rights jurisprudence, and would contribute to a perception of a greater coherence between the EU and the 'larger Europe'. The recommendations of the working party on human rights have been incorporated into the draft Constitution.

## II. Linking the Legal Orders: The Article 234 Procedure

Central to the success of the process of legal integration has been the relationship between the Court of Justice and the national courts. The latter's readiness to refer questions regarding the meaning of EC law to the ECJ through

[15] The issue of the granting separate legal personality to the *Union* (to replace those held currently by the Community and Euratom alone) and thus, for example, enabling it to be recognized as a separate legal actor on the international stage, has been advocated by Working Group III, on Legal Personality, see Final Report CONV 305/02, 1 October 2002.

[16] Opinion 2/94 [1996] ECR I-1759.

[17] Working Group II, Charter/ECHR, see Final Report CONV 354/02, 22 October 2002.

the Article 234 procedure has provided the ECJ with the opportunity to hand down judgments containing both apparently technical, mundane guidance, as well as constitutionally significant principles. In turn the national courts, charged with applying the law, have received, and, for the most part, respected the ECJ's responses, and the assumption has developed that the answers given to the referring court in a particular case set a precedent that *all* national courts are to follow.

In this way, the courts are involved in an ongoing, dynamic process of developing the law. The ECJ has itself been heavily involved in determining the mechanics of the operation of Article 234, 'colouring in' the text and settling questions as to which bodies may refer to it, and introducing guidelines as to when a reference is, or is not expected. In *Lyckeskog*,[18] the ECJ explained what is meant by the term 'a court against whose decision there is no judicial remedy in national law'. Such courts, according to Article 234 are under an obligation to refer questions to the ECJ about the meaning of the EU law provisions relevant to the case before them. But what of the court from which there is the possibility of appeal only on condition that a declaration of admissibility is made by the higher court? It was submitted that, under such conditions, the lower court should be considered as being under an obligation to refer, as requirement of a declaration of admissibility (and the prospect of it not being granted) constituted a potential obstacle to ensuring the uniform interpretation of Community law. The ECJ did not agree. The requirement of a prior declaration of admissibility by the supreme court was not such as to deprive the parties of a judicial remedy. The ECJ's response appears a logical one and also, given the heavy case load it is confronted with each year, an entirely pragmatic one. Requiring courts such as that referring here to submit requests for references could clearly increase the number of cases coming before it each year.

Also worthy of note this year is the case of *Arsenal* v. *Reed*.[19] The case is a signal reminder of formal limits of the ECJ's role in the Article 234 process, and of the difficulties in drawing a strict line between 'interpreting' and 'applying' the law – the former properly the task of the ECJ, the latter that of the national judge. The case concerned an action seeking to prevent a street trader from selling unauthorized merchandise bearing Arsenal FC trademarks. The national court wanted guidance as to whether a lack of confusion amongst purchasers as to the origin of the merchandise could act as a defence for the vendor. On a 234 reference, the ECJ held that trademark registrations are enforceable against unauthorized use, where the use of that trademarked symbol or logo affects the *function* of the trademark.

[18] Case 99/00 [2002] ECR I-4839.
[19] Case C-206/01, 12 November 2002.

It is clear from the ECJ's judgment that it considered that Mr Reed's use of the Arsenal badge on his merchandise *could* create confusion as to the origin of those products, that is, a belief that they were the genuine article (if not amongst immediate purchasers, then those encountering the products after they had left the stall). Thus, the function of the trademark would be breached, and, according to the ECJ, in such a case, the trademark proprietor could rely on the relevant EC law provisions to prevent the unauthorized use of the trademark. When the judgment was returned to the English High Court, however, the case was settled in favour of Mr Reed, the vendor.[20] The national court declared that it was under no obligation to apply the result reached by the ECJ, as the ECJ has made incorrect findings of fact (that there could be confusion as to origin) upon which it based its judgment.

Was this an incorrect finding of facts by the ECJ, or a different, and legitimate reading of the facts? Whichever, it is undoubtedly true that the ECJ often does 'apply' the law to the facts of the case before it, providing a very clear model for action for the national court. The 'rebellion' in Reed provides a challenge to this rather more flexible approach (and more hierarchical relationship between the courts) that the ECJ has sought to establish. Such cases are, we presume, exceptional, though there remains little in the way of systematic research on the reaction of national courts to bear this out.

## III. Access to Justice

In a note submitted to the Working Group on the Charter/ECHR in September 2002, Advocate General Jacobs expressed the view that, even if the proposed inclusion of the Charter, and accession to the ECHR went ahead, 'the fundamental rights so recognised or referred to, risk remaining an empty shell if there is no system of judicial remedies which guarantees the effective protection of those rights'.[21] And, according to the Advocate General, the EU legal system fails to provide such an effective protection as a result of the overly restrictive rules governing the circumstances in which individual applicants can come before the EU courts to challenge the legality of the Community legislation.

The Advocate General had made this argument already in 2002, this time in a professional capacity, in the case of *Unión des Pequeños Agricultores (UPA)*.[22] The *UPA* case presented the ECJ with the opportunity to revisit and, many hoped, to revise the restrictive rules on standing for applicants who, unless having the 'privileged' standing status of an EU institution or a Mem-

[20] *Arsenal* v. *Reed* (No. 2) [2003] All ER 137.
[21] Working Group II, Working Document 20, 'Le système des voies de recours judiciaries', 27 September 2002.
[22] Case C-50/00 P *UPA* v. *Council* [2002] ECR I-6677.

ber State, have to show *direct and individual concern*[23] in the measure which they are seeking to challenge. And, as developed by the ECJ and CFI (which is the court which first hears all 'non-privileged' applicants, with the possibility of a referral to the ECJ), this test is one which, in relation to general legislative measures, it is all but impossible for applicants to pass. In essence, the Courts' existing test (requiring, as a minimum, that the applicant is one of a closed class of those affected by the measure), by and large operated so as to allow challenges to narrowly directed, administrative-type decisions only.

The availability of other routes before the Court, such as through an Article 234 reference from a national court are, according to the AG, too unpredictable to be regarded as acceptable, adequate alternatives: there is not always the possibility of a reference, nor can a court be forced to refer. As a result, those whose rights are infringed by unlawful legislation could find themselves denied an effective remedy – which, according to the AG in *UPA,* would itself be in contravention of Article 47 of the EU Charter. On that basis, AG Jacobs recommended that the existing test should be replaced by one which would allow direct challenges wherever, by reason of the applicant's particular circumstances, the measure has, or is liable to have, a *substantial adverse impact* on their interests.

In the period between the delivery of the AG's opinion and the formal judgment of the ECJ, the CFI handed down the *Jégo-Quéré* judgment.[24] The judgment is clearly heavily influenced by the AG's reasoning in *UPA*, particularly on the issue of the possibility of infringement of the right to effective judicial protection and remedies. Making explicit reference to the 2000 EU Charter, the CFI itself presented a revised, liberalized test for standing, granting it wherever a measure restricts an applicant's rights or imposes obligations on him. This liberalization of the standing rules was not, however, to be continued by the ECJ. In the judgment subsequently handed down in *UPA,* the ECJ opted not to amend the existing test, either in the terms proposed by the AG or, indeed, in line with the CFI's test in *Jégo-Quéré.* Instead, the ECJ settled for the *status quo*, submitting that any revision of the standing rules should be undertaken not by the Court, but by the Member States in the context of a treaty amendment. Apparently chastened, the CFI, in subsequent cases where the issue of standing has been in question, made no direct reference to its decision in *Jégo-Quéré.*

Thus, the issue has appeared on the Convention's agenda. Whilst the weight of academic opinion[25] has tended towards favouring a liberalization of the

[23] Article 230(4) EC Treaty.
[24] Supra n.9.
[25] See the citations in Granger, M.P. (2003) 'Towards a Liberalisation of Standing Conditions for Individuals'. *Modern Law Review,* Vol. 66, p. 124.

standing rules so as to enable individuals' easier access before the Courts to challenge the lawfulness of both legislative and administrative measures, it would be a mistake to assume that there is unqualified support for this development across the EU. Member State traditions in relation to judicial review are quite different. As one current Judge of the European Court observed when speaking in a personal capacity, whilst challenges to the administrative acts of the executive are generally permitted across the Member States, the idea of allowing for the annulment of general legislative measures passed in accordance with democratic procedures is, according to some legal traditions, 'almost revolting'.

Clarification of the rules, with or without the liberalization for challenges to general legislative measures, is undoubtedly needed. The recommendations by the Simplification Working Group[26] to introduce into the Charter a new typology of legal instruments which, *inter alia,* makes a formal distinction between general legislative acts and administrative acts, could assist in the formulation of a clear and differentiated approach, should that be the route preferred by the majority of states.

## IV. Competence and Powers

### *Internal Competence*

The Union is based on the principle of attributed competencies: it may only exercise those powers which have been transferred to it by the Member States. Of course, over the years, there have been examples of 'competence creep', where the Community may have exercised powers which appear not to have been formally and explicitly attributed to it. The ECJ, through its policing role of determining whether a measure is properly inside Community competence, has contributed to fixing the limits of competence, though famously, of course, it was admonished by the German constitutional court for purporting to have the competence to determine the limits of Community competence.[27]

The Final Report of the Working Group on Complementary Competencies[28] recommended a clearer categorization of, and demarcation between, the types of competencies attributed to the Union. It has proposed a three-fold categorization of competencies, ranging from 'exclusive' Union competence, which precludes Member States from acting individually unless they are empowered by the Union; through 'shared', or concurrent competence, where Union activity (exercised in accordance with principles of subsidiarity and proportionality) will pre-empt national measures; to complementary, or sup-

[26] Working Group IX, Simplification, Final Report CONV424/02, 29 November 2002.
[27] *Maastricht (Brunner* v. *The European Union Treaty)* [1994] CMLR, Vol. 1, p. 57.
[28] Working Group V, Final Report CONV 375/1/02 REV 1, 4 November 2002.

porting areas, in which the EU has no power to introduce any harmonizing legislation. Further, controversial work is being undertaken within policy areas allocated to these categories. In addition, proposals have been made to tighten up the conditions for the use of the general 'catch-all' residual legal base, 308 EC Treaty, as one means of averting competence creep. A new *ex ante* power of oversight by national parliaments is also foreseen, allowing them to scrutinize proposals for their compliance with the principle of subsidiarity and, where sufficient concern is demonstrated, request the Commission to go further to justify its measure, or indeed, revise it.

Whether a clearer demarcation of the nature and scope of competencies will reduce the incidence of actions alleging a transgression of the limits of competence (or whether it makes them any easier for the ECJ to resolve) remains to be seen. Given recent experiences, it is to be doubted. In 2002, the ECJ was again faced with the task of adjudicating on the lawfulness of a measure which, according to its opponents, extended the community's legislative competence into an area from which it is explicitly excluded by the Treaty – the harmonization of national measures protecting human health. A case brought on these grounds resulted in the ECJ overturning the Tobacco Advertising Directive in 2000.[29]

Given the ECJ's findings in that case, the applicants seeking to challenge the lawfulness of the Tobacco Control Directive[30] must have been optimistic about their chances of success. Three challenges were launched against this directive, which imposes various controls on the sale, manufacture and presentation of tobacco products by the Member States (such as maximum limits for tar, nicotine and carbon monoxide, health warnings, and the banning of 'misleading' terms such as 'mild' and 'low tar'). Two challenges were brought directly under Article 230, and both of those failed on issues of admissibility – the German government's being rejected as being out of time,[31] the other by Japan Tobacco, failing before the CFI as the applicant could not show the requisite direct and individual concern.[32] The third challenge, *BAT*,[33] was brought before the ECJ on a reference from the UK court. Significantly, the reference was deemed admissible, even though the transposition date for the directive had not yet passed, and the national implementing legislation had not yet been adopted. The readiness of the ECJ to accept this reference in such circumstances (in the face of Commission opposition) is perhaps an example of the ECJ seeking to counter AG Jacob's criticisms in *UPA* about the

[29] Case C-376/98 *Germany* v. *Parliament and Council* [2000] ECR I-2247.
[30] Directive 2001/37/EC, (*OJ* 2001 L 194, p. 26).
[31] Case C-406/01 *Germany* v. *Parliament and Council* [2002] ECR I-4561.
[32] Case T-223/01 *Japan Tobacco* v. *Council and Parliament* [2002] ECR II-3259.
[33] Case C-491/01, *The Queen* v. *Secretary of State for Health, ex parte British American Tobacco Investments) Ltd and Imperial Tobacco Ltd,* 10 December 2002.

inadequacy of the Article 234 route as a meaningful complement and alternative to the restrictive Article 230 route.

Having succeeded in getting before the ECJ, the applicant's seven grounds for annulment of the directive could then be considered. Amongst these were breaches of the principles of subsidiarity, proportionality, the duty to give reasons, the fundamental right to property and, of course, the legal base issue – that the base used to introduce the measure (primarily Article 95 EC Treaty on the internal market) was inappropriate and inadequate. Following the ruling in *Tobacco Advertising*, the crucial tests would be whether the directive was designed primarily to facilitate the free movement of tobacco products throughout the EU, and whether it would indeed have a positive effect on interstate trade. Eight of the Member States presenting observations argued that Article 95 had been correctly used in this case. The ECJ agreed. The directive, it ruled, was indeed intended, and had the objective of facilitating the free movement of tobacco products. The standards it set would, for example, prevent the emergence of different national rules which *could* emerge if Member States were individually (in response to the dangers to health posed by tobacco) to fix permissible levels of carbon monoxide. A provision in the directive, stating that all products complying with the requirements would be entitled to free movement throughout the EU (such a clause being missing from the Advertising Directive) was highlighted as further confirmation of the directive's role in facilitating free movement.

As to the protection of health, the fact that it was a 'decisive factor in the choices to be made' was not enough to remove the measure from the lawful ambit of Article 95. Arguably, one could read the ECJ's ruling in this case as applying quite loosely the test it set out in the *Advertising* case – where 'abstract risks' of obstacles to free movement emerging were insufficient to justify recourse to Article 95. The difficulties the directive is overcoming here are, in some instances, hypothetical, future obstacles. Indeed, the directive may itself create obstacles, through the requirements of written health warnings on packs. Unless such warnings are to be presented on all packs in all of the Community languages, then these labelling requirements will segment the European market along linguistic lines. This issue was not addressed by the ECJ. In short, this case demonstrates that even apparently demarcated boundary lines can be fuzzy, and a constitutional allocation of competencies is unlikely to bring a final settlement of power between the constituent units of the Union.

### *External Competence*

With its 'open skies' actions, the Commission was seeking to establish recognition of an exclusive competence for the EU to negotiate air service agreements with third countries. The actions were brought against eight Member States that had, individually and independently, concluded bilateral agreements with the US, governing reciprocal access and landing rights.[34] The Commission argued that the Member States had thereby infringed the external competence of the EU, as their powers to conclude such agreements should properly be seen as having been transferred wholly to the EU, to be exercised by the Commission on behalf of the Union. Whilst this exclusive competence was not explicitly set out in the Treaty, the Commission suggested that it was necessary to recognize it in order to attain the objectives of the Treaty, because the introduction of autonomous rules by Member States would lead to distortions of competition, discrimination and disturbance of the EU market.

The ECJ did not accept that the Community had exclusive competence. Whilst clauses in the agreements which favoured the individual contracting state's national carriers were discriminatory, this could be countered through an application of the free movement principles (and the rules were found to breach Article 43 on freedom of establishment), rather than requiring the establishment of exclusive EU competence. The area is one of concurrent competence in which, in the absence of EU legislation, the Member States remained free to act autonomously. However, where the EU had already exercised its shared competence, it thereby occupied the field, pre-empting and prohibiting Member State action in that area. Finding that the EU had legislated in respect of fare setting, and computer reservations, these elements of the Member State agreements were also, in principle wrongfully concluded. The Commission is reported as remaining committed to establishing exclusive competence in this area, something which, for the past decade, it has been trying to secure through political negotiation and, as here, through judicial means.

## V. Development of Substantive Law

### *Free Movement of People and Citizenship Rights*

In 2002, the ECJ developed further its jurisprudence on EU citizenship, bringing within its protective scope wider categories of people who are thus able to lay claim to rights of non-discrimination. In *D'Hoop*,[35] a returning Belgian student, schooled in France, was able to rely on her status as an EU citizen to claim an allowance from the Belgian government which, under national law,

[34] The actions were brought against the UK, Germany, Sweden, Denmark, Finland, Austria, Belgium and Luxembourg, and all judgments were handed down on 5 November 2002 (see, e.g., Case 467/98 *Commission* v. *Denmark*.

[35] Case C-224/98, *D'Hoop* v. *ONEM* [2002] ECR I-6191.

was payable only to young people who had completed their schooling in Belgium. The conventional understanding of to whom, and in what circumstances, the protection of non-discrimination in relation to state benefits is applicable under EC law is under radical transformation.[36] No longer is it limited to those moving to another Member State and exercising their economic free movement rights (most obviously workers and their families). Ms D'Hoop's education in France was enough for the ECJ to bring her within the personal scope of the citizenship provisions, from which it drew the conclusion that her home state should not treat her less favourably than it did Belgian nationals who had not exercised their free movement rights.

In *Baumbast*[37], the ECJ further held that the citizenship provisions, which grant to all with Member State nationality the right to reside in another EU country, are directly effective. Whilst the ECJ accepted that the right to reside is subject to various conditions laid down in primary and secondary legislation, it gave a very robust, citizen-friendly re-reading of these conditions. The limitations on residence rights for the non-economically active set out in secondary legislation (for example, that the individual should have their own sufficient financial resources, and not be an unreasonable burden on the state) were read very narrowly. Indeed, the ECJ declared that non-fulfilment of such conditions would not be fatal to the citizen's right to remain – the Member State's response must be proportionate.

*Baumbast,* too, is authority for the principle that non-EU citizens may obtain, as a matter of EC law, a right of residence in a Member State where that right is derived from their children's right to be educated there. And that right is itself open to all children, whether EU citizens or not, where at least one of their parents has been an EU national exercising their rights to free movement, and regardless of whether that parent is still in the same Member State. *Baumbast* would certainly appear to be pushing the outer limits of the personal and material scope of EC law. It is also noteworthy for the role that the discourse of fundamental human rights played in this expansive reading of the law, and specifically for the significance accorded to the right for the respect for family life, contained in Article 8 ECHR. This Article was drawn upon again in the case of *Carpenter*,[38] which saw the ECJ rule that the Philippine-national wife of a UK national, was able to rely on EC law to obtain a right of residence in the UK (in the face of a deportation order). The right was derived from her husband's status as the provider of cross-border services (necessary to make this an EC law issue, rather than simply a national one).

[36] See also C-184/99, *Grzelczyk* [2001] ECR I-6193.
[37] Case C-413/99 *Baumbast and R* [2002] ECR I-7091.
[38] Case C-60/00, *Carpenter* v. *Sec State for Home Department* [2002] ECR I-6279.

Significantly, the ECJ was prepared to accept that very little, if any, physical movement from the home state was necessary to activate the protection of EC law – services could be provided for clients in other states without Mr Carpenter leaving the UK. Amidst some rather unconvincing reasoning that the deportation decision could constitute an obstacle to Mr Carpenter's right to exercise his fundamental freedoms, the ECJ presents a far more coherent, convincing justification, though one that is removed from what have been the traditional concerns (and ambit) of EC law: that the decision to deport constitutes an interference of the right to respect for family life as set out in Article 8 ECHR.

### *Free Movement: Establishment and Capital*

In a set of cases brought by the Commission against France, Portugal and Belgium,[39] the ECJ examined the lawfulness of the practice by the state of taking 'golden shares' in privatized industries (for example, the gas and petroleum industries). Golden shares grant to their holders special rights and powers, enabling the state to retain a degree of influence in privatized corporations beyond their financial stake. In the cases under consideration, justifications advanced by the states for granting themselves such shares included the need to safeguard supplies of petroleum in the event of a crisis.

The ECJ found that, although such arrangements impacted on national and non-national investors alike, they fell within the scope of the free movement of capital and establishment provisions, as they were liable to impede the acquisition of shares in undertakings, and dissuade investors from investing in the capital of those undertakings. As non-discriminatory hindrances, the arrangements could, in principle, be justified if they pursued a legitimate general interest objective and were proportionate, inasmuch as the same objective could not be attained by less restrictive measures. Whilst the Belgian system was deemed lawful, the Portuguese rules were found against, as they sought to further economic objectives (which can never serve as justification for obstacles to free movement), and the French rules, whilst pursuing a legitimate objective, were disproportionate as they granted the state too wide a discretionary power in relation to its exercise of its golden share rights.

### *Competition*

The CFI's use of the Charter in respect of the competition law case of *max.mobil* has already been mentioned.[40] Mention must also be made of the three merger

[39] Cases C-367/98, *Commission* v. *Portugal*; C-483/99 [2002] ECR I -4731, *Commission* v. *France* [2002] ECR I-4781, and C-503/99, *Commission* v. *Belgium* [2002] ECR. I-4809.
[40] Supra n. 8.

cases[41] which saw the CFI dramatically flexing its muscles, refusing to accept the factual assessments of collective dominance on which the Commission had based its decisions to prohibit mergers. The cases demonstrate a more robust and rigorous approach by the CFI to the Commission. In response, the latter has issued a package of measures, including a proposal for a new merger regulation, and draft 'best practice' guidelines,[42] as it seeks to rebuild some of the confidence lost in it through the cases, which present a damaging critique of the Commission's conduct.

Turning to the ECJ, in *Wouters,*[43] the Court ruled that, despite its anti-competitive effects, the Dutch Bar Council's prohibition on multidisciplinary partnerships (i.e. integrated legal and accountancy partnerships) was lawful. In arriving at this result, the ECJ appears to advance a reading of Article 81 which allows for the public interest to be taken into account when assessing whether or not that Article has been breached. In the case of the Dutch ban, the objective of the legislation (to ensure the integrity, independence and proper practice of the legal profession), was such as to justify the anti-competitive effects. The novelty with *Wouters* is that it could appear to have introduced a US-style 'rule of reason' in the operation of Article 81, a situation which traditionally has been formally rejected.

### *Environment*

In *Concordia Bus Finland*,[44] the ECJ was asked whether environmental criteria could be taken into account when authorities are at the stage of *awarding* contracts to the 'economically most advantageous' tender, under the public procurement rules. The ECJ ruled that environmental concerns (whilst 'secondary' to economic criteria) could be taken into account at the award stage. This is provided such criteria are linked to the subject matter of the contract, do not confer an unrestricted freedom of choice on the authority, are expressly mentioned in the contract documents or the tender notice, and comply with all the fundamental principles of Community law, in particular the principle of non-discrimination. In *Concordia*, the ECJ's advice would appear to suggest that it was thereby lawful for the public body to take into consideration ecological criteria such as the level of nitrogen oxide emissions or the noise level of the buses in its award decision. The fact that the awarding body's own transport undertaking was one of the few undertakings able to offer a bus fleet satisfying those criteria does not necessarily breach the principle of equal treatment, the ECJ further ruled.

[41] Case T-342/99, *Airtours* [2002] ECR II-2585; Cases T-310/01 and T-77/02, *Schneider* [2002] ECR II-4071; Cases T-5/02 and T-80/02 *Tetra Laval* [2002] ECR II-4381.
[42] See Commission Press Release IP/02/1856, 11 December 2002.
[43] Case C-309/99, *Wouters et al.* [2002] ECR I-1577.
[44] Case 513/99 [2002] ECR I-7213.

In *Alpharma* and *Pfizer,* [45] the CFI explored the application of the precautionary principle. Although Community institutions may take protective measures without having to wait until the reality and seriousness of the risk to health become apparent, and whilst they may adopt measures that seriously harm legally protected positions on the basis of as yet incomplete scientific knowledge, they cannot base such protective measures on 'mere conjecture which has not been scientifically verified'.

Risk assessment, the CFI recognized, is a task to be shared between a scientific evaluation of risk, and a political analysis of what is deemed to be unacceptable risk. A divergence between scientific advice and political decision is possible, as long as the political decision is taken with the objective of the protection of human health. The role of the courts is to conduct a review of the political decision against the standard of manifest error, or a misuse of powers. In these two cases, the Council's bans of certain antibiotics for animal foodstuffs was upheld.

*Sex Equality*

To finish, a case from the field of sex equality. In *Lawrence,*[46] the ECJ was asked whether, in an action claiming sex discrimination, it is necessary that both the applicant and the 'comparator' work for the same employer. The question arose in the context of an action brought by women workers who had previously been employed by a local council, but whose employment contracts had been transferred to a private undertaking. The workers sought to compare their position to that of continuing council employees engaged in work of equal value. The ECJ held that there was nothing in principle which precluded Article 141 EC Treaty from allowing the applicant and the comparator to be employed by different employers. However, to succeed, such an action has to show that any difference in pay is attributable to a single source – there has to be one body which is capable of being held responsible for the difference in pay. Such a single source for the differences in pay was not present in a case such as *Lawrence*.

## Conclusions

The cases noted above represent merely a small fraction of the work done by the ECJ and the CFI in 2002. From these, however, we get a view of a CFI which is growing in stature, gaining in confidence and developing its own

[45] Case T-70/99, *Alpharma* v. *Council* [2002] ECR II-3495 and Case T-13/99, *Pfizer Animal Health* v. *Council* [2002] ECR II-3305.
[46] Case 320/00 [2002] ECR I-7325.

distinctive voice – yet at the same time being reminded of, and responding to the ECJ's 'senior' role, as with the CFI's post-*UPA* case law. Both courts deal with the minutiæ of legal technicalities, as well as with issues of profound political significance, as they play their 'constitutional' roles. They also review the constitutionality of legal measures, assessing them against a seemingly increasing, ever more entrenched set of human rights. In addition, the ECJ polices the boundary disputes between the Member States and the institutions in the exercise of power.

Whilst the CFI and ECJ are undoubtedly constitutional courts for the European *Community*, their role within the wider *Union* has remained limited. How this is to be addressed by the Convention remains to be seen. Although there appears support for continuing to push the legal order of the third pillar closer towards the conventional 'Community' model, the approach to the CFSP appears very different. Given the impact the Court has had in the Community pillar over the last five decades, any reticence on the part of the 'masters of the Treaty' may be entirely understandable.

JCMS 2003 Volume 41. Annual Review pp. 97–114

# External Policy Developments

DAVID ALLEN AND MICHAEL SMITH
Loughborough University

## I. General Themes

2002 in retrospect represented a long period of waiting between the events of 11 September 2001 and the outbreak of the conflict in Iraq in March 2003. During this period, the EU became increasingly divided over Iraq and over its relationship with the United States. As the global situation worsened it became clear that the focus of decision-making on a number of external issues was shifting from Brussels back to the capitals of the larger Member States.

Nevertheless the EU's external activity was as wide ranging as ever and the Commission pressed ahead with its reform of the external service, focusing on the flexible rotation of posts. A new delegation was opened in Nepal and a new representative office in Afghanistan, so that by the end of the year the Commission was accredited to 158 countries and international organizations and represented by 104 heads of delegation in 131 external missions. At the Convention on the Future of Europe, plans for a network of EU embassies, staffed by a new EU diplomatic corps who would be trained at an EU Diplomatic Academy, were discussed. If these plans were eventually accepted, EU embassies would not replace those of the Member States but the Union would be able to provide consular services for member countries which did not have their own embassies in various capital cities.

### *Foreign and Security Policy*

The European security and defence policy (ESDP) made only faltering progress in 2003, with Greece's objections to the 2001 Ankara agreement, concerning EU access to Nato resources, preventing the planned autumn EU takeover of Nato's 'Amber Fox' operation in Macedonia. It was not until the Copenhagen European Council meeting in December that agreement was finally reached on EU–Nato relations. The EU developed its plans for crisis management, including signing consultation agreements with Canada, Russia and the Ukraine. The Commission's Rapid Reaction Mechanism called on a total of €25 million in order to handle situations in Afghanistan, Somalia, Ethiopia/ Eritrea and Sudan, and to provide emergency aid to the Palestinian Authority to replace infrastructure destroyed by Israel.

The Seville European Council produced a declaration on the role of the CFSP/ESDP in countering terrorism that prioritized political dialogue with third parties, intelligence-sharing and civilian protection measures. The Member States squabbled about how ESDP operations might be financed. France led a group of EU countries that were keen to charge common costs to the Union's budget. Britain and Germany countered with a preference for the Member States picking up costs 'where they fell'. A deal was eventually made at Seville with the Member States agreeing to two categories of common costs, one for the headquarters (HQ) and another for barracks and troop deployment. All EU countries, nevertheless, remained reluctant to increase their defence budgets in order to supply the EU force with the equipment it currently lacks. In April, however, eight Member States did manage to reach a preliminary agreement to build the A400M military transport aircraft in the face of considerable US opposition.

At the end of the year, France and Germany presented plans on the ESDP to the Convention. They called for a collective security doctrine equivalent to Nato's Article V and for decisions about some military actions to be taken using qualified majority voting (QMV) by a core of Member States working together on the basis of 'enhanced co-operation'. The British see these plans envisaging the creation of an integrated EU command capability as undermining their own conception of ESDP as a partner rather than a rival to Nato. Despite their reluctance to increase defence budgets, all the main players are keen to get better value for their defence spending and seem willing to work towards either a European Procurement Agency (the Franco-German proposal) or a Defence Capability Development Agency (the British proposal).

Most participants at the Convention in 2002 seemed to accept that the foreign policy roles played by the High Representative (currently Javier Solana) and Commissioner for External Relations (the Relex Commissioner, currently Chris Patten) need to be merged, along with their competing bureaucracies. Yet, disagreements continued as to whether the EU's 'foreign minister' should be based in the Commission or the Council. The larger Member States would like the post to be based in the Council, but also to have full access to the total resources available for EU external relations (at present, of the €3.2 billion allocated for external relations, only €30 million is allocated to the CFSP). The Commission and some of the smaller EU states would naturally prefer control of foreign policy and external relations resources to remain within the Commission.

Whilst the results of the Convention will not be known until late in 2003, the European Council did reach agreement in Seville on Solana's plans to reform the General Affairs Council (GAC) by separating out decision-making on EU external relations from the other GAC agenda items. Finally, it should be noted that the Union has been increasing the number of its special representatives, whilst significantly cutting their budgets in 2002. In particular Miguel Moratinos, the EU's envoy to the Middle East, has suffered a budgetary cut of some 37 per cent, with the result that he has claimed that his safety and security have been compromised. Also Klaus Peter Klaiber, the EU envoy to Afghanistan, is said to lack the funds to fly back to Brussels from his base in the run-down building in Kabul previously owned by the former East German government!

During 2002, the Union adopted 16 joint actions and defined 22 common positions. The EU adopted eight joint actions concerning the Western Balkans including the establishment of the European Union Police Mission (EUPM) in Bosnia and Herzegovina, and the appointment of Lord Ashdown as EU special representative there. There was one joint action in the Middle East extending the mandate of the EU special representative and another on the former Soviet Union relating to the Organization for Security and Co-opertion in Europe (OSCE) observer mission on the Russian–Georgian border. A further three concerned Asia, one related to Africa (extending the mandate of the EU special representative), and two defence joint actions dealt with ballistic missile proliferation, and small arms and light weapons.

The common positions related to the Western Balkans (one), the Middle East (one on the temporary reception by Member States of 12 Palestinians evacuated from the Church of the Nativity in Bethlehem), Asia (four including one on Myanmar) and Africa (11 including Angola, Liberia, Sierra Leone, Zimbabwe, Rwanda and the Democratic Republic of the Congo). The EU also adopted common positions on combating terrorism (three) and the International Criminal Court. The Union and the Presidency issued 182 declarations (as listed in the European Commission's 2002 General Report on the Activities of the European Union (European Union, point 762, Table 17)).

### *External Trade and the Common Commercial Policy*

As in 2001, work continued in the EU on the modification of the trade policy framework, although many of the most significant developments were to be found in the external and multilateral context. Commercial policy instruments were, as always, monitored and updated: in 2001, this activity covered a review of the anti-dumping and anti-subsidy provisions of the CCP, which led to clarification of their coverage. In this context, the Parliament welcomed the Commission's Annual Report on these issues, and stressed the need for clarity on their coverage and operation in the setting of the new Doha Round of World Trade Organization (WTO) trade negotiations.

In terms of the cases investigated and measures applied in anti-dumping, the Council was active in the updating process, and particularly in the recognition of Russia as a genuine market economy. Meanwhile, the Council imposed definitive anti-dumping duties in 25 new cases; it also confirmed or amended definitive duties in 32 proceedings, and closed 17 proceedings without renewing the measures. The Commission initiated 20 new investigations and 52 reviews; it also adopted 15 provisional measures and closed one investigation without taking action. In addition, it confirmed or amended definitive duties in three proceedings and closed one investigation without renewing the measures. Definitive duties were imposed by the Council in three new anti-subsidy cases. Although it confirmed or amended definitive duties in three proceedings, the Commission initiated three new anti-subsidy investigations, adopted two provisional measures, opened four reviews and closed three procedures, whilst confirming or amending definitive duties in two cases. A number of procedures were also initiated under safeguard measures and under the trade barriers regulation. The Commission also continued its work on customs co-operation under the 'Customs 2002' programme, and was involved in significant discussion of customs clearance procedures in the context of enhanced security measures after the 11 September 2001 attack on the World Trade Center.

As regards the broader framework of commercial policy, there was continuing attention to the generalized system of preferences (GSP), including the entry into force of a new regulation on tariff preferences on 1 February 2002. The Union also addressed itself to measures aimed at harmonizing its network of mutual recognition agreements with a number of industrial countries. In January the Commission addressed the issue of export controls, specifically in the context of equipment that might be used for purposes of torture.

In the context of the build-up to the Doha round WTO negotiations, the Parliament (through its trade committee) called in July for more detailed reporting on the progress of trade negotiations, and also for the right of assent. Whilst Parliament had been able to claim the right of assent to the Uruguay round agreements in the mid-1990s, this had only been possible because those agreements had created a new international organization, the WTO, with budgetary implications for the Community. Its new claim could also be viewed in the context of the build-up to the Intergovernmental Conference scheduled for 2003–04.

On another issue of authority and competence that had a fairly long history, the Commission continued its campaign during 2002 to establish its competence in the negotiation of 'open skies' agreements for European airlines. This campaign had been unsuccessful during the late 1990s. However, in 2002 it was pushed forward significantly by judgments, first of all, by the Advocate-General (in May 2002) and then by the European Court of Justice (ECJ) itself (in November), which seemed to confirm that the agreements reached bilaterally by a number of Member States were *ultra vires*. More will be said on this issue in the context of EU–US relations, yet it appeared that a turning-point had been reached on general competence issues (giving the Commission the right to negotiate on behalf of the Community and, by implication, also to require the unpicking of those agreements already reached).

As noted above, a key element in the development of the CCP during 2002 was preparation for the Doha round of trade negotiations under the WTO. In the early part of the year, there was much work to be done on the follow-up to the Doha meeting in November 2001, which had established a broad agenda needing a good deal of further definition. The Commission published a communication in September on 'Trade and Development – Assisting Developing Countries to Gain from Trade'. This linked, not only to the WTO context, but also to broader development policy issues.

More particularly, within the broad thrust of the round towards development issues, there were concerns over market access measures, over the making available of cheap generic versions of major pharmaceutical products to poor countries, and about the cluster of problems attached to 'sustainable development'. The latter led not only to discussions in the Doha process, but also to a major role for the Union at the Johannesburg summit in September. A crucial further dimension was added to the Doha follow-up by the need to initiate negotiations on agriculture, with a deadline of 31 March 2003 for agreement on a framework. This interacted inevitably and strongly with the EU's internal discussions on CAP reform, and with EU–US relations, as the EU moved towards a negotiating position by the end of the year. A number of questions also arose over the Doha process itself, concerning the chairing of the key negotiating committees and the development of the Union's negotiating position, not only for the negotiations on trade in goods, but also for those on services, intellectual property and investment.

At the same time, the EU was active in the WTO dispute settlement process, in terms of both its overall development through a new memorandum of understanding, and specific disputes. The most dramatic were those with the USA over steel and foreign sales corporations (see below). Yet the EU was also active in other areas involving (for example) cotton textile products with India. The Union also supported a number of countries moving towards membership of the WTO, including Chinese Taipei, Macedonia and Armenia, and most significantly Russia.

*Development Co-operation Policy and Humanitarian Aid*

2002 was the second full year of operation for the EU's EuropeAid Cooperation Office set up as part of Commissioner Patten's plan for the reform of EU aid dispersal. EuropeAid's first report (for 2001) was published in September and recorded the fact that in 2001 the EU had managed to spend €7.7 billion of the €9.7 billion committed for aid. EuropeAid handles the implementation of EU aid programmes under the direct control of Patten's Relex Directorate-General (DG), leaving a diminished Development DG to formulate programmes. Some 200 of the Development DG's staff have been transferred to EuropeAid (by 2005 Patten plans to have over 50 per cent of EuropeAid's Brussels-based staff deployed in recipient countries). The management of all trade with the Afro-Caribbean-Pacific (ACP) countries is now the responsibility of Pascal Lamy's Trade DG. Lamy has seized this opportunity to push ahead with plans for Economic Partnership Agreements (EPA) with the ACP countries as envisaged in the Cotonou agreements.

At the Barcelona European Council meeting the EU formally agreed to raise the percentages of EU GDP devoted to aid from 0.33 per cent to 0.39 per cent (still well below the UN target of 0.7 per cent, and requiring a large increase from countries like Germany whose aid budget currently represents just 0.27 per cent of GDP). In 2002 Oxfam produced a report that was highly critical of the EU's continued support for its textile and agricultural producers, claiming that the Union was the most protectionist of all the developed countries.

During 2002 the EU extended €1.149 billion of food security and food aid to the developing world. The European Community Humanitarian Office (Echo) allocated €537.845 million in humanitarian aid, with the largest sums once again going to the ACP states (€200 million) followed by the Southern Mediterranean (€57 million including €27 million for Palestine), the Western Balkans (€43 million) and the former Soviet Union (€40 million). The EU was active in a number of global development meetings, including the International Conference on Financing for Development that produced the 'Monterrey Consensus', the World Food Summit on Sustainable Development in Johannesburg and the World Food Summit in Rome.

## II. Regional Themes

### *The European Economic Area and EFTA*

Activity in the European Economic Area (EEA) and in relation to the European Free Trade Association (EFTA) continued largely on its established course in 2002. There were meetings of the EEA Council in October, a number of sessions of the EEA Joint Committee and of the EEA Parliamentary Committee in May and November. Although all this seemed very predictable, a number of evaluations during the year pointed to renewed interest in EU membership in two of the EEA member countries, Norway and Iceland.

Although there was increased public support in Norway, the government ruled out any early attempt to restart negotiations; in the case of Iceland, there was a marked swing in support, but issues such as the common fisheries policy (CFP) remained central to any potential talks. Both Norway and Iceland, in addition to their EEA membership, also gain from the Schengen agreement and other arrangements that give them at least some of the benefits available to EU Member States. No major disputes occurred with these two EEA members, although Norway was threatened in May with a probe into the pricing of its salmon exports, which cast a small shadow over the review of its general set of agreements with the Union.

There was no significant move towards rekindling the question of Swiss membership. Yet, a good deal of attention was paid to Switzerland itself, accompanied by some significant tensions. In the early part of the year, the Council finally adopted a decision on the agreements that had been negotiated over the previous few years with Switzerland. In June the former authorized the opening of negotiations in four new areas: the adoption of the Schengen *acquis*, the implementation of the Dublin convention on asylum and related issues, free trade in services and the audiovisual sector.

Alongside these positive moves, however, there was a good deal of friction. This centred especially on the EU's implementation of its agreements on exchange of information about savings and accompanying taxation issues, including tax fraud. If there is to be an EU-wide regime, there has to be an agreement with Switzerland, and the Swiss tradition of banking secrecy immediately becomes an obstacle. During the year, therefore, there was an escalation of pressure from EU finance ministers (with the British in the lead) and the Commission. This was designed to get the Swiss to offer as much information – if possible automatically – as was shared by EU Member States (not all of them were really enthusiastic about the measures in the first place). The Swiss countered by linking the issue to other areas of negotiation, a logical step but one not without risk, whilst also trying to produce proposals for strictly limited information–sharing in defined circumstances. Threats of financial sanctions from EU finance ministers escalated in the autumn. Yet, these had not been put into place by the end of the year; indeed, the search for a compromise was in progress.

*Western Balkans*

The Western Balkans have for a long time been symbolic of the failure of the EU's CFSP. Nevertheless, by the end of 2002, there were distinct signs that at last the EU might be beginning to pull together the political, economic, military, judicial and civilian aspects of its external policy into a coherent whole. Throughout the year, spurred on by threats of an imminent American withdrawal because of the controversies over the International Criminal Court, the EU sought to establish a European Union Policing Unit (EUPU) in Bosnia and Herzegovina. It was eventually agreed that the EUPU would take over from the UN International Police Task Force (that had been set up in 1995) on 1 January 2003. Some 900 people including 500 policemen drawn from all 15 EU Member States, as well as from 18 other European countries, will make up the EUPU (wearing national uniforms but also displaying berets and shoulder tags bearing the EU insignia). The EUPU will be responsible for training the 20,000 strong Bosnian police force in all aspects of police work. In 2002 the EU spent €14 million establishing the force and some €38 million has been committed for each of the next three years.

In addition, the Union has ambitions (via the ESDP) eventually to replace the 10,000 strong Nato intervention force in Bosnia and Herzegovina. If this comes to fruition, then the EU will be responsible under the authority of its Special Representative, Paddy Ashdown, for all aspects of international intervention and assistance in Bosnia. As a preliminary to more significant military intervention in Bosnia, the EU was also able at the end of 2002 to agree terms with Nato (under the Berlin-plus arrangements) for replacing (in early 2003) the 900-strong Nato force in Macedonia with an EU (ESDP) force.

In the Federal Republic of Yugoslavia, the EU was instrumental in 2002 in discouraging the establishment of a 'break-away' state of Montenegro, instead brokering the creation of a much looser and new federation of Serbia and Montenegro. In addition to the development of its ESDP, the EU has based its dealings with the Western Balkans on the stabilization and association process designed eventually to lead to EU membership for all the states in the region. In addition to the ongoing negotiation of stabilization and association agreements, the EU supported this process in 2002 with assistance worth €665 million under the Community Action for the Reconstruction, Development and Stabilization (Cards) process. At the end of 2002, Croatia was considering submitting an application for EU membership early in 2003, with a view to entering the Union at the same time (2007) as Romania and Bulgaria.

*Russia and the Soviet Successor States*

In 2002, Russia finally came to terms with the forthcoming reality of EU eastern enlargement. It concluded a serious negotiation with the Union over the status of Kaliningrad (which is due to become a Russian enclave within the EU once Poland and Lithuania join in 2004). In recent years, Russia has chosen to privilege its relationship with the United States and with selected Member States, such as the UK and Germany.

However, the Kaliningrad issue required direct negotiations between Moscow and Brussels and much of 2002 was taken up with this. At the EU–Russia summit in November, agreement was reached on a 'flexible facilitated travel document' process (a visa regime in all but name). This would allow Russians living in Kaliningrad to travel to and from Russia using documents issued by Poland and Lithuania, but paid for by the EU under its Schengen regime. The vital need to resolve this issue, which threatened to hold up enlargement, meant that Russia was able to keep any serious discussion of the Chechen issue off the agenda at both the EU–Russia summits in May and November.

Indeed, the November summit had to be moved from Copenhagen to Brussels because the Russians were displeased at the fact that the Danish government had permitted Chechen exiles to hold a Congress in Copenhagen shortly after the Chechen inspired siege at the Moscow Opera House. In 2002 the EU also recognized Russia as a market economy, which should ease its entry into the WTO. However, much still remains to be negotiated on the trade and energy front (at present some 40 per cent of Russian exports come to the EU, and after enlargement this could rise to 50–70 per cent).

EU relations with Belarus remained poor. They were not improved by the refusal of the Belarus government to allow an OSCE advisory and monitoring group (AMG) to enter the country. In November the EU threatened to ban the Belarus leader, Alexander Lukashenko, and 50 of his aides from travel to Europe because of a belief that Belarus was exporting defence equipment to Iraq. In the summer, EU enlargement Commissioner Gunter Verheugen publicly fell out with Ukrainian President Leonid Kuchma when he rejected the notion that the Ukraine might become a member of the EU in the near or even distant future. This was in spite of the fact that German Chancellor, Gerhard Schröder, had supported the idea on a recent visit to Kiev.

In 2002 the EU continued its regular (and fundamentally unsatisfactory) political dialogue with most former Soviet states under the partnership and co-operation agreements that were negotiated in the 1990s. Of more substance, however, was the €440 million that was given to the area in financial assistance under a new set of arrangements that limited each recipient state to support in just three of six potential fields.

*The Mediterranean and the Middle East*

The growing threat of war in Iraq and the increased conflict between Israel and the Palestinian Authority dominated the EU's relationship with this part of the world in 2002. The Israeli–Palestinian conflict significantly marred the April Euro–Mediterranean meeting in Valencia of the 'Barcelona process' (with both Lebanon and Syria refusing to attend). It became clear at this troubled meeting that the 'Barcelona process' needs peace in the Middle East rather more than the Middle East peace process needs the 'Barcelona process'. Nevertheless Algeria, Lebanon and Jordan all signed Euro–Mediterranean agreements in 2002. Thus, Syria was the only state not yet to have completed a bilateral agreement with the EU.

Javier Solana maintained a high profile in the Middle East, trying all the time to keep the EU itself united whilst seeking to keep the US interested in pressurizing Israel into moderating its increasingly intolerant behaviour towards the Palestine Authority. Israel strongly resisted the Union's attempts to bring economic linkages to bear on the political relationship. The EU was handicapped in its contemplation of economic sanctions by the fact that, whilst the EU is Israel's most important trading partner (taking 34 per cent of Israeli exports), Israeli exports to the EU are worth $7.6 billion compared to EU exports to Israel amounting to $13.9 billion.

In addition, Israel made it clear that any attempt to apply political conditionality under the terms of the 1995 EU–Israel trade agreement would result in the exclusion of the EU from the Middle East peace process. In 2002, Solana was twice denied access to Yasser Arafat by Israel and, during one meeting between Arafat and EU special representative Miguel Moratinos, Arafat's headquarters came under fire from Israeli helicopters. Solana, however, did succeed in maintaining the Union's profile in the peace process, in particular via the role that he played in the work of the 'quartet' consisting of the EU, the UN, Russia and the US. In October, this group announced a new peace initiative based primarily on EU proposals for free Palestinian elections, the establishment of a Palestinian state and a negotiated settlement to be reached by the end of 2005.

However progress towards a Middle East peace settlement was overshadowed by the growing determination of the US to effect regime change in Iraq. The EU struggled in 2002 to preserve its own unity, with Britain, Germany and France in particular all taking diametrically opposed stances on the need for military action. In 2002 the Union held its collective line on demanding that the UN remain at the centre of all deliberations about the fate of Iraq. Yet, when the crunch eventually came, the major Member States would be fundamentally divided over how to react to unilateral US action.

Relations with Israel were also soured by a failure to resolve the ongoing dispute about the 'origin' of certain Israeli exports to the EU, with Commissioner Patten arguing that goods produced in the occupied territories were not entitled to enter the EU under the preferential terms of the 1995 agreement. In 2002, there were also demands from within the Union that Israel be sued for the damages that it had inflicted on Palestinian assets (that had been previously paid for by the EU). Inside Israel, legal moves were taken by individuals arguing that EU funds to the Palestinian Authority had been diverted into terrorist hands.

The relationship between the EU and Iran was of continuing interest during the year, particularly in the context of the 'war against terror' and the United States' identification of Iran as part of the 'axis of evil'. Despite US suspicions, the EU continued to pursue its critical dialogue with Tehran (in March Javier Solana met with Iranian President Mohammed Khatami), and moved towards the opening of formal negotiations on a trade and co-operation agreement. EU foreign ministers agreed on the opening of negotiations in June, and they began formally in December; perceptions of significant opportunities for EU companies in Iran were qualified by the recognition that human rights issues in particular would be difficult to overcome.

Finally, as the enlargement process reached its 'end game' at the Copenhagen summit, an uneasy settlement was reached with Turkey over the 'Berlin plus' arrangements for the European Rapid Reaction Force's proposed role in Macedonia. In return Turkey did not succeed in extracting a date from the EU for the start of its own accession negotiations; instead it merely received a promise that the situation would be reviewed at the end of 2004. This will be after Cyprus has joined the Union, yet also probably before a solution is found to the ongoing division of the island; in 2002 the UN tried and failed to resolve the situation and thus ease the context within which Cyprus enters the Union. The delicate negotiations with Turkey towards the end of 2002 were not made any easier by the comments by the President of the Convention on the Future of Europe, Valéry Giscard d'Estaing, who said in November that Turkey's membership would represent 'the end of the EU'.

### *Africa*

In 2002 problems in Robert Mugabe's Zimbabwe came to a head with the result that the EU was forced to withdraw its election observers and impose targeted sanctions on Zimbabwe in February before the March elections (which were then condemned by the European Parliament as being 'deeply flawed').

The Mugabe government had accepted an EU observer team only on the condition that it included no participants from several Member States (including the UK and Germany). The EU was inhibited in its attempts to influence the Zimbabwe government by its desire not to alienate neighbouring African governments who did not support the EU sanctions. In the summer the sanctions were extended as the Mugabe government increased its intimidation of both white farmers and the opposition Movement for Democratic Change.

However, EU foreign ministers were criticized in October for 'undermining their own sanctions' by agreeing to switch a meeting between the EU and the Southern Africa Development Community (SADC) from Copenhagen to Mozambique so that Zimbabwean ministers, who were banned from travelling to Europe, could attend.

The EU was unable to implement fully the Cotonou Agreements in 2002 because not all the Member States had ratified them. As in 2001, the EU was forced to fall back on transitional arrangements in order to apply political conditionality to Zimbabwe and several other African states, as well as to dispense some €2 billion of European development fund (EDF) funds. In July the African Union was officially launched to replace the Organization for African Unity (OAU), and the EU was swift to offer support and funds from the EDF for the new Union's conflict settlement mechanism.

In Nigeria, the EU worked hard with other members of the international community in order to prevent the execution (by public stoning) of a pregnant woman Satiya Huisani Tungar-Tudu. The EU was sharply criticized by conservationists for the open-ended fishing agreements that it has negotiated with a number of African states. These agreements, which give EU fishing boats access to West African waters (with no quotas imposed), have led to a serious degradation of fish stocks in recent years.

*Asia*

The relations between the EU and Asia during 2002 at the multilateral level centred on the fourth Asia–Europe Meeting (ASEM) in Copenhagen in late September, for which there had been a number of preparatory meetings, including one of foreign ministers held in Madrid during June. The foreign ministers' agenda was dominated by issues such as terrorism, human rights and migration. It also touched on the thorny issue of ASEM membership, particularly a possible extension to South Asia. Other preparatory meetings for the ASEM included those on environment, migration, finance and economic policy. The ASEM itself generated broad agreements on the pursuit of an open and transparent global trading system and on dialogue between cultures and civilizations. Yet, much of the rest of its business was routine; statements were adopted on terrorism (including an agreed action plan) and the Korean peninsula.

Bilateral relations were initially dominated by those relating to South Asia, especially in the context of the war in Afghanistan and its regional spillover. The EU played a key role in the management of aid efforts for Afghanistan, including the second ministerial 'pledging' conference held in Tokyo during January, and a further pledging conference in Bonn in December 2002. The Union promised development aid of €1 billion for the period 2002–06 in addition to humanitarian assistance (whilst it was reported that, out of a total commitment of €830 million for 2002, €755 million had been spent by early December).

Meanwhile, the Union's special representative in Kabul from 1 July was Francisc Vendrell, replacing Klaus-Peter Klaiber. The Union remained concerned about tensions between India and Pakistan over Kashmir; there were also potential tensions between the EU and India, created by the production in April of a report on riots in Gujarat. Interestingly, this report had been compiled jointly by the EU embassies in New Delhi, and it implicated the Indian government in efforts to 'purge' Moslems in Gujarat and elsewhere. Despite these issues, Javier Solana undertook a productive tour of India, Pakistan and Afghanistan during July, on his way to the ASEAN Regional Forum in Brunei. Furthermore, the third EU–India Summit held in October passed off without incident. In the case of Pakistan, the Union organized observers for the elections in October, and they registered some dissatisfaction with the electoral process.

EU relations with Southeast Asia during 2002 largely followed established patterns. The process of opening new Commission offices in the region continued, deepening relations with a number of new partners. Sanctions on the regime in Burma (Myanmar) remained in place, but there were two visits by the EU troika – in March and September – linked to the gradual opening up of relations in the wake of the release of opposition leader Aung San Suu Kyi. The Union lent its political and financial support – to the tune of €2.3 million – to an agreement between the Indonesian government and rebel groups in the province of Aceh, whilst there were trade disputes with Thailand covering products such as tuna, chicken and prawns. The troika was involved in the post-ministerial conference linked to the Asean Regional Forum that took place at the end of July.

Relations with China during 2002 saw the adoption of strategic priorities for the period 2002–06, followed by a visit to Beijing from Commissioner Patten during April. The Fifth EU–China summit took place in Copenhagen at the time of the ASEM, producing a joint statement. There were relatively few commercial tensions with China during the year. The most intriguing were those over tourism agreements that hinged on the provisions for 're-admission' of those tempted to overstay their tourist visas in the EU. Otherwise, both the Union and China found themselves affected by US policies over trade in steel (see below), although the Chinese were exempted from many of the US sanctions.

During 2002, the EU committed €374 million for financial and technical co-operation with Asia, of which €127.5 million related to Afghanistan. At the same time, the Union allocated €99 million to the region for political, economic and cultural co-operation.

*Latin America*

The central inter-regional event of 2002 for EU–Latin American relations was the Madrid conference, held in May, and which was the first follow-up meeting to the Rio conference held in 2000. That conference had established the framework for a 'strategic partnership' between the two regions, both at the inter-regional level and in the context of WTO negotiations. The Madrid meeting attempted to consolidate the partnership, but came up against a problem of conflicting priorities. Whereas the EU and its Member States focused strongly on issues of anti-terrorism and security in the wake of 11 September 2001, the Latin American partners wanted the emphasis to be on development issues. Another conditioning factor was the renewed financial crisis centred on Argentina, which threatened to spread and to curtail the mutual gains from economic relations. As a result, whilst the final declaration from the conference stressed common values in the general sense, it could not gloss over the key areas of tension.

Progress was made, however, on two key processes stemming from the search for inter-regional trade enhancement. In July, there was agreement that formal negotiations should be launched with the Mercosur group (Argentina, Brazil, Uruguay and Paraguay) with the aim of reaching a free trade pact. Later, in November, a free trade agreement was signed with Chile, covering €8 billion of trade, encompassing large cuts in tariffs on industrial goods and opening up trade in services.

Contacts continued during 2002 with other established Latin American partner groups. The dialogues with the Andean Community, with Central American countries, and with the San José Group were maintained, and in the latter two cases there were moves towards broader agreements on co-operation and political dialogue; in the case of the San José Group this was seen as the first step towards a free trade agreement. At the bilateral level, perhaps the most notable step, in addition to the agreement with Chile, was the opening of a (one-person) Commission office in Havana. Although the EU's position on relations with Cuba remained unchanged, there was increasing talk of the Cubans' willingness to sign up to the Cotonou process (a move opposed by some key EU Member States). The financial crisis in Argentina produced a muted EU response: little was forthcoming in the way of financial assistance, and the most concrete steps were temporary increases of some import quotas on Argentine beef.

During 2002, €23 million were committed to financial and technical co-operation with Latin America, and €126 million to economic co-operation, including educational and other cultural programmes. Latin America was also included in the proposals for a new framework for co-operation between Asia and Latin American countries (the ALA countries), tabled by the Commission in July 2002.

*The United States, Japan and other Industrial Countries*

It would be difficult to imagine a more challenging year for the EU in its relations with other industrial countries. This was almost entirely due to the evolution of relations with the United States in the aftermath of 11 September 2001, not only in terms of the 'war on terror', but also in relation to a host of other connected issues. Security relations dominated, with real signs of a major rift by the end of the year. In terms of the war on terror, the EU and its Member States stood firm with the USA in the initial stages.

Yet, as 2002 unfolded, a host of, more or less, fundamental tensions became apparent: over the treatment of Taliban and Al-Qaeda suspects in Guantanamo Bay; concerning the willingness of the Member States to extradite suspects to a country that practised the death penalty; relating to the compatibility of US demands for sharing of information (for example, on air travellers) with EU directives on data privacy; and over broader processes of judicial co-operation between the Eurojust organization and US authorities. The tensions extended, for example, to competition issues raised by US treatment of air carriers affected by the post-11 September decline in traffic and to the potential uses of the EU's proposed Galileo satellite system. The Americans were moving slowly towards an agreement with the EU on Galileo use, but one which might overlap and conflict with US satellite intelligence operations.

Alongside this set of tensions went the development of the momentum behind the confrontation with Iraq. From the moment when George W. Bush declared in his State of the Union address that there was an 'axis of evil' centred on Iraq, Iran and North Korea, there was a sense of inevitability about the gathering storm. At the Barcelona European Council in March, the split between Britain and Spain, and most of the other Member States was apparent, and it deepened as the year went on. The tensions within the EU became transferred to the United Nations, as debate on successive resolutions and the role of the organization extended into the autumn and winter. It was also clear that this split – and attitudes towards US predominance – was likely to infect other issues, such as, enlargement. During the later part of the year, as the Copenhagen European Council approached, US pressure on France and Germany (especially to give an early date for Turkish entry) became linked strongly with the general issue of American leadership.

Tensions with the USA on matters of international security also affected transatlantic relations in terms of what might be termed international regimes. Most directly, it became apparent during 2002 that the EU and the USA differed fundamentally on their approaches to the proposed International Criminal Court (ICC). Whilst all Member States (including the UK) were strongly signed up to this plan, the American administration denounced it in May 2002. The latter spent the rest of the year trying to reach bilateral deals on exemption for US service personnel, a number of them with potential members of the EU such as Romania.

The Union itself reluctantly conceded that such deals could be concluded. Yet, the EU continued to react strongly against attempts by the USA effectively to blackmail others into conceding immunity (for example, when in June the US threatened to allow UN resolutions on peace-keeping in Bosnia and other areas to lapse because the immunity of their personnel might be threatened).

A different type of issue, but still one demonstrating the growth of tensions, was the ratification of the Kyoto protocol on climate change. As noted in previous *Reviews*, this was a highly contentious issue, but again one on which EU Member States agreed. Collective EU ratification in June 2002 boosted the prospects of the protocol in general. However, in the absence of US participation, its entry into force depended on pretty much every other industrial country ratifying it (and thus to a degree on the success of the EU in persuading countries such as Russia to do so). Tensions surrounding this area of policy were also linked to frictions over issues of 'sustainable development' that were apparent at talks on environment and development in Bali during June and at the Johannesburg summit in August.

At the same time as these global issues continued to focus EU–US tensions, there were major disputes at the bilateral level, several of which threatened to put pressure on global bodies such as the WTO. In March, President Bush announced 30 per cent import tariffs on a wide range of steel products, including many in which the EU was the dominant supplier. Whilst the Union applied safeguard measures to counter the diversion of steel exports from third countries, and immediately complained to the WTO, both the Commission and some Member States spent much of the year arguing for exemptions on a bilateral basis, with considerable success. As a result, by the end of the year there was a sense of at least some de-escalation of the dispute, although the EU was still pursuing the WTO dispute process.

Alongside this major dispute went further development of the EU–US dispute relating to foreign sales corporations (see previous *Reviews*). From the beginning of the year, the WTO disputes panel made clear its acceptance of the EU's case, and at the end of August its arbitration panel announced that the EU could retaliate with up to $4 billion of sanctions. Although the Commission made clear that it was developing the list of proposed sanctions, their application was delayed whilst attempts were made to legislate in Washington. Above all, Pascal Lamy, the Trade Commissioner, and his counterpart Robert Zoellick, the US Trade Representative, were anxious not to link this dispute with the steel issue or with broader EU–US troubles.

As noted earlier, EU–US trade problems also infected the follow-up to the Doha development agenda. This was primarily through production of competing proposals on agriculture that threatened to paralyse the development of an agenda for multilateral talks, a situation exacerbated by the passing of the US Farm Bill, with increased subsidies, and by the inability of the EU to make progress in reform of the CAP.

As in previous years, a number of developments in EU and US internal policies made for tensions. Two examples will suffice here. First, in the wake of the Enron scandal and American efforts to deal with fraudulent accounting, the US Congress produced the Sarbanes-Oxley Act, imposing new demands for accounting – a measure that automatically affected EU companies with operations in the USA, and which led to intensive lobbying on Capitol Hill by the Commission and others. Second, as the EU moved towards approval of new regulations on genetically modified organisms (GMOs), there was fierce US pressure to prevent the introduction of what were seen as onerous labelling requirements for food products, and to achieve the end of the effective moratorium on the commercial growing of GMOs in the EU. In addition, mention has already been made of the interaction between the Commission's activities on 'open skies' and US interests.

By comparison, as always, relations with other industrial countries were comparatively low key. This was especially the case with Japan, where the EU–Japan summit in Tokyo affirmed the effective working of the action plan, and where the travails of the Japanese economy preoccupied its government rather than relations with the EU.

With South Korea, the dispute over subsidies for shipbuilding continued, and the WTO ruling on the EU's complaint was awaited. In the meantime, the Council approved limited state aids for EU shipbuilders pending the judgment. For the Korean peninsula as a whole, the main EU concern was the North Korean defection from the agreements that had established the Korean

Peninsula Energy Development Organization. There was also the threat of nuclearization of the Korean conflict – a matter that involved the USA, but which was effectively, if only temporarily, sidelined by their preoccupation with Iraq during 2002. Both the shipbuilding and the nuclear issues were raised at the first EU–Korean summit held in Copenhagen alongside the ASEM (see above), which reaffirmed the EU–Korean Framework Agreement for Trade and Co-operation.

For the rest, there were two EU–Canada summits in May and December, that (as before) identified a number of common EU–Canada interests in both commercial and security areas (the latter including crisis management operations). There was also an EU–Australia ministerial meeting in April, but many of the most significant EU–Australia contacts were to be found in the negotiations over agriculture at the WTO, in which context Australia is one of the leaders of the Cairns Group of agricultural exporters; and despite some tensions with New Zealand over the introduction of restrictive new EU wine-labelling regulations, there was little of note to report.

JCMS 2003 Volume 41. Annual Review pp. 115–17

# Enlarging the European Union

JULIE SMITH
Royal Institute of International Affairs

In December 2002 the European Council finally made the decision that ten would-be EU members had been waiting to hear: they would be able to join the Union on 1 May 2004. Cyprus, the Czech Republic, Estonia, Hungary, Poland and Slovenia, which had started accession negotiations in 1998, along with Latvia, Lithuania, Malta and Slovakia, which had begun their negotiations in 2000, were deemed ready to accede (European Council, 2002b, p.1). Two more candidates, Romania and Bulgaria, had already declared that their goal was to join in 2007 and the Council gave its support for this objective, offering those countries additional EU assistance to help them secure it (European Council, 2002b, pp. 4–5). Finally, in recognition of its progress towards meeting the 'Copenhagen criteria', Turkey was given a 'date for a date': if it met the political criterion by December 2004, then accession negotiations would begin 'without delay' (European Council, 2002b, p. 6).

Copenhagen was the scene for the EU's momentous decision on enlargement, just as it had been the venue for the European Council that set the criteria for accession back in December 1993; this symmetry seems fitting given Denmark's consistent support for the process of enlargement right from the start. Moreover, the conclusion of negotiations with the ten accession countries required a considerable amount of tenacity on the part of the Danish Presidency of the Union, as well as the European Commission. In October 2002 several apparently intractable problems were still on the table: the budget, direct payments to farmers and Kaliningrad.

At their Seville summit in June, Heads of State and Government failed to come to an agreement on financing enlargement and deferred their decision to a special European Council held on 24–25 October. The Member States were deeply divided between net contributors, such as Germany, the UK and the Netherlands which wanted reform of the common agricultural policy (CAP) before agreeing a deal on financing enlargement, and the net beneficiaries of CAP led by France, that would not contemplate reform before 2006 (Euractiv.com, 2002a). Additionally, some candidate states were concerned by the prospect of being net contributors to the EU's coffers upon accession.

The re-emergence of the Franco–German axis ensured that agreement on financing enlargement was reached at Brussels, albeit at the expense of a spat between the UK and France (Horsley, 2002). The deal reached was that new Member States would receive only a proportion of the levels of direct payments for agriculture that the existing Member States received (rising from 25 per cent in 2004 to 100 per cent in 2013, but with total agricultural spending held down after 2006). There would also be temporary budgetary compensations for new members to ensure that they would not become net contributors. The budgetary ceiling set at the Berlin Council in 1999 would not be breached, however (European Council, 2002a; Euractiv.com, 2002b).

The Kaliningrad question, which revolved around the need for easy access between the Russian enclave and the rest of the Russian Federation, had been a source of contention between the EU and Russia for over two years. A proposal put forward at the Brussels summit to permit Russians to travel to and from Kaliningrad through new EU neighbours, Poland and Lithuania, provided they held a Facilitated Transit Document was accepted by Russia and the EU on 11 November 2002 (Commission, 2002b). Coupled with the budgetary agreements, this paved the way for the completion of accession negotiations with the ten in Copenhagen on 13 December.

Yet, if 2002 saw the end of negotiations for ten would-be members, it did not mark the end of their preparations. In its regular reports on the 13 candidate states presented on 9 October 2002, the European Commission indicated that it believed ten states would be ready to join in 2004. However, it argued that there should be an ongoing monitoring process in order to ensure that there was no backsliding in the implementation and enforcement of the *acquis* (Commission, 2002a). In contrast to past practice, in 2002 the Commission extrapolated from the experience of transposition and implementation of the *acquis* to date, in order to assess what countries were likely to have achieved by the time of accession. Thus, the 2002 reports assessed states' 'track record in implementing the commitments made in the negotiations and the degree of alignment and implementation of the *acquis*' (Commission, 2002a, p. 16).

The Commission noted that candidate states had reached high overall levels of alignment with the *acquis* as they had been transposing it into national law. There had also been 'steady' progress in building up the necessary administrative and judicial capacity for implementing and enforcing the *acquis* (Commission, 2002a, p. 17). However, it pledged to monitor implementation until the signing of the Treaty and report back to the Council, a suggestion that the Council accepted at Copenhagen. The Commission, in its guise as the 'guardian of the treaties', also committed itself to continuing to monitor implementation between the time the candidates signed the Treaty of Accession and their actual joining, as well as post-enlargement. Additionally, it proposed a safeguard mechanism to ensure the continued implementation of the internal market and in the area of justice and home affairs (Commission, 2002a, p. 26).

Despite the need for this continued monitoring, it was clear by the end of 2002 that the EU was committed to accepting ten new members on 1 May 2004. Thus, while there could still be delays associated with ratification, not least since most of the candidate countries had committed themselves to holding referendums on accession, it seemed that enlargement would finally happen. However, Copenhagen did not mark the beginning of the end of the accession process: Croatia put in its application for membership on 18 February 2003, with the Former Yugoslav Republic of Macedonia indicating it would also apply in 2003. With Romania and Bulgaria still negotiating, and Turkey awaiting a date to start talks, it seemed that enlargement would remain on the EU's agenda for several more years.

## References

Commission of the European Communities (2002a) 'Towards the Enlarged Union. Strategy Paper and Report of the European Commission on the Progress towards Accession by Each of the Candidate Countries'. {*SEC* (2002) 1400–1412} Brussels, 9.10.2002, *COM*(2002) 700 final.

Commission of the European Communities, Relex-Feedback (2002b) *Special News Digest – EU and Russia Reach Deal on Kaliningrad.* Email briefing, 13 November 2003.

Euractiv.com (2002a) 'Chirac and Schröder Give Green Light for United Europe'. 25/10/02, available at «http://www.eurativ.com».

Euractiv.com (2002b) 'Brussels Summit'. 28/10/02, available at «http://www.euractiv.com.

European Council (2002a) *Presidency Conclusions, Brussels European Council, 24 and 25 October 2002* (Brussels, SN 300/02).

European Council (2002b) *Presidency Conclusions, Copenhagen European Council, 12 and 13 December 2002* (Brussels, SN 400/02).

Horsley, W. (2002) 'Summit's Hot Air and High Drama', 25 October, available at «http://news.bbc.co.uk/1/hi/world/europe/2362681.stm».

JCMS 2003 Volume 41. Annual Review pp. 119–35

# Justice and Home Affairs

JÖRG MONAR
University of Sussex

## Introduction

After the hectic activity of the first months following the 11 September 2001 terrorist attacks the year 2002 marked, to some extent, a return to normal for the development of EU justice and home affairs (JHA). Several of the rapid steps forward agreed in the last quarter of 2001 took until June to be legally formalized, but the threat of international terrorism ensured that some of the momentum gained in police and judicial co-operation in criminal matters was not lost.

Progress in the areas of asylum and immigration policy was again slow, with the staunch defence of individual national positions and the unanimity requirement causing further delay in the implementation of the ambitious agenda set three years before by the Tampere European Council. The impact of illegal immigration issues on the French Presidential elections played a major role in making EU action in this domain the central issue of the Seville European Council in June. This set a number of priorities for the implementation of a comprehensive action plan already decided in February. The challenges of both illegal immigration and security at the new post-enlargement external borders made the EU move closer to an integrated management of external borders, although the idea of a European border guard remained controversial.

While there were difficult negotiations on the development of the role of Europol, its judicial counterpart, Eurojust, finally came fully into being. The reform of EU justice and home affairs became one of the major themes of the work of the Convention on the Future of Europe, with a dedicated working group making substantial proposals for change at the end of the year.

## I. Developments in Individual Policy Areas

*Asylum*

Under the impact of the persisting unanimity requirement, most of the European Commission's proposals aimed at implementing the Tampere objective of a 'common asylum system' struggled to make any substantial progress in the Council. In June the Seville European Council felt it necessary to re-emphasize the Tampere targets. It also set 2003 as a deadline for the Council to adopt such key legislative measures as the directives on: common minimum standards regarding procedures for granting or withdrawing refugee status; the approximation of rules on the recognition and content of the refugee status; and subsidiary forms of protection. Germany was one of the Member States least willing to compromise. It maintained, *inter alia*, reservations on prosecution by non-state agents giving right to refugee status, and on the granting of refugee status to persons exposed to persecution because of political opinions which they have only started to proclaim after leaving their country of origin.

The adoption of the directive on common minimum conditions for the reception of asylum-seekers, originally scheduled for approval in April 2001, moved closer. At the end of the year the only outstanding problem remained Sweden's objection to a proposed British amendment that would allow Member States to remain free not to grant aid to persons who have failed to declare themselves as asylum-seekers on entering national territory. Germany successfully insisted that its Länder remain free to decide on access of asylum seekers to the labour market. A positive note was set by the UK's notification to participate in this directive, although both Denmark and Ireland made use of their opt-outs.

In December, political agreement was reached on the Dublin II regulation which further defined the criteria and mechanisms for determining the Member State responsible for examining an asylum application presented in another Member State. This regulation, however, was intended only to remove gaps and inaccuracies in the existing Dublin convention and brought no really innovative elements. The agreement became possible on the basis of a Danish Presidency proposal that a Member State shall be responsible for up to 12 months after entry for processing the asylum application of any asylum-seeker who has irregularly entered its territory.

A 'common asylum system' hardly seems possible without a common analysis and evaluation of the challenges in the asylum domain. Following on from the Council's decision to put an end to the largely inefficient Centre of Information, Reflection and Exchange on Asylum (CIREA) in July the Commission created a European Union network for asylum practitioners (Eurasil).

This was a step towards a more comprehensive system of information exchange on asylum and immigration developments including the monitoring of countries of origin.

*Immigration*

On migration issues, the year was clearly dominated by an increasing emphasis on the fight against illegal immigration. On 28 February, the EU Council adopted a 'Comprehensive Action Plan to Combat Illegal Immigration and Trafficking in Human Beings' (Council, 2002c) which followed – with unusual speed and no parliamentary scrutiny – the Commission's Communication on Illegal Immigration of November 2001 (*COM*(2001)672).

The action plan took up all areas for action suggested in the Commission's communication. On visa policy, it provided for improving security standards on the uniform visa format and increased consular co-operation, adopting a longer-term approach than the Commission, however, on the establishment of integrated consular offices and a European visa identification system. The Commission's recommendations on stepping up information and intelligence exchange, including the improvement of the existing early warning system (EWS) as well as more common analysis, were broadly endorsed.

On pre-frontier measures, the action plan provided for more mutual advice and support by liaison officers in the fight against illegal immigration, but was rather evasive as regards financial and technical support for action in third countries, including awareness-raising campaigns. Regarding arrangements at external borders, the action plan placed great emphasis on controls at sea borders and the need for a coherent strategy which would also have to take into account other elements such as customs controls and the prevention of the entry of illegal goods. The plan followed the Commission's suggestions on common training measures and on the strengthening of the liaison officer system, but not on the establishment of a European border guard.

In the area of readmission and return, the action plan came out in favour of common standards for return procedures, specific measures, such as the introduction of rules on the transit of returnees, and the conclusion of new readmission agreements with third countries. The action plan also envisaged a stronger role for Europol, especially regarding trafficking and smuggling of human beings. As regards the introduction of new penalties in the fight against illegal immigration, the action plan reflected the much more reluctant approach of the Member States. It placed emphasis on ensuring adequate implementation and a careful study of existing legislation in areas such as the fight against illegal employment and carrier sanctions, rather than on new legislation.

In the weeks following the adoption of the Council action plan, illegal immigration rapidly moved higher on the Union's agenda. A major reason for this was the huge politicization of illegal immigration issues in the French presidential election campaign in April and May. The unexpected appearance of Jean-Marie Le Pen from the far-right National Front in second place – ahead of the French Prime Minister Lionel Jospin – in the first round of the elections in May appeared to be largely due to his effective capitalization on French citizens' concerns about illegal immigration. In several EU countries this reinforced the determination to engage in effective common action at the European level as one way of not leaving problems in this area to political extremists and racist groups.

With this background, the Spanish Presidency of the EU decided to put illegal immigration as a central issue on the agenda of the Seville European Council (to be held on 21 and 22 June). Welcoming this move, on 16 May Prime Minister Tony Blair wrote to the Spanish Prime Minister José-Maria Aznar in which he deplored the lack of progress on the Tampere agenda in the area of asylum and immigration. Blair also expressed his hope that a 'strong push' be delivered by the Seville European Council. He asked, in particular, for urgent action to strengthen the Union's external borders, a tougher approach towards countries of origin on returns, and the examination of the scope of Community funding for encouraging stronger EU frontiers and the creation of an equitable asylum system.

Even before this letter, in April the Council had already adopted conclusions on the fight against illegal immigration by sea which indicated a tougher approach. In the run-up to the Seville summit, disagreements emerged between those EU Member States such as the UK and Germany who advocated stronger pressure being put on non-co-operative countries of origin – including potential cuts in EU economic and financial aid – and those such as France who preferred to use 'carrots' rather than 'sticks'. It was in the end the latter approach that prevailed at the Seville meeting. The Council introduced the notion of 'joint management' of migration flows together with third countries that were promised technical and financial assistance.

Paragraph 36 of the Presidency Conclusions, however, opened the door to the use of negative measures in both the CFSP and EC context in case a country of origin showed an 'unjustified lack of co-operation' – an interesting new example of 'cross-pillarization' in EU justice and home affairs. The European Council also decided to speed up the negotiation and conclusion of readmission agreements, and to introduce as soon as possible a common identification system for visa data. They also decided to to adopt a repatriation programme and put pressure on the Council rapidly to adopt a number of legislative measures on combating trafficking in human beings and the facilitation of unauthorized entry (Council Document SN 200/02). As part of the strategy against illegal immigration, the Heads of State and Government also set targets for the gradual introduction of a co-ordinated, integrated management of external borders (see below).

The impetus provided by the Seville European Council – already the second EU summit after Tampere to focus largely on justice and home affairs issues – facilitated the adoption by the Council in June of the framework decision on combating trafficking in human beings (Council, 2002c) which had been under negotiation since December 2000. The framework decision provides for a common definition of trafficking and establishes maximum penalties of at least eight years' imprisonment for traffickers if their victims have been endangered or subjected to violence.

As part of the new emphasis on repatriation, the Council agreed at its 28 November meeting on the basis of a previous Commission Green Paper on returns (Commission, 2002b) a plan for the return of Afghan refugees of whom around 100,000 were estimated to be in the EU. The plan provided for co-operation on both voluntary and non-voluntary return including contacts with Afghan authorities, the organization of return flights and hosting arrangements. The adoption of the plan caused some embarrassment for the Commission. It could not come up with appropriate funding arrangements in time, as a major disagreement between Commissioners Vitorino (Justice and Home Affairs), Patten (External Relations) and Nielson (Budget) arose over the appropriate funding basis, Nielson being opposed to allocations from the European Refugee Fund being used for financing expulsions.

During the entire year the EU kept the negotiation of readmission agreements at a sustained pace: readmission agreements were signed with Hong Kong on 27 November and initialled with Macao on 30 May and with Sri Lanka on 18 October. By the end of the year, negotiations were well under way with Morocco, Pakistan, Russia, Sri Lanka and the Ukraine, and in November the Council adopted negotiating mandates for readmission agreements with Albania, Algeria, China and Turkey.

Seville and the range of measures taken during the year clearly meant that the EU was moving sharply towards a more restrictive approach in its management of migratory flows, being more willing than ever before to use external relations instruments to tackle challenges in this domain. This reinforced emphasis on control and restriction came out all the more distinctly as very little progress was made in the same period on key legislative measures on legal immigration. The proposed directives on conditions of entry and residence for the purposes of family reunification, study or vocational training, paid employment and self-employed economic activity, all continued to be subject to protracted negotiations in the Council. The only element of progress was the adoption in December of a Council regulation extending the social security rights of EU workers laid down in Regulation (EEC) No. 1408/71 to third-country nationals residing lawfully in the territory of a Member State.

### *External Border Management*

It was to be expected that co-operation on external border management would be one of the priorities during the year. The Laeken European Council in December 2001 gave the Council and the Commission a mandate to work on co-operation between services responsible for external border control, and to examine the possibility of common services to control external borders. Yet, by the start of the year, the feasibility study on the establishment of a European border guard, started under Italian leadership in October 2001 by Belgium, France, Germany, Italy and Spain, was well under way. The strong emphasis on co-operation at external borders was very much driven by the growing awareness that the external border control capabilities of the future new Member States were not going to fulfil EU/Schengen standards by the time of accession in 2004 and that substantial help by the EU would be needed beyond the time of accession.

This, and more general concerns about external border security, as well as the increased salience of the fight against illegal immigration reinforced by the events of 11 September 2001, led several Member States to support the idea of setting up a common European border police. The main arguments in favour of such a move were that it would provide an instrument of solidarity for sharing the burden of controlling external borders in the enlarged Union, and allow for better use of personnel and technical resources as well as available expertise, while at the same time also marking a step forward for political integration. Other Member States, including the UK, shared the view that greater co-operation on external border issues was needed, yet expressed reservations about the idea of creating a European border police force.

In response to the Laeken mandate, on 7 May the European Commission presented a communication 'Towards an Integrated Management of External Borders' (Commission, 2002c). Based on an analysis of the main challenges at external borders and the current state of co-operation between Member States, this communication proposed a gradual move towards a common management of external borders. This would start with a consolidation and codification of common rules and standards for external border controls, continue, *inter alia*, with the creation of an 'External Borders Practitioners Common Unit' and various other co-operation mechanisms, leading then to financial burden-sharing mechanisms and – finally – a 'European Corps of Border Guards'.

With its more long-term approach to the creation of a European border guard, the Commission clearly made an effort to satisfy both the advocates and the sceptics of such a project, placing much emphasis in the meantime on the practical progress which could be achieved in various fields. As all the Member States could find much in the communication that they were able to support, the reception was broadly positive. However, several Member States rejected the Commission's view that integrated border management should ultimately lead to the creation of a European border guard.

On 29 and 30 May the Italian-led feasibility study on the creation of a European border police was presented at a ministerial conference in Rome under the auspices of the Spanish Presidency. The feasibility study was based on the input of a larger number of national experts, most of whom tended to defend their national methods and organizational structures. This partially explains why the feasibility study – rather than coming out clearly in favour of the creation of a fully fledged European border police – advocated instead a complex network of national border police forces which would be partially fused by a number of uniform structures, such as special 'centres' as 'knots' of the network, common units for special tasks, common risk analysis and financing mechanism and a core curriculum. The study was filled with detailed operational and organizational assessments and proposals. Yet, it was lacking in clarity and forceful central ideas. Even some of the participating Member States were not fully satisfied, and a Brussels source seems even to have dismissed the entire study as '80 pages of waffle' (*Guardian*, 31 May).

In the meantime, the Council had come under serious pressure to act because, in the joint letter of 16 May mentioned above, Tony Blair and José-Maria Aznar called for more measures at external borders in the fight against illegal immigration. On 13 June 2002, the Council therefore agreed on a 'Plan for the Management of the External Borders of the Member States' (Council Document No. 10019/02). The plan took up most of the analysis and proposals in the Commission communication, merging it with some of the more practical elements of Italian-led feasibility study.

The Council plan, which was endorsed by the Seville European Council in June, was different from the Commission communication mainly in that it placed less emphasis on common legislation and financing in the field of border controls. It also refers only in rather vague terms to a later 'possible decision' on the setting up of a European Corps of Border Guards that would support, but not replace, national border police forces.

Yet, it left the door open for the eventual development of such a corps and provides for a very broad range of short and medium-term measures. These include: enhanced common operational co-ordination and co-operation mechanisms; moves towards a common integrated risk analysis; co-operation on training and inter-operational equipment; the gradual development of a common corpus of legislation – obviously to be based on the Schengen *acquis* – and burden-sharing between the Member States and the Union which, in the longer term, could include the funding of the acquisition of common equipment.

Many of the measures of the action plan were linked to precise deadlines, and some were clearly quite ambitious, going some way in the direction of the gradual establishment of a European border guard. This applies, in particular, to the envisaged creation of 'common units' – within five years – at especially sensitive land and sea borders (in the context of which, border guard officers of other Member States could even be vested with the competence to control persons and conduct joint patrols together with national officers).

Towards the end of the year it seemed that most of the Member States were favouring a 'network' model. This would leave national border guard forces in charge of their own border yet subject to common guidelines, training and equipment standards defined by a special Council body. It would also lead to the formation of a common rapid reaction force consisting of specially trained national units which could be deployed at particular 'hot spots' of external borders when requested by a Member State. As there are clearly major differences between national positions on the eventual creation and shape of a European border guard force, this issue could in the longer term emerge as an area for 'enhanced co-operation' involving initially only some of the Member States.

## II. Judicial Co-operation

Judicial co-operation in civil matters continued to develop rather slowly throughout the year. The one major element of progress was the political agreement reached in the Council on 28–29 November on a regulation concerning jurisdiction and the recognition and enforcement of judgments in matrimonial matters and those of parental responsibility, which is of particular importance in cases of child abduction. Member States had been divided over the question of the automatic return of a wrongfully removed or retained child to its usual country of residence because of its psychological implications, especially in cases of a very long stay in another Member State. The agreement reached in the Council established as a principle that, in the case of the wrongful removal or retention of a child, the courts of the Member State of origin keep their jurisdiction until the child has acquired a habitual residence in another Member State. This element of clear progress contrasted, however, with the Council's repeated failure to reach agreement on the framework decision on drug trafficking, the Netherlands still refusing to accept the principle of prison sentences for the possession of small amounts of soft drugs.

A major step forward for judicial co-operation in criminal matters was marked by the formal establishment of Eurojust following a Council decision of 28 February (Council, 2002a). As a result, the provisional unit, located in Brussels, could finally be formally replaced by the permanent Eurojust, located in the Hague, although organizational problems meant that it took several weeks before this office became fully operational. Composed of one member nominated by each of the EU countries plus supporting staff, Eurojust has been vested with the task of facilitating judicial co-operation between prosecutors and magistrates in the Member States. This is principally through the co-ordination of the competent authorities and the facilitation of the implementation of international mutual legal assistance and extradition requests. Mike Kennedy, a British Crown Prosecutor, was appointed as its first President, which may partly be seen as recognition of the very active role played in recent years by the UK in the judicial co-operation domain.

Depending on the type of action, Eurojust can either act through its national members or collectively as a college. Yet, it can only come into action if an investigation or prosecution case involves at least two Member States, and if it fits into one of the categories of 'serious crime' defined in Article 2 of the Europol Convention (including, *inter alia*, terrorism, drug trafficking and money-laundering) and Article 4 of the Eurojust decision (including, *inter alia*, computer crime, corruption and fraud). While this imposes certain restrictions on the scope of Eurojust's activities, the new structure could potentially play a more 'active' role than Europol, as it has been vested with the power to ask national prosecution authorities to undertake an investigation or prosecution, or to set up a joint investigation team. Eurojust can also request a Member State to consider whether another Member State might be in a better position to conduct an investigation or prosecution in a specific case of serious cross-border crime. In comparison with the existing European Judicial Network (EJN), with which it has to co-operate and which is mainly focused on improving contacts and bilateral co-operation, Eurojust has clearly been given a much more operational and multilateral set of tasks.

Data protection was a major issue in the negotiations on Eurojust right up to the final Council Decision in February. It can process data only on persons who are the subject of an investigation, on victims and on witnesses, and even the types of data which can be used are limited to the person's identity and the nature of the alleged offences. These data are accessible only to the national members, their assistants and authorized Eurojust staff, all of whom have been made subject to monitoring by the Joint Supervisory Authority. Concerns remained, however, over the restrictions on the rights of individuals to know and correct data relating to them and the different levels of liability – according to national laws – of Member States in case of a violation of data protection rules. Serious criticisms continued to be raised also on the inequality of powers of the national members of Eurojust – which vary according to the powers the respective prosecutor, judge or police officer has within its own territory and could be a source of confusion – and on the absence of jurisdiction of either the European Court of Justice or the European Court of Human Rights in relation to action taken by Eurojust as a college (see, e.g., Justice, 2002).

After the removal of several parliamentary reservations, both the framework decision on combating terrorism and the framework decision introducing the European arrest warrant were finally adopted by the Council on 13 June (*OJ* 2002 L 164 and *OJ* L 2002 L 190). This formally completed the two major elements of legislative breakthrough achieved in response to the 11 September terrorist attacks towards the end of 2001 (see the previous *Annual Review*). The lists of terrorist organizations and individuals subject to a freezing of their assets were several times amended and added to during the year, *inter alia*, to include the successor organization to the Kurdish PKK (KADEK) and the Popular Front for the Liberation of Palestine (PFLP).

## III. Police Co-operation

The further development of Europol continued to be an important issue on the Council's agenda during most of the year. Police organizations extended tasks in monitoring and analysing terrorist threats. The aftermath of the events of the 11 September 2001 had clearly given a new impetus and enhanced importance to Europol. This was reflected in an increase in Europol's budget for 2002 by 49.5 per cent which was justified by additional tasks in the fight against terrorism, the build-up of its information system and the new Europol liaison officers at Interpol and in the US. Yet Member States' views on the further development of Europol continued to differ and made building compromises in the Council extremely laborious.

After lengthy negotiations, the Council was finally able to agree (on 28–29 November) on a protocol to the Europol convention. The protocol enables Europol to participate in a supporting capacity in 'joint teams' led by the Member States, and to request national authorities to initiate and co-ordinate investigations in specific cases of serious cross-border crime. It also puts Europol in a position to take part in the possible creation of joint investigation teams involving authorities of two or more Member States for limited periods of time which the Council had approved through a framework decision on 13 June (Council, 2002b).

Another set of important reforms was seriously delayed, however. In July, the Danish Presidency introduced a set of proposals to amend the Europol convention, aimed at extending the scope of the police organization's remit, opening up access by other national law enforcement authorities to Europol and enhancing parliamentary scrutiny of Europol's work (Council Document 10307/02). As regards Europol's remit, the Danish Presidency went for a 'catch-all' concept by proposing to replace the current list of 25 offences by a general competence for 'serious international crime'. While this would have had the advantage of allowing Europol to address newly developing forms of cross-border crime quickly and without having to wait for a Council decision adding offences to the existing list, it entailed the risk of significant differences in interpretation being given to the concept of 'serious international crime' by individual Member States. The new classification would, however, reduce data protection standards, as the exchange of personal data would then no longer need to be justified on the basis of specifically identified criminal offences. As a result there was much opposition to the proposed change in the Council. Since a compromise proposal to extend the remit to 'international organized crime' raised similar concerns about the lack of clarity, the Danish Presidency revised its proposal in November to come back to a formula rather similar to the current Article 2 of the convention with its list of offences. On this basis the Council was able to reach political agreement (on 19 December) on a limited extension of the remit which would enable Europol to act also in case of mere suspicion and not only a factual indication of organized international crime.

The Danish Presidency equally failed to get sufficient support for its proposals to allow other national 'competent authorities' (such as individual police forces) to supply Europol with information, to respond to information requests and to request information and analysis from Europol. This would clearly have brought Europol into closer contact with the variety of national police forces in the Member States, from which it remains fairly remote under the current system. However, several Member States took the view that such a bypassing of the 'national units' (that are currently in charge of centrally co-ordinating and channelling all information flows to and from Europol at the national level) would reduce the quality and control of the information flows and create risks of confusion and contradictions between different sources.

There was also the argument that the current centralized system would ensure a greater degree of discipline and effective control of data flows in view of the large number of new Member States with their persisting structural weaknesses. As a result, the Danish Presidency had to come back to a formula – endorsed by the 19 December Council meeting – under which

Europol national units would remain the central liaison bodies between Europol and national authorities. This solution gives the Member States only slightly more flexibility in allowing direct information flows between other national authorities and Europol under the control of the national Europol units.

The Danish Presidency was more successful in getting support for its proposals on strengthening parliamentary scrutiny of Europol which were largely based on a far from revolutionary Commission communication in February on 'Democratic Control over Europol' (Commission, 2002a). Member States were able to agree on the regular forwarding to the European Parliament of the annual non-confidential reports of Europol and the Europol management board, as well as the analytical reports on data protection of the joint supervisory body. They also accepted an obligation for the Council to consult Parliament before Europol-related measures are adopted on certain specified matters such as the processing of personal data, their forwarding to third countries, relations with other bodies and the organization of Europol. Yet the Parliament's position emerging from the consultation will have no binding effects on the Council; and the Danish Presidency had to drop initial proposals under which the Director of Europol would have had to appear in his own right before the European Parliament and a potential joint committee consisting of representatives of the European Parliament and national parliaments set up specifically for the scrutiny of Europol activities. At the end of the year all of these changes still needed to be codified in a further protocol to the Europol convention.

By the end of the year, the political compromises reached on the issues of remit, relations with other national authorities and parliamentary scrutiny still needed to be formalized in another protocol to the Europol convention which would then be subject to national ratification. This brought out again the cumbersome process of amending this intergovernmental legal instrument, with the Member States still being unable to arrive at a consensus on replacing the Europol convention by a Council decision which would have done much to simplify the process.

A Commission proposal for a Council decision to establish a legal base for the funding of Europol out of the EC budget – initially €5 million for 2002 for activities related to the fight against terrorism – failed to be adopted by the Council in spite of strong support (379 to 29 votes) by the European Parliament. Some Member States felt that this would gradually transform Europol from an intergovernmental institution into a Community institution subject to some degree of control by both the Parliament and the Commission, and that it would complicate decision-making and priority-setting for Europol.

The various controversies regarding the further development of Europol did not prevent the police organization from making further progress in its relations with third countries, signing a new co-operation agreement with the Czech Republic and starting negotiations with a number of other countries. The most difficult new agreement to negotiate was – unsurprisingly – the second agreement with the United States on the exchange of personal data which was to complement the agreement of 6 December 2001 on the exchange of strategic and technical information and liaison officers. A range of NGOs had expressed major concerns about a potential undermining of EU data protection rules, and several Member States were not satisfied with the initial guarantees offered by the US regarding their data protection rules that are significantly lower than in the EU. A further problem was the question of Europol's immunity in the case of US citizens seeking compensation for injury suffered as a result of transfers of data by Europol. After the US government had given additional reassurances in a letter clarifying the content of relevant US legislation on data protection, the Council authorized the Director of Europol to sign the agreement with US representatives on 20 December in Copenhagen (Council Document No. 15231/02).

During the previous year, the newly created police chiefs' task force (PCTF) had been widely criticized for failing to provide leadership and continuity on the further development of EU police co-operation. In response to these criticisms, in April the PCTF set up a supervisory committee consisting of representatives of the past, present and future Presidencies of Europol, the Council and the European Commission. The new supervisory committee was given the task of improving the preparation of and the follow-up to PCTF meetings. Yet, it remains to be seen whether its existence will make much of a difference, as the work of the PCTF continues to be affected by a poorly defined function, a lack of operational powers and wide differences between the national status and competencies of its members.

## IV. Reforming JHA: The European Convention's Working Group Report

The debate on the further development of the 'area of freedom, security and justice' reached a new intensity during the year as a result of the launching of the European Convention. In its deliberations the Convention gave considerable room to justice and home affairs issues and set up a dedicated working group ('X'). From September to November the working group, which was chaired by former Irish Prime Minister John Bruton, held nine meetings and took evidence from a number of experts, mainly senior officials from national law enforcement authorities and EU institutions. On 2 December the group then submitted its final report with a range of reform proposals in view of a Constitutional Treaty of the EU (CONV 426/02).

The proposals of working group X were based on two 'golden rules'. The first was the introduction of a common legal framework for justice and home affairs – meaning effectively the removal of the first/third pillar division – which would, however, allow for some variations in procedures to take into account the particularities of this domain. The second was the separation, wherever possible, between 'legislative' and 'operational' tasks, a distinction justified on the grounds of the ever increasing importance of mechanisms and structures of practical co-operation between police and judicial authorities within the EU.

As regards future EU legislative action in the current areas of the first pillar, the group's final report recommended the application of qualified majority voting (QMV) and co-decision to legislation on asylum, refugees and displaced persons, immigration matters, visa policy and civil law co-operation. The latter incorporated as an exception most areas of family law. This appeared as a clear enough move towards majority voting, but the report left some questions unanswered – for example, that of the voting rules on border management legislation – and contained some rather complex solutions, such as maintaining family law under the unanimity rule, but not matters of parental responsibility. Some doubts were also left regarding the scope of the proposed new formal treaty objective of a 'common policy on immigration' as the report suggested that Member States would remain largely responsible for the admission and integration of third country nationals. This seemed slightly at odds with the recommendation that qualified majority voting and co-decision should apply to legislation in the whole immigration policy area, a proposal which is not without problems as long as some Member States continue to be exposed to much higher immigration pressures than others.

Regarding police and judicial co-operation in criminal matters, the group came out firmly in favour of replacing the current third pillar instruments (framework decisions, decisions and common positions) with the EC instruments of directives, regulations and decisions and abolishing conventions. This could indeed make a major contribution to legal coherence and the effectiveness of legislative action in these areas. The group followed the 'Tampere philosophy' by suggesting that the principle of mutual recognition of judicial decisions should be formally enshrined in the Constitutional Treaty. Yet it also accepted the need for the approximation of certain elements of criminal procedure and specific aspects of criminal law.

The report tried to reduce the potential tension between these different approaches by making legislative action on approximation dependent on a number of criteria, the most important of which was the 'serious nature' of the crime in question and its cross-border dimension. A majority of the working group felt it necessary for the scope of EU action to be limited by an exhaustive list of the crimes fulfilling these criteria (to be amended only by a unanimous decision of the Council). This would obviously entail a similar problem of rigidity as a fixed catalogue of competencies would for the EU as a whole. A rather curious criterion proposed was that of a potential justification of legislative approximation by the need to generate 'sufficient mutual confidence'. While mutual trust is certainly a most important commodity in constructing the area of justice, it would seem extremely difficult to define both such trust and its sufficient extent in a legal sense. The report was very clear, however, on the need for a legal basis permitting the adoption of common rules on elements of criminal procedure with transnational implications. This would indeed fill an existing *lacuna* and facilitate the full application of mutual recognition of judicial decisions. The group felt that the existing provisions on police co-operation were broadly adequate, but suggested a strengthening of the legal basis for taking action on crime prevention. This reflects the need for a better balance at EU level between preventive and penal action that had been increasingly recognized in recent years.

On the question of the voting rules to be applied in the current areas of the third pillar the group – unsurprisingly – failed to reach consensus. A majority of the members were willing to recommend QMV and co-decision on quite substantial matters. These included constituent elements and sanctions for the identified types of serious cross-border crime (see above), and common rules on specific elements of criminal procedure, such as the admissibility of evidence throughout the EU. Consensus was reached on applying QMV and co-decision to measures improving the effectiveness of Europol, but some members felt unable to agree to a similar recommendation regarding Eurojust. There were obviously some concerns about a proliferation of new EU bodies in the third pillar domain, as the group came out in favour of the setting up of such bodies – which would include a potential European border guard – being subject to unanimity in the Council. Rather interestingly the group proposed a continuation of the current sharing of the right of initiative between the Commission and Member States, this however in the form of a threshold of EU countries being required for a Member States' initiative to be admissible. This could indeed help to prevent a multiplication of initiatives with too much of a national bias and to create from the outset a 'critical mass' in the Council. Yet, the proposed maintenance of both unanimity in the substantial areas of police and judicial co-operation in criminal matters, and of a right of initiative of Member States, made the group's strong insistence on a full merger of the current first and third pillar areas in a common legal framework slightly less convincing.

As regards operational co-operation, the group suggested a streamlining of the current working structure in the Council, possibly under a single senior committee with executive responsibilities, to deal more effectively with all aspects of operational co-operation between police and judicial authorities. The group regarded the management of the EU's external borders as a priority area in the operational co-operation sphere. It came out in favour of financial solidarity and the gradual development of a common system of external border management including from a longer-term perspective, the 'possible' creation of a European border guard.

The report's consideration of the further development of co-operation through Europol and Eurojust revealed the difficulties of the suggested distinction between legislative and operational tasks. The group proposed that the Constitutional Treaty should open up the possibility of granting Europol powers relating to intelligence, co-ordination and carrying out of investigations, as well as the participation in operational actions. All this, however, would require legislative action in the operational domain. A significant number of members of the group supported the idea of creating a legal basis for a European public prosecutor responsible for detecting, prosecuting and bringing to judgment the perpetrators of crimes against the financial interests of the EU. This, however, was far from ripe for consensus, and members also disagreed on whether or not to enable Eurojust on a medium to long-term basis to bring cases before national courts.

Under the heading of 'horizontal questions', the group advocated the introduction of a provision on the technique of 'mutual evaluation' in order to ensure high standards in the implementation of EU justice and home affairs policies. This recommendation, clearly based on the long-standing use of the technique within the Schengen context, was at least partially a response to widespread concerns about implementation standards in the future new Member States. The group also suggested giving the Commission full powers for infringement proceedings before the Court of Justice in case of breaches of Member States' obligations in this domain, and recommended – more generally – the removal of any remaining restrictions on the role of the Court.

The Convention's working group report was by far the most comprehensive and analytical based set of reform proposals emanating from an EU body in recent years. While some commentators regarded it as over-ambitious, for instance on the European public prosecutor issue, others saw it as too conservative, for example on maintaining unanimity on many third pillar issues. What became perfectly clear, however, from both the report and the debates in the Convention's plenary was that there was a large consensus in this unique assembly about the ever-growing importance of this domain of EU policy-making. There was also accord over the need for the EU to arrive at a better match between its ambitions and capabilities to act.

## References

Commission of the European Communities (2002a) 'Communication … Democratic control over Europol'. *COM* (2002)95, 26 February.

Commission of the European Communities (2002b) 'Green Paper on a Community return policy on illegal residents'. *COM* (2002)175, 10 April.

Commission of the European Communities (2002c) 'Towards an integrated management of external borders'. (*COM*(2002) 233), 7 May.

Council of the European Union (2002a) 'Council Decision … setting up Eurojust with a view to reinforcing the fight against serious crime'. *OJ C* 58, 5 March.

Council of the European Union (2002b) 'Council Framework Decision … on joint investigation teams'. *OJ L* 161, 19 June.

Council of the European Union (2002c) 'Council Framework Decision … on combating trafficking in human beings'. *OJ L* 203, 1 August.

European Convention (2002) Final Report of Working Group X 'Freedom, Security and Justice'. Document *CONV* 426/02, Brussels 2 December.

Justice (2002) 'Eurojust. A Justice Briefing to MEPs'. London February.

JCMS 2003 Volume 41. Annual Review pp. 137–55

# Developments in the Member States

MICHAEL BRUTER
London School of Economics and Political Science

## Introduction

This section of the *Annual Review* will analyse the major political developments in the 15 European Union (EU) Member States in 2002, and their implications for European integration. This year was particularly rich in electoral terms for the European Union, with major elections taking place in no fewer than seven of the Member States. At the same time, public opinion was monitored very carefully as a new referendum on the Nice Treaty in Ireland was expected to have a major impact. The Swedish Parliament also announced a referendum on the euro (to take place on 14 September 2003).

Major debates occurred across the Member States on the forthcoming draft of the new EU Constitutional Treaty, with Germany and France attempting to forge common positions, and small countries and the UK also trying to have their own say in a heated and seemingly very open manner.

For these reasons, we shall pay particular attention to the electoral and opinion-related developments in the Member States in 2002, and to the national contribution to the debate on the Convention on the Future of Europe, as well as to the policy and legal aspects of integration.

## I. Elections: Calm Waters or Earthquake?

Two of the 'large' countries of the European Union – France and Germany – conducted important elections in April/May, June and September 2002. Austria, Ireland, the Netherlands, Portugal and Sweden were also to hold general elections during the year.

*Portugal: The Collapse of the Left*

The first national election to take place in the EU, in March, also brought the first *coup de théâtre* of the year to the Union's political scene. Portugal's long-standing socialist government (in office since 1995) ended up being narrowly defeated by the centre-right Social Democrats and their allies in the 17 March elections (see Table 1). The Socialist Party's vote was reduced to 37.9 per cent (and 96 seats), while the Social Democrats progressed to 40.1 per cent of the votes (and 105 seats). The 14 seats (8.8 per cent of the vote) gained by their coalition partner, the conservative *Partido Popular,* were sufficient to give the centre-right an absolute majority in the 230-seat *Assembleia da Republica.*

*France: Political Earthquake and Resurgence of a Politicized Youth*

In France, most observers expected a 'formal' first ballot of the presidential election (on 21 April) that would leave the two main contenders, Gaullist President Jacques Chirac and Socialist Prime Minister Lionel Jospin, fighting it out in a close race in the second ballot (on 5 May).

Apart from a few anecdotes (such as the Centrist candidate, François Bayrou, slapping a young boy trying to steal his wallet while he was visiting a rough suburban area, and the Greens changing candidates very late in the run-up to the elections), the campaign was largely unspectacular. The two main candidates preferred to defend their records in office rather than discuss new policy proposals. A few days before the first ballot of the elections, however, it seems that, after looking at the recent polls and at the reactions she was experiencing on the streets, Chirac's wife, Bernadette, expressed her belief that a Chirac–Le Pen second ballot would be far from impossible. Her comments provoked rather contemptuous reactions from the pollsters and the President's own communication team. The advisers of the Socialists were

Table 1: The Portuguese Elections (17 March 2002)

| *Party* | *Ideology* | *Votes* | *2002–1999* | *Seats* | *2002–1999* |
|---|---|---|---|---|---|
| Partido Social Democrata | Centre-right | 40.1 | +7.1 | 105 | +25 |
| Partido Socialista | Socialist | 37.9 | –7.0 | 96 | –16 |
| Partido Popular | Conservative | 8.8 | +0.3 | 14 | –1 |
| Coligacao Democratica Unitaria | Greens + Communists | 7.0 | –2.2 | 12 | –5 |
| Bloco de Esquerda | Extreme-left | 2.8 | +0.3 | 3 | –1 |
| Total | | 100 | | 230 | 226 |

Table 2: The French Presidential Elections

| *Candidate* | *Party* | *First* | *Second* |
|---|---|---|---|
| Chirac (incumbent) | RPR, Conservative | 19.9 | 82.2 |
| Le Pen | FN, Extreme-right | 16.9 | 17.8 |
| Jospin (Prime Minister) | PS, Socialist | 16.2 | |
| Bayrou | UDF, Centrist | 6.8 | |
| Laguiller | LO, Extreme-left | 5.7 | |
| Chevènement | PR, Left | 5.3 | |
| Mamere | Verts, Ecologist | 5.2 | |
| Other | | 24.0 | |
| Turnout | | 71.6 | 79.7 |

equally dismissive. Some party activists, for example, complained that the Socialist Party was not really campaigning hard enough on issues and was taking its candidate's fortune for granted.

On the night of the election, a small deviation from the pollsters' latest prediction created a political earthquake in the country and, to a large extent, around Europe. By 0.7 percentage points, the National Front xenophobe, Jean-Marie Le Pen, beat Jospin for second place (behind Chirac) amidst an unprecedented number (16) of candidates, and a record rate of abstention (28.4 per cent). Le Pen therefore qualified for the final round of the election in a run-off against Chirac. Despite Chirac's pole-position, the result of the first round was interpreted as a slap in the face for traditional political parties. For the first time, the incumbent President secured less than 20 per cent of the votes, while the left failed to be represented in the second ballot of the presidential race for the first time in three decades.

With the notable exception of Jospin who (along with a few extreme-left candidates) refused to express his voting preferences for the second ballot, almost the entire French political, intellectual and social elite called on voters to mobilize in a 'Republican Front' against intolerance and racism on 5 May. A few hours after the results of the first round were known, spontaneous demonstrations by teenagers and students took place across the country. They went on to be a regular daily feature between the two ballots, with increasing numbers of participants each time. Attempts by the political parties, trade unions and pressure groups to hijack the youth's demonstrations failed, as did the extreme-right's attempts to provoke the demonstrators into violence.

The French youth of 2002 became the symbol of a generation often accused of political cynicism and apathy, and one that had largely abstained in the first round. Yet, by the time of the second ballot, they expressed a desire to save democracy from intolerance, and dissatisfaction with traditional French political forces, providing a fresh challenge for established politicians, starting with the likely winner Chirac himself.

On 5 May, the worst fears of most commentators were proved wrong. President Chirac secured 82.2 per cent of the vote for his 'Republican' candidacy, Le Pen performing less well than even the two extreme-right candidates in the first ballot. Participation also increased by 8.1 percentage points (in spite of there being little suspense in the second ballot), with turnout measured at 79.7 per cent of the voters. Right away, the re-elected President Chirac admitted to having benefited from a large number of voters who did not support his policies and/or record, yet wanted to express their rejection of extreme-right ideology. He appointed centre-right Jean-Pierre Raffarin as Prime Minister, and asked the French people to support his political project further when voting for a new *Assemblée Nationale* in June.

Between early May and mid-June, political mobilization continued to be intense and the right, left, and extreme-right tried to refine their strategies. The moderate right argued that the main reason for the strong performance of Le Pen and the lack of enthusiasm for traditional parties was due to *cohabitation* (with a President and parliamentary majority belonging to different ideologies), and the poor focus of the mainstream parties on the issues of central concern to citizens. According to the presidential majority, French citizens were concerned with 'insecurity' (crime and, albeit to a limited extent, social difficulties in some French regions, as well as immigration). A clear attempt was also made to force the various parties of the centre-right to merge into a single pro-presidential party. This provoked the anger of the centrist UDF, whose leader, François Bayrou, performed much better than expected in the presidential election. On the other hand, the Socialist Party, now led by the not very charismatic François Hollande tried to play down their pre-presidential election criticisms of *cohabitation*.

The legislative elections (9 and 16 June) resulted in a sizeable majority for Jean-Pierre Raffarin, with the new '*Union pour la Majorité Présidentielle*' (UMP) securing 33.7 per cent of the votes in the first ballot and 357 out of 577 parliamentary seats. The Socialist vote collapsed to 24.1 per cent, giving them only 140 seats, whilst the UDF managed to survive and keep a parliamentary group of 29 (plus a few defectors from the UMP).

Just a month and a half after their big breakthrough, the National Front's vote fell to 11.3 per cent – not enough to make it to the second ballot in nearly as many constituencies as in 1997. The Party ceased to be viewed as a serious electoral trouble-maker by many analysts. The Greens could salvage only three parliamentary seats, and the Communists 21 (with less than 5 per cent of the vote). The latter's result, combined with the appalling performance of

Table 3: The French Legislative Elections

| *Party* | *Votes 1st* | *2002–1999* | *Seats* | *2002–1999* |
|---|---|---|---|---|
| UMP (Conservative) | 33.7 | +8.6 | 359 | +149 |
| UDF (Centrist) | 4.8 | * | 31 | * |
| PS-PRG-DG (Socialist) | 25.6 | –2.7 | 154 | –110 |
| FN (Extreme-right) | 11.3 | –3.8 | 0 | 0 |
| PCF (Communist) | 4.8 | –5.1 | 21 | –14 |
| Verts (Ecologist) | 4.5 | –0.9 | 3 | –12 |
| Divers Droite (Right) | 3.7 | * | 9 | * |

*Note*: * In the 1997 elections, the RPR, UDF, and most 'divers droite' competed together. Totals do not match because small lists are not counted and 13 seats were empty before the 2002 election.

Robert Hue in April, led the Communist Party to experience its most significant internal crisis since the collapse of the Communist bloc in 1990.

In June, the French political landscape was, therefore, returned to a rather paradoxical normality, with a clear right-wing majority, a more or less single party left-wing opposition, and still no National Front members in Parliament. The effect of the 21 April earthquake, however, was to be measured in another currency than sheer electoral results. A whole generation of new, active, yet politically apathetic citizens had just sent its loudest warning since 1968 to the whole way of 'doing politics' in France.

*The Netherlands: Hercule Poirot and the Fortuyn Mystery?*

Even if the French presidential election had resulted in the expected Chirac–Jospin battle, the forthcoming Dutch election (15 May), involving the charismatic leader, Lijst Pim Fortuyn, threatened to be the talk of the day in all the intellectual, political, and journalistic circles in Europe. Moreover, if Fortuyn had done well in the Dutch election and, given Le Pen's breakthrough in France (on 21 April), many would have argued that there may be a re-emergence of the far-right in Europe.

Pim Fortuyn, the young, homosexual and charismatic Mayor of Rotterdam and leader of the country's new Right-Populist party was shot dead by one of his enemies just a few days before the elections, creating a wave of controversy in one of the oldest European democracies. The other parties discussed the possibility of delaying the elections, before deciding against the measure. They clearly paid the price of voters' sympathy for the deceased. Pim Fortuyn's list secured 17 per cent of the votes, making it the second largest parliamentary group in the new *Tweede Kamer*.

Table 4: The Dutch General Elections

| *Party* | *Votes* | *Change* | *Seats* | *Change* |
|---|---|---|---|---|
| CDA (Christian Dem.) | 27.9 | +9.5 | 43 | +14 |
| LPF (Right Populist) | 17.0 | n.a. | 26 | n.a. |
| VVD (Liberal) | 15.4 | –9.3 | 24 | –14 |
| PvdA (Labour) | 15.1 | –13.9 | 23 | –22 |
| GL (Green) | 7.5 | –0.5 | 10 | –1 |
| SP (Socialist) | 5.9 | +2.4 | 9 | +4 |
| D66 (Social-Liberal) | 5.1 | –3.9 | 7 | –7 |
| CU (Conservative) | 2.5 | n.a. | 4 | n.a. |
| SGP (Christian Cons) | 1.7 | n.a. | 2 | n.a. |
| LN (Populist) | 1.6 | n.a. | 2 | n.a. |
| Total | 100 | | 150 | |

With the Labour Party having received one of its lowest scores ever, discussions were held between the representatives of the centre-right, right and occasionally the extreme-right parties represented in Parliament. However, no viable coalition could be found and, after a long period of uncertainty (not unusual in Dutch politics), new elections were finally called for February 2003.

### *Ireland: Calm Before the Tempest?*

If the major political event of the year in Ireland, viewed from the rest of Europe, was its October second referendum on the Nice Treaty, the Irish were undoubtedly more interested in the general elections for the lower chamber of Parliament, the *Dail Eireann*, held on 16 May.

In many ways, the elections were a non-event. The incumbent *Fianna Faíl*, a conservative party, slightly improved its parliamentary representation, gaining four more deputies (and a total of 81 out of the 166 members of the lower chamber). Their main challengers, *Fine Gael*, lost a large chunk of their electoral share, resulting in their parliamentary representation being reduced from 54 to 31. The Labour Party (21 instead of 17), Progressive Democrats (8 as against 4), and Greens (now 6 deputies) all increased their seats in Parliament. However, the main event was probably the confirmed emergence of the *Sinn Fein* who gained five representatives. In an unprecedented, worrying way, they came fourth in the list of voters' first preference with 6.5 per cent of the votes.

The 'No' vote to the Nice Treaty referendum in 2001 and the emergence of *Sinn Fein* as a new radical force in Irish politics were enough to make some

Table 5: The Irish General Elections

| *Party* | *Vote* | *Seats* | *Change* |
|---|---|---|---|
| Fianna Faíl (Conservative) | 41.5 | 81 | +4 |
| Fine Gael (Christian Democrat) | 22.5 | 31 | –23 |
| Labour | 10.8 | 21 | +4 |
| Sinn Fein (Extremist) | 6.5 | 5 | +4 |
| Progressive (Liberal) | 4.0 | 8 | +4 |
| Green | 3.8 | 6 | +4 |
| Other | 11.0 | 14 | +2 |

political commentators suspect that this may represent a significant change in Irish politics after several decades of apparent stability.

*Sweden: The Revenge of Social Democracy*

Spring 2002 was, therefore, as hectic in terms of national elections in the Member States as it was hellish for the European left. Indeed, left-wing parties or coalitions lost their majorities in Portugal, France and the Netherlands, failed to make the second round of the French presidential elections, and made no breakthough in Ireland.

The next elections after an eventless summer took place in Sweden in mid-September. They contrasted with the experience of left-wing incumbent governments in the spring. In the first place, they were utterly predictable. Second, the Social Democrats increased their majority by 3.5 percentage points while the conservative Moderate Party lost 7.7 percentage points, with the latter's votes largely being transferred to the Liberals.

The context of the elections was marked by four main questions: a continued economic downturn in the country and a persistently weak currency, the question of a possible referendum on future participation in the euro, the popu-

Table 6: The Swedish General Elections

| *Party* | *Votes* | *Change* | *Seats* |
|---|---|---|---|
| Social Democrats | 39.8 | +3.5 | 144 |
| Moderate (Conservative) | 15.2 | –7.7 | 55 |
| People's Party (Liberal) | 13.3 | +8.7 | 48 |
| Christian Democrats | 9.1 | –2.6 | 33 |
| Left (Socialist) | 8.3 | –3.6 | 30 |
| Centre Party | 6.1 | +1.1 | 22 |
| Greens | 4.6 | +0.1 | 17 |

larity of the incumbent Prime Minister, Göran Persson, and immigration. The campaign was relatively low key, even though observers were also keen on monitoring the performance of the extreme-right *Sverigedemokraterna*, that was hoping to build on the recent successes of ideologically close parties in Denmark and Norway.

However, the party obtained only 1.4 per cent of the votes and failed to secure any representation in Parliament. All in all, Sweden signed up for a further four years of Social Democratic government with a referendum on the euro likely to be called for the autumn of 2003. As for political commentators, they were already turning their eyes to the far more disputed German election to follow a week later.

*Germany: Much Ado About Nothing?*

By the start of the summer, the incumbent 'Red–Green' coalition of Chancellor Gerhard Schröder's Social Democrats and Foreign Minister Joshka Fischer's Greens had fallen to rather low levels of popularity amongst German citizens. The economy looked gloomier than ever. Equally, the weak performance of the euro on the world's currency market was partly attributed to Germany's fragile economic policy, a factor not helped by criticisms by the European Commission. Furthermore, the integration of the East German Länder seemed everything but successful, whether economically, socially or politically.

In order to counter this already ageing SPD–Green coalition, and fearing that their liberal FDP partners might fare poorly in the coming elections, the main parties of the German right, the Christian Democratic CDU-CSU, chose shock tactics and ran under the leadership of the conservative Bavarian Prime Minister, Edmund Stoiber. The CDU-CSU campaign was accused of incorporating nationalistic and anti-immigration themes that have been largely avoided in mainstream German politics in the post-war period. Throughout the winter and the following spring, the Christian Democrats gradually built

Table 7: The German General Elections

| *Party* | *Vote* | *2002/199* | *Seats* | *2002/1998* |
|---|---|---|---|---|
| SPD (Social Dem.) | 38.5 | –2.4 | 251 | –47 |
| CDU (Christian Dem.) | 29.5 | +1.1 | 190 | –8 |
| CSU (Social Christians) | 9.0 | +2.3 | 58 | +11 |
| Grüne (Greens) | 8.6 | +1.9 | 55 | +8 |
| FDP (Liberal) | 7.4 | +1.2 | 47 | +4 |
| PDS (Ex-Communist) | 4.3 | –0.8 | 2 | –34 |

up a significant lead in public opinion polls. By the beginning of the summer of 2002, the return to power of the German Christian Democrats (utilizing a very different political style from that of Helmut Kohl's largely centrist leadership) looked more than likely.

Nevertheless, the course of events in summer 2002 somewhat modified these expectations. Germany fell victim to severe flooding and weather problems that, strange as it might sound, seem to have marked the beginning of the Christian Democrats' misfortune. On the one hand, the Chancellor was perceived as sympathetic to the needs of the flood victims (urgently visiting the worst hit areas, and seen in public comforting and assuring them of state support). In contrast, Stoiber refused initially to interrupt his holidays to comment on the catastrophe. He was quickly branded as heartless and unsympathetic by the media and especially by the influential German tabloids.

Right away, the gap between the two camps closed. A head-to-head debate between the two Chancellor candidates was held on 25 August for the first time in German history. It attracted 15 million viewers. While it was mostly perceived to be superficial and uninteresting, the Prime Minister seemed to fare marginally better than his rival who continued to lose public sympathy. A second debate (8 September), just two weeks before the election led to a similar outcome.

The last few weeks of the campaign were particularly dull. On election day, the Social Democrats (SPD) and the Christian Democrats (CDU-CSU) polled almost identical scores (about 38.5 per cent of the votes each). This represented a rise of 3.4 percentage points for the Christian Democrats (+1.1 for the CDU, and +2.3 for the Bavarian and more conservative CSU) and a fall of 2.4 percentage points for the SPD (who also lost 47 seats as compared to 1998). However, in terms of seats, the Social Democrats still gained three more than the main right-wing alliance, to which they could add the 55 deputies of the Greens (the Greens secured 8 more seats, and a 1.9 percentage point increase in their voting share). This gave the 'Red–Green' government a majority of 306 of the 603 members of the *Bundestag*, one of the tiniest parliamentary majorities in contemporary German history.

In direct contrast to most forecasts, the liberal FDP also saw their voting share surge to 7.4 per cent (up 1.2 percentage points and gaining four extra seats). In contrast, the ex-communist PDS lost 0.8 percentage points, falling under the key 5 per cent threshold for parliamentary representation and thereby resulting in a drop in seats from 36 to a mere 2 representatives. The extreme-right parties that made fairly significant gains in 1998 in terms of votes (although not securing representation in the *Bundestag*) lost some ground. The *Republikaner* obtained only 1.3 per cent of the votes, the openly neo-nazi

NPD barely 0.4 per cent of the votes and the newer PRO an insignificant 0.8 per cent of the vote.

Given his slimmer parliamentary majority, the margin of manœuvre for Chancellor Schröder and his 'Red–Green' coalition government is extremely limited. Indeed, shortly after the election, the popularity of the Chancellor and his government started plummeting once again. The prospect of very difficult regional elections in several key Länder made it likely that Schröder will have to handle a right-wing controlled *Bundesrat*, and a majority of unsympathetic state governments that could further reduce his political and governmental options over the next four years.

*Austria: Running from Haider's Ghost?*

In 1999, Austria stunned the world when the conservative ÖVP and the extreme-right FPÖ formed a coalition government under the leadership of the ÖVP leader, Wolfgang Schüssel. The new coalition was based on a new 'black-blue' majority in Parliament (with both ÖVP and the FPÖ controlling 26.9 per cent of the votes and 52 of the 183 seats in the Austrian Parliament). The Social Democratic SPÖ, usually regarded as the most dominant political party in Austrian politics (and with 33.2 per cent of the vote and 65 seats), formed the principal opposition.

The initial response on the part of the other Member States was to impose diplomatic sanctions as a means of showing their disapproval of the new Austrian government being reliant upon the support of the FPÖ. Yet, after several months, the Union came to realize that nothing could be done to reverse the situation in Austria, and the country returned to its rather quiet political life, in spite of the criticisms of many intellectuals and journalists (some of whom, like Anton Pelinka, were sued by the FPÖ).

In September 2002, however, with the FPÖ performing poorly in public opinion polls, Jörg Haider, the populist and charismatic leader of the FPÖ, questioned the electoral outcomes of the party's coalition strategy. He decided to precipitate a political crisis in Austria by persuading his party to leave the coalition, thereby prompting early general elections (called for 24 November).

The election campaigns were fairly tense. Given the poor showing of the FPÖ in the polls, there was intense campaigning on the part of the SPÖ and ÖVP. Chancellor Schüssel claimed that the benefit of having the far-right in a coalition was that it would moderate its political demands (and thus lose some credibility in certain quarters of its normal electoral support). In contrast, the Social Democrats blamed Schüssel for having compromised Austria's reputation in Europe by relying on a political party that hardly tried to hide its anti-immigrant and xenophobic rhetoric.

Table 8: The Austrian General Elections

| *Party* | *Votes* | *Change* | *Seats* | *Change* |
|---|---|---|---|---|
| ÖVP (Conservative) | 42.3 | +15.4 | 79 | +27 |
| SPÖ (Social-Dem.) | 36.5 | +3.3 | 69 | +4 |
| FPÖ (Extreme Right) | 10.0 | –16.9 | 18 | –34 |
| Die Grünen (Greens) | 9.5 | +2.1 | 17 | +3 |
| Liberal Forum (Lib) | 1.0 | –2.7 | 0 | n.a. |
| Communists | 0.6 | +0.1 | 0 | n.a. |
| Total | 100 | | 183 | |

On election day, the Conservative ÖVP secured 42.3 per cent of the vote, (up 15.4 percentage points since 1999), making them the largest parliamentary party by some margin. The Social Democrats (SPÖ) obtained 36.5 per cent of the votes (an increase of 3.3 percentage points). Haider's party registered 10 per cent of the vote (a decline of 16.9 percentage points), with the Greens having 9.5 per cent (up 2.1 percentage points). In terms of parliamentary seats, however, the 79 (out of 183) representatives of the ÖVP would not allow the Conservatives to govern on their own. After the election, no coalition combination (with the 69-seat strong SPÖ, as in the old times, with the 18-seat strong FPÖ, as in 1999–2002, or even with the leftist Greens and their 17 representatives) was excluded by incumbent Chancellor Schüssel. His position was stronger this time, given that no coalition could possibly be created without his party.

After several months of unsuccessful negotiations with the Social Democrats followed by brief, if ill-fated discussions with the Greens, Chancellor Schüssel ended up forming a redesigned coalition with the FPÖ in February 2003. The far-right party obtained slightly fewer portfolios than in the last government, yet retained some key governmental positions such as Vice-Chancellor/Minister of Justice (Dieter Boehmdorfer), which was heavily criticized under the first coalition government. The new government was sworn in on 28 February 2003 with the democratic world being not nearly so vocal in its criticisms as four years earlier.

### *Conclusion: Electoral Developments in the Member States in 2002*

2002 proved to be an important year in Europe in electoral terms. The two historical pivots of European integration (France and Germany) held no fewer than three major national elections, and Portugal, Austria, the Netherlands, Sweden and Ireland contributed to a heavy electoral calendar.

By and large, the year (particularly the first half) was largely beneficial to Europe's political right with the respective parties assuming power in France, Portugal and the Netherlands (and usurping the previous dominance of the left) and asserting their electoral domination in Austria and Ireland. After a catastrophic start, the left retained its presence as the leading political force in Sweden (where the Social Democrats traditionally dominate) and in Germany (where the SPD and the Greens continued to deny the Christian Democrats).

As far as 'new politics' were concerned, the results were mixed, especially for the Greens (who resisted fairly well and even gained ground in Germany, Sweden, and Austria, yet collapsed in France). As for the extreme-right, the picture is even more difficult to characterize. The Austrian FPÖ ended up retaining its participation in one of the few EU national governments where the far-right had a role in spite of losing nearly 60 per cent of their share of the vote in the national elections. In contrast, extreme-right forces performed rather poorly in Germany, Sweden and the French legislative elections. Nevertheless, the breakthrough of extremist parties in Ireland and Portugal, the impressive second position of the Pim Fortuyn list in the Netherlands (after the death of its leader), and the astonishing *coup de théâtre* of the French presidential elections in which National Front leader Jean-Marie Le Pen made it to the second ballot, were enough to reinforce the profile of the far-right as the main threat to the established European democracies.

The growing cynicism of the European electorates was also reflected in the record low turnout rates of many of the elections held this year. A record 28.4 per cent of the French electorate abstained for the first ballot in the presidential elections, while 36 per cent and 39 per cent failed to vote in the two ballots of the legislative elections respectively. Abstention also reached 37 per cent in Ireland, and passed the symbolic 20 per cent mark in both Germany and the Netherlands.

Particularly interesting was the lack of motivation of young voters, partly blamed for the relatively good results of the extreme-right in several national elections. Many parties, intellectuals and organizations started to search for ways in which the electorate in general and young citizens in particular could be motivated to 'rejoin' the political life of their Member State. Proposed solutions ranged from suggested reforms of the electoral system (such as in France) to the modernization of political parties and electoral campaigns, through to the greater involvement of ethnic minorities, immigrants and youth in the political debate. Several reforms, both at national and party level, sought in the coming years to improve participation and also correct the lack of democratic satisfaction apparent in public opinion polls taken in 2002.

## II. Public Opinion in the Member States

### *The Irish Referendum: Requiem for a Treaty?*

In 2001, the traditionally 'pro-European' Ireland stunned the European Union by rejecting the Nice Treaty in a public referendum. Although the Treaty was supposed to pave the way for Union to enlarge, it clearly failed to motivate Irish voters in a positive way. The Treaty was heavily criticized in Ireland for encompassing confused reforms that would fail to address the institutional weaknesses of the European Union. As well as including reforms of the Union and its decision-making system to prepare for expansion of the Union from 15 to 25 countries, the Treaty incorporated the new Charter of Fundamental Rights and the European Rapid Reaction Force. Yet, the status of the Charter and the Force was fairly unclear and the institutional reforms were largely suspected of making the Union's decision-making even more complicated and obscure than ever before.

The 2001 referendum was primarily characterized by a very low turnout and a perceived attempt by citizens to express their general dissatisfaction with Irish politics. The 'No' camp was, in effect, a surprised victor in this largely uneventful race. While the low turnout was undoubtedly to the disadvantage of the 'Yes' camp, the result probably reflected the unease of the Irish (and public opinion in other Member States) with the enlargement process. Beyond the Treaty itself, and its occasional lack of clarity, the Irish were being asked to approve an enlargement process that would modify their status within the European Union. It would formally change Ireland's role from being one of the poorer states and main beneficiaries of EU funds, to that of being a 'richer' Member State that should contribute more financially.

The Irish public clearly expressed its sympathy for enlargement (see below) but remained wary of any impact on Ireland's position with regards to several key EU policies. Similar reactions could be witnessed in other countries, such as in Spain, Portugal or Greece. In one sense, the Irish 'No' probably showed rather graphically a major internal conflict within European public opinion. On the one hand, citizens were faced with the 'need' to enlarge the European Union and facilitate the 'natural' geographical and cultural reorientation of Europe. Yet, on the other hand, they were scared of an enlargement process that would at the same time probably impose discernible economic costs on the current EU-15 and a greater political risk of a less integrated process involving ten more Member States.

Nonetheless, arguing that the low participation was a clearly misleading factor, the Irish government decided to organize a second referendum on the Nice Treaty, thereby upsetting the Eurosceptics throughout Europe, still startled at their unexpected victory in Ireland. The referendum date was set for 21 October.

The referendum campaigns were more dramatic than a year earlier. On the one hand, the 'No' camp protested loudly at the lack of 'democratic fairness' in an Irish government organizing a second referendum on the Nice Treaty merely because it did not like the answer given in the first. On the other hand, the 'Yes' camp insisted on the need to make sure that Ireland would not become the 'shame' of Europe by being labelled the country that made enlargement to central Europe and the Mediterranean impossible.

Interestingly enough, the results of *Eurobarometer* 58 (autumn 2002), show that, in 2002, the Irish were the EU citizens that thought that their country benefited most from EU membership (82 per cent against 9 per cent who thought that it did not). The figures also indicate that the Irish were the second best (after Luxembourg) supporters of their country's EU membership status (74 per cent as opposed to only 7 per cent against), and the third most (after Greece and Denmark) in favour of further enlargement (67 per cent in favour and barely 15 per cent against). Fifty-eight per cent of Irish *Eurobarometer* respondents even thought that enlargement should be a priority of the Union (again, the third highest score among the EU-15). In these circumstances, all 'rational' expectations should have been for a 'Yes' vote in the second referendum.

Unlike June 2001, the 21 October 2002 referendum took place amid substantial media coverage and international pressure. Partly as a result, the number of voters turning out increased by more than 50 per cent (from 973,000 in 2001 to 1,494,000 in 2002). In other words, turnout increased from just above one-third to half of the Irish electorate. Virtually all this mobilization benefited the 'Yes' camp. Indeed, while the 'No' only gained 14,000 votes, the number of voters saying 'Yes' more than doubled from 453,000 to 960,000. In 17 months, the country therefore switched from a 54 per cent majority saying 'No' to 63 per cent in favour. On this basis, Ireland became the fifteenth and final Member State to ratify the Nice Treaty which therefore came into effect.

### *Sweden, Denmark, the United Kingdom and the Euro*

Another long-standing question of interest for pollsters has been the attitude of public opinion towards the euro in the three EU countries that still do not participate in the single currency, namely Denmark, Sweden and the UK.

In the United Kingdom, the landslide victory of Tony Blair's Labour Party in 2001 (see previous *Annual Review*) raised some expectations that a British referendum on the euro may be held in the early years of the new parliamentary session. However, the likelihood became increasingly remote as 2002 progressed. The influence of the relatively Eurosceptic Chancellor chequer, Gordon Brown, increased and the assessments of the rather vague 'five economic tests' (proposed by the Blair government as a precursor to holding a referendum) had yet to be completed by the year's end.

Throughout 2002, contradictory comments seemed to be made by both the Prime Minister and various Cabinet members, whilst public support for the euro failed to rise significantly even after the 12 Member States of the euro area celebrated the launch of the new currency's notes and coins. Undoubtedly, this was one of the primary reasons for the Prime Minister to delay the prospective referendum, Yet, there were also growing criticisms of the government's strategy of 'waiting' in recognition of the lukewarm public opinion (as opposed to taking a forthright pro-euro stance in front of the voters).

In Sweden and Denmark, however, things started to look more positive for the single currency in 2002. After the September general election, the Swedish government announced that a referendum on the single currency would be scheduled for autumn 2003 (to be held on 14 September). However, public opinion on joining the euro remains volatile in Sweden.

In Denmark, positive views finally started clearly to outweigh negative ones in the opinion polls. According to *Eurobarometer* 58, 55 per cent of Danes were now in favour of Denmark joining the euro, with only 40 per cent against. The most liberal parties within the Danish right-wing coalition (traditionally in favour of European integration), toyed with the idea of reviewing the status of Denmark's opt-out on EMU, although much would also depend on the government's performance when holding the EU Council Presidency in late 2002. However, the presence of more conservative parties in the coalition, and the fear of repeating the catastrophic scenario of the first Maastricht referendum (in 1992), encouraged the Fogh Rasmussen government to take a little more time before calling for a plebiscite on this issue.

### *Governments, Public Opinions, the Constitution and Enlargement*

2002 was also the year that saw final clarification of which countries would be likely to join the European Union on 1 May 2004. This clear deadline was perceived as having a very direct influence on the need for the European Union to reform its institutions and probably to adopt its first Constitutional Treaty. The Convention on the Future of Europe, chaired by former French President, Valéry Giscard d'Estaing, prepared proposals for a new constitution and several national governments have tried to influence the debate by agreeing on possible paths of institutional and policy modernization.

On the policy front, the main news from the Member States was undoubtedly the reaching of agreement on the modernization of the common agricultural policy (CAP) between France and Germany before the December 2002 Copenhagen summit. This agreement between France, the main beneficiary of the CAP, and Germany, the primary contributor to the EU budget, had long appeared remote. Yet, the agreement clearly unsettled the British government that counted on Franco–German disagreements to avoid any further questioning of the UK budgetary rebate. The accord between France and Germany opens the way for the renegotiation of the CAP after 2006 and implies that the continuation of the British rebate (as a significant oddity of the EU budget) may need to be reviewed as well. The Blair government claimed that the stance was unacceptable and fought an emerging 'grand coalition' against the rebate. However, most Member States were mostly relieved to avoid a pre-enlargement crisis that would be related to the CAP.

In terms of developments in the Member States, however, this pre-Copenhagen agreement was first and foremost a sign of a revival of the Franco–German 'special relationship', only a few years after the 'third way' project shared by Tony Blair and Gerhard Schröder seemed to suggest a possible restructuring of diplomatic alliances within Europe. Indeed, the fact that this renewal took place between a left-wing German government and a right-wing French administration was also to be taken as a further indication that the European project still largely goes beyond the left–right ideological debate.

The same was true for the debates in many Member States with regard to the discussions on the Convention on the Future of Europe. However, given the fact that, in relation to the Convention, the European Commission and the European Parliament were trying to lead the 'think tank' battle, the national governments often preferred to remain on the sidelines in the actual preparation of the future Constitutional Treaty.

The British Foreign Minister, Jack Straw, wrote (on 10 October) a long editorial in the *Economist* discussing the need for a European Constitution and the form that he thought it should assume. He insisted that the Constitutional Treaty should be brief (taking the US constitution as a model), and clarify the limits of EU competencies. In his words, it should specify that the EU is a community of sovereign states, and detail the 'purpose, principles, then organs and institutions – the "why" and the "how" first, then the "what" in terms of broad policies, after that' while stressing the role of national parliaments in the European decision-making process. Regardless of his essentially intergovernmental stance, the official approval of the very principle of a European Constitution by the British Foreign Secretary has come as a surprise to many observers.

As regards this 'constitutional' debate, the French and the German governments once again tried to come up with a common approach. Chirac and Schröder met (on 14 December) to discuss the future Constitutional Treaty and any common proposals about what it should include. The most notable idea was that of a dual Presidency of the European Union. A new President of the European Council would be elected by Council members for a period of two and a half years with the possibility of a second mandate (instead of the six-monthly rotating Presidency).

The two leaders also proposed that the Foreign Affairs High Representative be given a 'double' Council/Commission cap, implicitly opening the field of the common foreign and security policy (CFSP) to Community rule. The President of the European Commission would see his powers reinforced and would be elected directly by the European Parliament alone. This proposal was tentatively approved by Spain and the United Kingdom. Yet, the smaller Member States were more apprehensive. In particular, the Netherlands led a group of those who want to maintain the rotating Presidency. Greece seemed to also support this approach. The Commission was happy at the idea that its President would be elected directly by the European Parliament. It remained, however, rather sceptical about the sensibility of having two 'equal' Presidents sharing power in the Union.

At this stage, the Member States were somehow trapped; between the proposals of the various actors preparing the new Convention's constitutional drafts and the stances of the citizens they claim to represent. This chapter will finish, therefore, with a survey of citizens' attitudes throughout Member States on the eve of the adoption of the first European Constitutional Treaty.

### *Conclusion: Public Opinion, the Union and its Future Constitution*

Since the mid-1990s, European public opinion has followed a strange path. On the one hand, public opinion became more sceptical in its assessment of the concrete benefits of European integration for EU members. On the other hand, support for European integration has kept increasing and it is becoming more and more clear that a mass European identity is emerging. The year 2002 confirmed this evolution. According to the results of *Eurobarometer* 58 (autumn 2002), the proportion of citizens between spring 2000 and autumn 2002 who perceived that EU membership brought them advantages decreased by two points, while the proportion of citizens having a positive image of the EU increased by seven points during the same period.

In exactly the same way, ratings on the perceived benefits of membership decreased slightly for the third year in a row. However, there is still a majority of 50 per cent against 28 per cent who do not believe their country has benefited from being in the Union. Overall public support for European integration also rose (building on two consecutive years where there was an increase) to reach an EU average of 55 per cent (up 7 percentage points since 2000). Indeed, those citizens who thought that their country's full membership was 'a bad thing' represented only 10 per cent of the total. Moreover, the desired speed of further integration was also on the increase for the sixth year running.

The countries where support for European Union membership was the highest were Luxembourg (83 per cent) Ireland (74 per cent) and the Netherlands (69 per cent). The lowest rating was recorded for the UK where only 31 per cent of the British public thought full membership was 'a good thing'. Yet, in all 15 Member States, including the United Kingdom, many more people perceived European Union membership as 'a good thing' rather than as a bad one (only 19 per cent of the British public viewed full membership as 'a bad thing').

In 2002, support for the various policies of the European Union was also improving in all Member States. There was a public majority (67 per cent) supporting a common foreign policy, 74 per cent in favour of a common defence policy, and 67 per cent for economic and monetary union (EMU). Support for the euro also increased significantly, recording a 75 per cent approval rating in spring 2002 in the euro area, and 67 per cent for the European Union as a whole. These results are respectively 9 and 8 percentage points higher than a year before.

Finally, public 'trust' in the EU institutions also increased significantly in 2002, opening the way for further institutional reform and democratization. Except in Britain, the European Parliament received 'trust' scores of between 52 per cent (Sweden) and 75 per cent (Luxembourg) in the Member States (for instance, 69 per cent in Belgium, 62 per cent in France, 74 per cent in Italy, 58 per cent in Germany, 65 per cent in the Netherlands). The EU average for 'trusting' the European Parliament was 59 per cent.

Similarly, the European Commission seems to have finally overcome the scandals of the 1990s. The 'trust' of the public in the Commission in the various Member States was reasonably good, recording, for example, percentage ratings of 64 per cent in Belgium, 59 per cent in Spain, 67 per cent in Ireland, 74 per cent in Luxembourg, and 65 per cent in Italy. Average EU 'trust' rating in the EU-15 was 53 per cent. In more and more countries, these 'trust' scores are now higher than for equivalent national institutions, and not only in Belgium, Italy and France as was the case ten years ago.

In this context, it is not surprising that the European public should be widely in favour of radical modernization and democratization of the European political system, which could also dramatically increase the democratic legitimacy of the European Union (one of the reasons why Member States resist such change).

Indeed, in 2002, 48 per cent of citizens against 36 per cent (43 per cent against 37 per cent in 2000) were already satisfied with the way 'democracy' functions in the European Union. However, most were ready for an acceleration of the EU democratization process that goes much beyond the will of the Member State governments. In particular, by the end of 2002:

- 65 per cent of citizens across the EU were in favour of a European constitution (9 per cent against). National variations ranged from 49 per cent against 9 per cent, compared to 79 per cent against 5 per cent in Italy);
- a directly elected President of the European Commission was by far the preferred institutional arrangement for EU citizens (40 per cent in favour of this option – out of four possible answers). It was the case in all Member States except Finland and Sweden;
- an overwhelming majority of citizens in all countries were still in favour of increasing the powers of the European Parliament.

All in all, public opinion in the EU seems to have reached a new level of maturity in its attitudes towards further European integration, demanding more control and scrutiny over the way the decisions are made. To some extent, this positivism in favour of a more democratic European Union seems in contrast with the continuing rise in abstention by voters in national elections and the good performance of extreme-right parties and candidates in several Member States. This paradoxical evolution of citizens – navigating between cynicism and idealism – may indicate a potentially longer-term tendency in most Member States in the twenty-first century.

JCMS 2003 Volume 41. Annual Review pp. 157–72

# Developments in the Applicant States

KAREN HENDERSON
University of Leicester

## Introduction

2002 was the year in which the EU finally decided which of the current 13 candidate states would be invited to join in 2004 in the first wave of 'eastward enlargement'. Appropriately, the decision came at the Copenhagen European Council of December 2002, nearly ten years after the Copenhagen European Council of June 1993 had first taken the decision in principle that 'the associated countries in Central and Eastern Europe that so desire shall become members of the Union', and established the economic and political conditions necessary for membership. Ten states were invited to join: Cyprus, the Czech Republic, Estonia, Hungary, Latvia, Lithuania, Malta, Poland, Slovakia and Slovenia. Bulgaria and Romania had themselves conceded that they would not be ready by 2004, although they were making reasonable progress in accession talks, and negotiations with Turkey had yet to begin.

The later stages of the accession process have increasingly thrown the spotlight on the importance of the domestic political situations in the candidate states. This new chapter of the *Annual Review* has been designed to examine developments in the internal politics of each candidate state that were significant for the EU, as well as the state of public opinion on EU membership which was to become crucial in 2003, when most of them were to put the accession treaties to the test of a public referendum.

## I. Elections in the Applicant States

2002 was a particularly important election year domestically for the accession states. The four central European Visegrád countries – the Czech Republic, Hungary, Poland and Slovakia – are the most populous of the states due to join the EU in 2004, and national elections took place in all of them except Poland. There were also parliamentary elections in Latvia and Turkey, and presidential elections in Slovenia. In most cases, the prize for the victor was considerable: a place in the history books as the leader who took their state into the European Union.

*Hungary*

The Hungarian parliamentary elections of April 2002 were the most bitterly contested since the fall of communism. This was reflected in the exceptionally high voter turnout of 71 per cent in the first round, and over 73 per cent in the second round. While not particularly remarkable by European standards, this contrasted markedly with the exceptionally low turnouts in all other post-communist Hungarian elections, including the first held in 1990. What was also notable about the elections was that the first round held on 7 April confounded opinion poll predictions of a win by the incumbent conservative right *Fidesz* Party of Prime Minister, Viktor Orbán, with the second round on 21 April finally giving a 10-seat majority to the Hungarian Socialist Party in coalition with the far smaller Alliance of Free Democrats. Both the unexpected outcome of the first round, and the closeness of the result were instrumental in sharpening the political battle and increasing turnout between the two ballots, which is unusual in two-round elections anywhere.

The alternation of government brought about by the 2002 election fitted into a Hungarian pattern of more than a decade's duration. This was a pattern

Table 1: Results of the Hungarian Parliamentary Elections, 7 and 21 April 2002

| *Party* | *Seats* | *% of Vote (First Round Lists)* |
|---|---|---|
| Government coalition | | |
| Hungarian Socialist Party (MSZP) | 178 | 42.1 |
| Alliance of Free Democrats (SzDSz) | 20 | 5.5 |
| Total government coalition | 198 | 47.6 |
| Opposition | | |
| *Fidesz*-Hungarian Civic Party/ Hungarian Democratic Forum (*Fidesz*-MPP/MDF) | 192 | 41.1 |
| Others | 0 | 11.3 |
| Total opposition | 192 | 52.4 |

*Note:* The Hungarian electoral system is complex. The first round comprises a proportional representation element, with 5 per cent threshold, for 140 seats awarded to party lists at county level, as well as a vote for a candidate in a single member district. The second round vote is for candidates in single member districts where no candidate obtained an absolute majority in the first round, after which national list mandates are awarded on a compensatory basis.

in which broadly left (yet economically reformist) secular cosmopolitan governments, led by the social-democratized communist successor party that had crafted the country's smooth exit from communism in 1989, were followed by governments led by more conservative nationally oriented parties. The fact that the country was one of the most stable in the post-communist world had been reflected by the unusual ability of governments to remain in power for the full four-year parliamentary term, as well as a much higher degree of continuity in the party system than elsewhere.

The major shift that had taken place in this period was in the nature of the right, which from 1998 to 2002 had become dominated by *Fidesz*, the Alliance of Young Democrats. This was a younger and more dynamic proponent of Hungarian national interest than the 1990–94 government of the Hungarian Democratic Forum. The right had traditionally shown far more concern than the left about the situation of ethnic Hungarians in neighbouring countries. During its last year in power, it had become embroiled in bitter arguments with both Romania and Slovakia over its new 'status law' by which the Budapest government granted ethnic Hungarians in both countries, and other neighbouring states, special cultural, and – most controversially – economic rights. While the Socialists did not openly contest the law in principle, they argued over the details, and the Alliance of Free Democrats criticized it for opposing the spirit of European integration. This argument had some validity since, while the international community was loathe to become involved in arguments between Hungary and its neighbours and merely exhorted the government to reach agreement with them, the EU was clear that Hungary, once a member, would not be able to differentiate between citizens of other EU Member States on the grounds of their ethnicity.

The EU itself was not a major issue in the election campaign, in spite of the fact that accession was imminent. Hungary had consistently been a front-runner for EU membership among the countries of central and eastern Europe (CEECs) from 1989 onwards, and the likelihood and desirability of its gaining membership was barely questioned at either domestic or international level. Although foreign ownership of land was a contentious issue in negotiations with the EU, the Independent Smallholders Party that campaigned most heavily on the issue had fractured internally and failed to re-enter Parliament in 2002. The more xenophobe Hungarian Justice and Life Party likewise failed to enter Parliament again, despite toning down its rhetoric in a vain attempt to make itself a possible coalition partner for *Fidesz*, which was its only chance of gaining any government power.

The battle between the Socialists and *Fidesz* was therefore fought mainly on domestic issues such as corruption and the economy, but with an acerbic intensity that was ideological rather than programmatic. Underlying policy issues was an introspective argument about the meaning of national identity and the right to rule. Orbán was initially loathe to accept his election defeat and assume the role of a constructive opposition, trying to mobilize extra-parliamentary protest. He was also prepared to promote a degree of Euro-scepticism by attacking the conditions for membership accepted by the Socialist-led coalition in the end game of accession negotiations, although not the principle of membership. While Hungary's chances of EU membership were never seriously called into doubt it was, nevertheless, a state deeply preoccupied with domestic disputes rather than constructive engagement with visions about the shape of a future European Union.

*Czech Republic*

For the parliamentary period from 1998 to 2002, the Czech Republic was in an unusual position for a post-communist state. Firstly, it met with the approval of many in the west because it was ruled by a 'real' Social Democratic party that was not the reformed successor party of a Soviet-era ruling communist party. The Communist Party of Czechoslovakia had spawned the Communist Party of Bohemia and Moravia which, as its name suggests, had been slow to renounce its communist-era history. This left the way clear for a party claiming the legacy of the relatively successful inter-war Social Democrats to gain a political foothold and, in the 1998 elections, to become the largest parliamentary party. Secondly, the Social Democrats formed a one-party government, which was unusual in a part of Europe where proportional representation made coalitions the norm. It was also a minority government which lasted a full term in office. This was similarly rare in the conflictual and volatile first decade of post-communism where even governments that started with a parliamentary majority often collapsed mid-term.

The key to the Social Democrats' survival was the 'opposition agreement' with Václav Klaus's rightist Civic Democratic Party (ODS) that had been the major government party from 1992 to 1997. United by a dislike of both the communists and the smaller, more centrist parties in parliament, the two largest parties agreed after the 1998 elections that ODS would refrain from bringing down the Social Democrats' minority government. They would, however, amend the electoral law in a fashion likely to eliminate their smaller opponents, thereby leading to alternation of one-party governments formed by the two largest parties in perpetuity. This somewhat disreputable intention was stymied by the Constitutional Court, which protected the principle of proportional representation enshrined (unusually) in the constitution of the Czech Republic against a new electoral law aimed at what can best be described as 'unproportional representation'. The *status quo* was also ably defended by the electorate, which voted against the two major parties in the 2000 elections for a third of the upper chamber (Senate) with sufficient determination to rob them of the exceptional majority that would have enabled them to change the constitution.

As a consequence, the parliamentary election of June 2002 was held under the existing system of proportional representation with a 5 per cent clause for entry into Parliament, amended only slightly to favour larger parties. An initial opinion poll lead for the opposition ODS was eroded shortly before the election and the Social Democrats again emerged as the largest single party. The major distinguishing feature of the result, however, was voter disdain for the way politics had been conducted during the previous four years. While the bitter contestation of the Hungarian elections had led to the highest turnout ever, the shoddy compromises of the 'opposition agreement' and the failed attempt at establishing 'partocracy' via instrumental electoral reform in the Czech Republic led to the lowest turnout ever, which sunk to 58 per cent from 74 per cent in 1998. Contrary to expectation, the beneficiary of small reductions in the Social Democratic and ODS vote (2 per cent and 3 per cent respectively) was not the centrist Liberal–Christian Democrat 'coalition', which also lost support, but the Communists, whose vote increased to 18 per cent from 11 per cent. They had gained the protest vote of economically discontented 'transition losers', some of whom in 1998 had opted for the Social Democrats.

The outcome of the election was that the Social Democrats remained in power, but took on a smaller centrist coalition partner instead of ruling alone in a minority government. The Prime Minister also changed from the rather

Table 2: Result of the Czech Parliamentary Election, 14–15 June 2002

| *Party* | *Seats* | *% of Vote* |
|---|---|---|
| Government coalition | | |
| Czech Social Democratic Party (ČSSD) | 70 | 30.2 |
| 'Coalition' (Freedom Union and Christian Democratic Union–Czechoslovak People's Party) | 31 | 14.3 |
| Total government coalition | 101 | 44.5 |
| Opposition | | |
| Civic Democratic Party (ODS) | 58 | 24.5 |
| Communist Party of Bohemia and Moravia (KSČM) | 41 | 18.5 |
| Others | 0 | 12.5 |
| Total opposition | 99 | 55.5 |

unpredictable Miloš Zeman to the Social Democrats' new leader, Vladimír Spidla. Since the first Social Democratic government had done well in conducting EU accession negotiations for the previous four years, there seemed no possible impediment to the country's membership. Although the government lost its Senate majority in the November 2002 election for a third of the upper chamber, Czech politics also showed signs of stabilization as the Communists were increasingly treated as a legitimate opposition to be integrated into the parliamentary system rather than eliminated from it.

In spite of sometimes lukewarm popular attitudes to the EU, support for membership by the major political parties was strong, with the Communists the only parliamentary party hostile to 2004 accession. ODS, which again became the largest opposition party after the 2002 election, was renowned for being Eurosceptic – or 'Eurorealist' as they preferred to call it – but its voters were more solidly pro-EU accession than those of the Social Democrats, and the ODS politicians did not oppose EU membership. They merely tried to project themselves as the equals of politicians in current Member States by engaging in a complex debate on aspects of future EU policy and decision-making.

*Slovakia*

Slovakia's chequered political history during the 1990s made election year more tense than in the Czech Republic, with the issue of EU and Nato accession a much clearer focus of the election campaign. In 1997, both the Commission and the European Council had concluded that the third Mečiar government (1994–98) did not fulfil the Copenhagen political criteria, and that it should therefore be excluded from the first group of CEECs to begin detailed accession negotiations. This mirrored the Nato decision of the same year not to admit it in the first wave of eastward expansion. Although Slovakia had caught up admirably in the accession 'race' under the subsequent government of Mikuláš Dzurinda elected in 1998, there was a widespread awareness in 2002 that the country could not afford to make any more mistakes. No significant party entered the campaign opposing EU membership, but the issue was prominent for another reason. The ruling parties were relentlessly vocal in reminding the electorate of the failures of Vladimír Mečiar's Movement for a Democratic Slovakia and its erstwhile coalition partner, the Slovak National Party, in matters of European integration. Their efforts in this direction were fully endorsed by a wide array of politicians from EU Member States and the USA, who were almost indelicately blunt about the fact that the return of Mečiar's party to government in any imaginable coalition constellation would lead to renewed international isolation and destroy Slovakia's chances of early EU and Nato membership.

However, two major domestic factors complicated the election. The first was that, despite the foreign policy successes of the Dzurinda government, many citizens regarded it as an economic failure, most notably because it had presided over an increase in the unemployment rate that at its high point edged towards 20 per cent. The second was that the party system was still in a state of flux. The first Dzurinda government had been a broad 'coalition of coalitions' embracing a wide spectrum of parties from left to right, of which only the Party of the Hungarian Coalition, representing the country's largest ethnic minority, managed to remain intact until the 2002 election. The electorate expressed its discontent with the government by turning not to the parliamentary opposition parties, who had been 'integration failures' when in government, but through support of new parties, most notably the rather populist but also vaguely centre-left *Smer* ('Direction') party of Robert Fico. Overconfidence in the accuracy of public opinion polls led many analysts to predict that Fico would become the new Prime Minister, and he was heavily lobbied by the international community to make sure that, in order to lead Slovakia into the EU and Nato, he would choose acceptable coalition partners, and not form a government with the Movement for a Democratic Slovakia.

In the event, the election result was very much clearer than predicted and produced a surprise victory for Prime Minister Dzurinda. He was able to remain in office since his Slovak Democratic and Christian Union was the largest of four centre-right parties who together gained a narrow parliamentary majority with just 42.5 per cent of the vote. The right had been strengthened

Table 3: Results of the Slovak Parliamentary Election, 20–21 September 2002

| *Party* | *Seats* | *% of Vote* |
|---|---|---|
| Government coalition | | |
| Slovak Democratic and Christian Union (SDKÚ) | 28 | 15.1 |
| Party of the Hungarian Coalition (SMK) | 20 | 11.2 |
| Christian Democratic Movement (KDH) | 15 | 8.3 |
| Alliance of the New Citizen (ANO) | 15 | 8.0 |
| Total government coalition | 78 | 42.5 |
| Opposition | | |
| Movement for a Democratic Slovakia (HZDS) | 36 | 19.5 |
| *Smer* ('Direction') | 25 | 13.5 |
| Communist Party of Slovakia (KSS) | 11 | 6.3 |
| Others | 0 | 18.2 |
| Total opposition | 72 | 57.5 |

by the fact Slovakia has a proportional representation electoral system, and 18 per cent of the vote was 'wasted' on parties that did not gain the 5 per cent required in order to be allotted seats. While, in the mid-1990s, it had often been the right that fell at the 5 per cent hurdle, in 2002 the main victims were parties affected by fragmentation in the nationalist wing and the centre-left of the party spectrum.

Slovakia therefore ended 2002 with a new government that demonstrated the highest degree of both programmatic coherence and policy continuity in the country's short history. Dzurinda's second government was staunchly pro-EU, and even the opposition was lukewarm rather than overtly hostile to membership. Mečiar's Movement for a Democratic Slovakia favoured European integration at a declaratory level, even if both the party and its leader remained unacceptable to the west. Its influence was also on the decline, for while it was still the largest single party in the 2002 elections, its support was waning among both the electorate and, it was soon to emerge, its own parliamentary deputies. Fico's *Smer* showed some measure of Euroscepticism, but also sought acceptance by Europe's Social Democrats. Even the unreformed communist left represented by the Communist Party of Slovakia, which had managed to enter Parliament for the first time since independence, was not prepared to ride against the wind by openly opposing the EU. In short, the elections had left Slovakia excellently placed to pursue the goal of EU membership.

### *Latvia*

The Latvian parliamentary election of October 2002 differed from those in the three Visegrád states in two major respects. Firstly, the country still suffers from major controversy about citizenship and electoral rights, with over one-fifth of its permanent residents comprising non-citizens – mainly Russians – who are excluded from voting. The issue is particularly sensitive because, by the end of the Soviet period, barely half the population of Latvia was ethnically Latvian, largely as a result of the number of Russians who had been settled there after the Soviet takeover at the beginning of the Second World War. Secondly, the party system still demonstrated a high level of volatility. The largest single party in the new parliament (*Saeima*), the centre-right 'New Era' of former central bank governor and incoming Prime Minister Einars Repse, had been established only the previous February. At the same time, the largest party in the previous parliament, Latvia's Way, failed to gain the 5 per cent necessary to enter Parliament, as did the largest of the Social Democratic parties.

The outcome of the election was a four-party coalition of a broadly centre-right nature, which represented a level of political continuity notwithstanding

Table 4: Result of the Latvian Parliamentary Election, 5 October 2002

| *Party* | *Seats* | *% of Vote* |
|---|---|---|
| Government coalition | | |
| New Era | 26 | 23.9 |
| Union of Greens and Farmers (ZZS) | 12 | 9.4 |
| Latvia First Party (LPP) | 10 | 9.5 |
| Fatherland and Freedom Union (TB-LNNK) | 7 | 5.4 |
| Total government coalition | 55 | 48.2 |
| Opposition | | |
| For Human Rights in a United Latvia (PCTVL) | 25 | 19.0 |
| People's Party (TP) | 20 | 16.6 |
| Others | 0 | 16.2 |
| Total opposition | 45 | 51.8 |

the fact that only one of the parties (the Fatherland and Freedom Union) had participated in the previous three-party government. This pattern of government formation was determined in part by the fact that those Russians permitted to vote inclined towards the left and were thus unacceptable government partners.

The new government has declared its support for EU membership. However, while successive Latvian governments had demonstrated a reasonable level of competence in preparing the country for EU accession, political elites have not been entirely successful in carrying their electorates with them. The Russian 'problem' has led to some manifestations of extreme nationalism among Latvians, and attitudes to European integration are marked by varying degrees of hostility, ignorance and indifference among approximately half the population. Latvia remains, therefore, one of the most Eurosceptic of the candidate states.

### *Turkey*

Of all the candidate states that held elections in 2002, Turkey produced the most dramatic change at the ballot box. The Turkish parliament called early elections for November 2002 after the collapse of Bülent Ecevit's government coalition in July. This had been precipitated by both deep economic crisis and concern over the state of health of the 77-year-old Prime Minister.

The elections were surrounded by early controversy as the Supreme Election Board ruled in September that the leader of the Justice and Development Party (AKP), former Mayor of Istanbul Recep Tayyip Erdogan, would be barred from standing because of a 1999 conviction for inciting hatred on religious grounds. This was followed by unsuccessful attempts to have both the AKP banned from the election and the date of the election delayed. It was clear in advance that several major parties were in severe danger of failing to re-enter Parliament, and that the AKP was almost certain to win the election and form a government.

Opinion polls were largely accurate, and the AKP won a landslide victory that left it just four seats short of the two-thirds majority necessary to change the constitution without a referendum. The electoral annihilation of ruling political elites was a result not merely of widespread public discontent caused by the economic crisis, but also of the electoral system, whereby a political party required 10 per cent of the vote to enter Parliament. A 5 per cent clause of the type common in the CEECs would have permitted a further five parties to enter Parliament, but would not have saved Ecevit's Democratic Left Party, which obtained a mere 1.2 per cent of the vote – more than 20 per cent less than in 1999.

Since AKP leader Erdogan had not been able to stand for election, the premiership went initially to the party's deputy chair, Abdullah Gül. However, a constitutional change in December 2002 paved the way for Erdogan to stand in a by-election and become Prime Minister. Although the AKP was a conservative Islamic party distrusted by the military, it favoured EU membership and attempted to portray itself as the Turkish equivalent of a western Christian Democratic party. It was committed to constitutional change and the improvement in Turkey's human rights record necessary for EU accession, and hoped to obtain a starting date for negotiations in December 2002. However, British and US support for its membership was not universally shared, and both the EU Convention President Giscard d'Estaing and the German opposition leader Edmund Stoiber made outspokenly hostile comments opposing Turkish EU membership in principle. In the event, the Copenhagen European Council merely committed itself to review Turkish progress towards satisfying the democratic criteria for membership in December 2004, and to start negotiations without delay if the result was positive.

Turkey's relationship with the EU was a particularly difficult balancing act because of its role in achieving a resolution of the Cyprus question. How-

Table 5: Result of the Turkish Parliamentary Election, 3 November 2002

| *Party* | *Seats* | *% of Vote* |
|---|---|---|
| Justice and Development Party (AKP) | 363 | 34.3 |
| Republican People's Party (CHP) | 178 | 19.4 |
| Independents | 9 | 8.6 |
| Others | – | 37.7 |

ever, by the end of 2002 its importance in this regard was rapidly becoming overshadowed by the fact that it was the only Nato member to share a border with Iraq. It remained to be seen whether Turkey's domestic or foreign policies would eventually emerge as the more crucial in determining the fate of its application to join the EU.

*Slovenia*

Direct elections for the Slovene Presidency took place in November and December 2002. While the Slovene Head of State has a ceremonial rather than an executive role, the elections were interesting as they embodied both the end of an era and a high degree of continuity in Slovene politics. The former Communist leader, Milan Kučan, who had presided over the country's successful transition from communism, its international recognition as an independent state and its subsequent reintegration into European structures, finally stood down after more than 12 years in office because he was ineligible to stand after completing two full five-year terms. However, his successor Janez Drnovšek of the ruling Liberal Democracy Party of Slovenia was, like Kučan, a one-time communist, and had been Slovene Prime Minister for most of the previous decade.

The only surprise of the election was the strong second round showing of Drnovšek's major opponent, the independent Barbara Brezigar who was backed by the Social Democratic Party and the New Slovenia Party. Both were, contrary to the former's name, more conservative parties than the leftist Liberal Democrats.

Since Drnovšek was the incumbent Prime Minister at the time of the election, Parliament was required to appoint a new one. His replacement was Anton Rop, the former Finance Minister and, like Drnovšek, a Liberal Democrat. The change of office-holders therefore had little bearing on Slovenia's high chances of EU membership, and served largely to emphasize the country's political stability.

Table 6: Slovene Presidential Election, 10 November and 1 December 2002

| *Candidate* | *Party* | *% of Vote (First Round)* | *% of Vote (Second Round)* |
|---|---|---|---|
| Janez Drnovšek | Liberal Democratic Party of Slovenia (LDS) | 44.4 | 56.5 |
| Barbara Brezigar | Independent | 30.8 | 43.5 |
| Others (7) | | 24.8 | – |

## II. Public Opinion in the Applicant States

Public opinion on the EU in most of the applicant states has been measured by the European Commission for more than a decade, first in its *Central and Eastern Eurobarometers*, and more recently in the *Applicant* and *Candidate Countries Eurobarometers*, which also include Cyprus, Malta and Turkey. It is a common subject of investigation in domestic opinion polls in most of the states concerned, but such polls, while often more detailed, present problems of comparability since the precise questions often differ. As a consequence, the *Eurobarometers* are the most widely cited source of public opinion data.

Although many caveats can be made about the usefulness of survey data in explaining the dynamic interplay of domestic politics and the EU accession process, the *Eurobarometers* permit some interesting comparisons of attitudes towards the EU in different candidate states. Table 7 shows the percentages of respondents who stated that they would vote in favour of EU membership in a referendum in the *Central and Eastern Eurobarometer* surveys conducted in late 1996 and 1997, and the *Candidate Countries Eurobarometer* surveys conducted in late 2001 and 2002. However, there is considerable variation between the proportion of other respondents who stated that they would actually vote against membership, and those who did not know, would not go to vote, or gave no answer at all. Therefore, the table gives a second figure in brackets which represents the percentage of those in favour of membership *minus* the percentage of those who would vote against membership. This figure can be regarded as a rough indicator of 'net support' for EU membership at the given point in time.

This somewhat complex table shows that some candidate countries have consistently demonstrated high or low support for EU membership, while elsewhere there have been notable shifts in attitudes over the last six years, which encompassed the publication of the European Commission's original opinions *(avis)* of July 1997. It is possible to suggest some explanations for discrepancies in attitudes that, while containing a degree of speculation, also indicate some of the underlying factors which influence national attitudes to the EU.

In late 2002, five states had 'net support' for EU membership above 50 percentage points. Of these, three – Romania, Bulgaria and Turkey – did not belong to the 'Laeken 10' states due to accede to the EU in May 2004. Here, accession had the attraction of being a currently unattainable aspiration. The *Eurobarometer* report notes that the majority of people in the candidate countries have a positive image of the EU mainly for economic reasons: 'The Union is seen as the source of prosperity and the guarantee of richness' (Commission, 2002a). It is thus highly relevant that these are the economically

Table 7: Percentage of Respondents who would Vote Positively in a Referendum on EU Accession

| *Country* | *2002* | *2001* | *1997* | *1996* |
|---|---|---|---|---|
| Romania | 84 (82) | 85 (82) | 71 (65) | 80 (78) |
| Hungary | 77 (69) | 70 (60) | 56 (47) | 47 (32) |
| Bulgaria | 74 (67) | 80 (76) | 57 (53) | 49 (45) |
| Turkey | 71 (53) | 68 (48) | n/a | n/a |
| Slovakia | 69 (58) | 66 (55) | 62 (54) | 46 (37) |
| Slovenia | 62 (41) | 56 (34) | 57 (39) | 47 (32) |
| Poland | 61 (43) | 54 (28) | 63 (57) | 70 (63) |
| Cyprus | 58 (33) | 62 (37) | n/a | n/a |
| Lithuania | 53 (37) | 50 (30) | 40 (27) | 35 (29) |
| Czech Republic | 50 (31) | 54 (36) | 49 (36) | 43 (32) |
| Malta | 47 (15) | 40 (4) | n/a | n/a |
| Latvia | 45 (13) | 46 (14) | 40 (27) | 34 (21) |
| Estonia | 39 (8) | 38 (11) | 35 (21) | 29 (12) |

*Sources:* Commission, *Candidate Countries Eurobarometer*, Report No. 2002.2, December 2002; *Applicant Countries Eurobarometer* 2001, Results summary, December 2002; *Central and Eastern Eurobarometer,* No. 8, March 1998; *Central and Eastern Eurobarometer,* No. 7, March 1997.

*Note:* Figures in brackets show percentage point difference between positive and negative responses.

weakest of the candidate states, and that Turkey and Romania are also two of the three largest. In the Romanian case, support for the EU has been consistently high. It must be remembered that the experiences of the late communist period were particularly unpleasant under the Ceauşescu regime, leaving little room for nostalgia for the past. In addition, the post-communist political elites have not proved particularly competent at mastering the difficult tasks of transition, so that the alternative vision of a future in European structures appears particularly attractive.

In Hungary, Bulgaria and Slovakia, on the other hand, there has been a marked increase in support for EU membership over the last six years. In the Slovak case, this appears to have been triggered by the shock of rejection by the EU in 1997, when it became manifest how far the country was lagging behind the other three Visegrád states. In Bulgaria, support increased after the change in government in 1997, when the economy gradually began to improve, and optimism about a future in Europe increased further as negotiations with the EU began in 2000.

The rise in support for EU accession in Hungary is less readily explained, since it has been a consistent leader in both transition and post-communist reform and European integration since the late communist period. It is an exception in being the only state where public opinion is strongly pro-EU in spite of the fact that its chances of early EU accession have never been in doubt. The mid-1990s were, however, pervaded by a degree of pessimism as tangible economic progress for the ordinary citizen seemed slow, and the relatively liberal regime of the late communist period lessened the perceived need to escape 'back to Europe'. It is possible that the generational change brought about by the new government in 1998, which entered office at the time accession negotiations started, helped cement a widespread view that EU membership was the natural course for a modern state in the heart of Europe.

The Polish trajectory of declining support for EU membership has been the opposite of the Hungarian. This initially seems curious, given that the two countries formed a pair in leading the transition from communism. However, their internal political dynamics have always been different. The communist period was a manifest failure in Poland, providing a strong impetus to integrate westward as the antithesis to the Soviet-dominated past. By the late 1990s, however, Poland was the first candidate state in which Euroscepticism took root. As the largest of the post-communist candidate states, and one of the most ethnically homogeneous, it had a stronger sense of national sovereignty, and once protected from 'the east' by Nato membership, it could afford to look in detail at what EU membership entailed.

Anti-EU feeling crystallized around two major issues. One was an agenda of conservative Catholicism and 'family values' that was portrayed by some as being in opposition to the decadent and secular modernity of western Europe. The other was the agricultural lobby of small farmers, which was particularly strong because Poland had been the only Soviet bloc state where agriculture was not collectivized. Since Polish society was both overwhelmingly Catholic and relatively rural, there was scope for internal political division among both these (in any case overlapping) groups, and anti-EU factions within them were thus able to obtain parliamentary representation, allowing party-based Euroscepticism to articulate popular reservations about the EU.

The third state which had pioneered the transition from communism, the ex-Yugoslav Slovenia, maintained a far more consistent middle-of-the-road trajectory of EU support in line with its high level of political stability during the 1990s. While not immune to concerns about national sovereignty, it had been forced to leave the Yugoslav federation primarily because its 1980s' aspirations for democratization and European integration were thwarted by the upsurge of communist-led Serbian nationalism at the end of the decade, and its precarious position on the edge of the 'Balkan abyss' thereafter provided a lasting incentive to join the EU, whatever reservations existed.

Cypriot support for EU membership appears from the 2001 and 2002 *Eurobarometers* to be at a fairly similar level to Poland and Slovenia, but it is imperative to note that data relate solely to the Republic of Cyprus. For the future of Cyprus as a member of the EU, the most crucial data are contained in a separate report on public opinion in Northern Cyprus based on a survey conducted in September 2002 (Commission, 2002b). This indicates 87 per cent support, and net support of 80 per cent, for Turkish Cypriot membership of the European Union. In other words, Turkish Cypriots demonstrate very strongly pro-EU attitudes on a par with the Romanians, and generally typical of economically deprived Europeans for whom EU membership is an aspiration rather than an expectation. Perceptively, respondents also considered politicians the group *least* likely to have advantages from EU membership. For talks on the future of Cyprus, these findings are of immense significance.

A final distinct group in terms of public opinion is represented by the five states with consistently lower levels of support for EU membership, which is, however, internally heterogeneous. Two of them – the Czech Republic and Estonia – belonged to the first group of states to begin detailed accession negotiations in 1998, while the economically less successful Lithuania and Latvia, and also Malta, belonged to the second group that began negotiations in 2000.

It is notable that the first two are characterized by concerns that the economic protectionism of the EU could be detrimental to their national interests. Both the Czech Republic (as the Czech part of Czechoslovakia) and Estonia were relatively prosperous inter-war countries whose post-war development was severely constrained by the backwardness of Russian-dominated communism, forcing them for decades to watch formerly poorer neighbours like Austria and Finland forge ahead. Since Estonia had been part of the Soviet Union, and Czechoslovakia was a stultifyingly orthodox Warsaw Pact state from 1968 until 1989, both rose to the task of economic reform in the 1990s with a frantic pent-up surge of historical self-confidence lacking in states such as Hungary and Poland that had been able to experiment with change in the 1980s. At the same time, however, such rapid reform led to social division and existential fears among the economically weaker members of society (older people, the less educated, rural dwellers, women and the unemployed), who generally hold lower expectations of benefit from EU membership (Commission, 2002a). This creates a second pool of potential Eurosceptics. The three Baltic states – most notably Estonia and Latvia, where EU support is lowest – also suffer from a widespread perception that politicians are the group most likely to be advantaged by EU membership (Commission, 2002a). This suggests an uncoupling of the elites successfully negotiating EU accession from their countries' citizens as a whole.

The final factor influencing the four Eurosceptic post-communist states is their sense of national identity. Among the Baltic states, it is notable that reservations about the EU are most prevalent in Estonia and Latvia, with their large Russian minorities, whereas Lithuania is nearer to converging with the levels of EU support in Poland or Slovenia. While the Czech Republic, which was the dominant partner in a communist federation, should not suffer from such concern, the country is surrounded on three sides by economically stronger German-speaking EU Member States. This conjures up pre-communist fears of external domination that have been manifest in arguments over nuclear power (with Austria) and the 'Beneš decrees' expelling Czechoslovak Germans after the Second World War (with Austria and Germany).

The last Eurosceptic country is a completely different case. Malta, the smallest of the candidate countries, has been the most profoundly divided of all on the issue of EU membership, which reflects its general domestic political polarization. It began negotiations together with the 'second group' of post-communist states purely of its own volition, since the socialist government defeated in the 1998 elections had previously suspended the country's application for membership. Unlike attitudes to the EU in the post-communist states, this division of opinion is more likely to be of permanent import.

Opinions on the EU in the candidate countries therefore differ for a wide variety of domestic reasons. Some relate to general or specific calculations of economic self-interest, while others tap into deeper insecurities about national identity. What will, however, increasingly become crucial is mapping the views of the current candidate states on questions regarding institutional structures and modes of policy-making within the EU. Their participation in the Convention on the Future of Europe has confronted parliamentarians and government members with the need to articulate views on the controversial issues that form the core of most EU-related domestic arguments within Member States. This will, in turn, gradually permeate public discussion on the EU. The dominant discourse that affects images of the EU will change from an evaluation of the pros and cons of membership to a more complex debate on the sort of European Union to which they wish to belong. Likewise, international interest in public opinion in central and eastern Europe will focus not on whether they want to join, but rather on the sort of Member States that they will become.

## References

Commission (2002a) *Candidate Countries Eurobarometer: Public opinion in the countries applying for European Union membership*, Report No. 2002.2, December, pp. 50, 83, 93, 94.

Commission (2002b) *Public Opinion Survey 2002: First results – Northern Cyprus.*

JCMS 2003 Volume 41. Annual Review pp. 173–89

# Developments in the Economies of the European Union

NIGEL GRIMWADE
South Bank University

## I. Overview

After the slowdown of the EU economy in 2001, there were strong hopes that 2002 would see a recovery with resumption of more normal conditions. Evidence that a recovery might be underway existed in the first quarter of the year, as GDP bounced back after declining in the final quarter of 2001. By the second and third quarters, however, it had become clear that the recovery had stalled. Far from accelerating, the growth rate bumped along a more or less flat path and, in the final quarter, fell. In the autumn, the best estimates of the European Commission were that the growth rate for the year would be only 1 per cent (0.8 per cent in the euro area), significantly below the rate of 1.7 per cent achieved in the previous year (both for the EU as a whole and the euro area) (Commission, 2002). By April 2003, the Commission's estimate for growth in 2002 had increased slightly to 1.1 per cent (0.9 per cent in the euro area), yet was still below what the Commission had forecast 12 months earlier (Commission, 2003).

By way of contrast, growth in other advanced industrialized countries proved stronger in 2002 than in the previous year, although there were signs that growth was slowing towards the end of the year. Estimates by the International Monetary Fund (IMF) show that, during 2002, world GDP grew at a rate of 3 per cent, compared with 2.3 per cent in the previous year (IMF, 2003). In the United States, GDP grew by 2.4 per cent (compared with 0.3 per cent in the previous year) reflecting, in part, the effects of cuts in short-term interest rates made in the wake of the events of 11 September (2001) and of discretionary fiscal stimulus. In Canada, the economy grew still faster at a rate of 3.4 per cent (compared with 1.5 per cent in the previous year). Growth was also strong in the emerging nations of Asia, where the growth rate was

6.5 per cent (compared with 5.7 per cent in the previous year). Growth in the euro area, however, was sluggish. Germany, which accounts for about one-third of output, was the slowest growing economy of all, with a growth rate for the year of only 0.2 per cent. Growth rates for France and Italy were estimated at 1.2 and 0.4 per cent respectively (compared with 1.8 per cent each in the previous year). Outside Europe, only Japan, with a growth rate of 0.3 per cent, had a comparable performance.

With few exceptions, however, global output growth was far from robust. A key factor was uncertainty over the political situation in the world – in particular, the prospect of a possible war in Iraq. This, in turn, was a contributory factor behind the rise in world oil prices, with a barrel of Brent oil rising from under $20 at the start of the year to over $30 by the end. Higher oil prices, however, were also driven up by the disruption to supplies caused by the strike in Venezuela, and by increased demand due to adverse weather conditions in the northern hemisphere and fast economic growth in Asia. Weak equity markets continued to weaken private domestic demand, while world trade grew at a slow rate. In the EU, recovery in the first three quarters of the year was based largely on the external sector, with imports declining in the first quarter and exports picking up in the second and third quarters. After declining in the first quarter, private consumption grew a little more strongly in the second and third quarters. Investment spending, however, fell over the year as whole. In the final quarter of the year, a distinct weakening in export demand was apparent, the result of both a slowing down in world trade and an appreciation of the euro against the US dollar (equivalent to roughly 24 per cent over the year as a whole).

In the face of sluggish demand, the fiscal and monetary authorities were constrained in their ability to combat this weakening by creating additional stimulus through an easing of fiscal and monetary policy. Inflation remained stubbornly high in the EU throughout 2002. Although the Harmonized Index of Consumer Prices (HICP) rose by only 2.2 per cent compared with 2.4 per cent in 2001, this was above the European Central Bank's (ECB's) ceiling of 2 per cent. Moreover, throughout the year, core inflation (which excludes energy prices and unprocessed food) was consistently above the HICP rate. This limited the scope for the ECB to cut interest rates below the 3.25 per cent rate set in the final quarter of 2001, although a 0.5 per cent reduction was forthcoming at its December meeting. At the same time, the constraints of the Stability and Growth Pact (SGP) meant that several Member States were obliged to engage in further fiscal tightening.

## II. Main Economic Indicators

### *Economic Growth*

Table 1 sets out the annual average rates of growth of real GDP for the individual Member States since 1961 and includes forecasts for the current year. Substantial variations existed between the economic performances of different Member States. Broadly, countries outside the euro area (the UK, Sweden and Denmark) performed better than those inside. Within the euro area, a clear division existed between the larger economies such as Germany, France and Italy, all of whom experienced sluggish growth, and a group of smaller countries which enjoyed much faster rates of expansion. Greece, Ireland and Spain continued to enjoy above-average rates of economic growth, although growth rates were lower in Greece and Spain than in the previous year. Between these two extremes, Austria, Belgium, the Netherlands, Luxembourg and Portugal all experienced relatively slow growth.

Table 1: Annual Average Percentage Change in Gross Domestic Product (measured in volume terms) for Individual Member States 1961–2003

| | *1961 –90* | *1991 –95* | *1996 –2000* | *1998* | *1999* | *2000* | *2001* | *2002 Estimate* | *2003 Forecast* |
|---|---|---|---|---|---|---|---|---|---|
| Belgium | 3.4 | 1.6 | 2.7 | 2.0 | 3.2 | 3.7 | 0.8 | 0.7 | 1.2 |
| Denmark | 2.7 | 2.0 | 2.7 | 2.5 | 2.6 | 2.8 | 1.4 | 1.6 | 1.5 |
| Germany | 3.1 | 2.0 | 1.8 | 2.0 | 2.0 | 2.9 | 0.6 | 0.2 | 0.4 |
| Greece | 4.5 | 1.2 | 3.4 | 3.4 | 3.6 | 4.2 | 4.1 | 4.0 | 3.6 |
| Spain | 4.6 | 1.5 | 3.8 | 4.3 | 4.2 | 4.2 | 2.7 | 2.0 | 2.0 |
| France | 3.8 | 1.1 | 2.7 | 3.4 | 3.2 | 3.8 | 1.8 | 1.2 | 1.1 |
| Ireland | 4.2 | 4.7 | 9.8 | 8.8 | 11.1 | 10.0 | 5.7 | 6.0 | 3.3 |
| Italy | 3.9 | 1.3 | 1.9 | 1.8 | 1.7 | 3.1 | 1.8 | 0.4 | 1.0 |
| Luxembourg | 3.7 | 3.9 | 6.8 | 7.5 | 6.0 | 8.9 | 1.0 | 0.4 | 1.1 |
| Netherlands | 3.4 | 2.1 | 3.7 | 4.3 | 4.0 | 3.3 | 1.3 | 0.3 | 0.5 |
| Austria | 3.6 | 2.0 | 2.8 | 3.9 | 2.7 | 3.5 | 0.7 | 1.0 | 1.2 |
| Portugal | 4.8 | 1.7 | 3.9 | 4.6 | 3.8 | 3.7 | 1.6 | 0.5 | 0.5 |
| Finland | 3.8 | -0.6 | 4.8 | 4.9 | 3.4 | 5.5 | 0.6 | 1.6 | 2.2 |
| Sweden | 2.9 | 1.3 | 3.3 | 3.6 | 4.6 | 4.4 | 1.1 | 1.9 | 1.4 |
| UK | 2.5 | 1.8 | 2.9 | 2.9 | 2.4 | 3.1 | 2.1 | 1.8 | 2.2 |
| EU-15 | 3.4 | 1.5 | 2.6 | 2.9 | 2.8 | 3.5 | 1.6 | 1.1 | 1.3 |
| Euro area | 3.6 | 1.5 | 2.6 | 2.9 | 2.8 | 3.5 | 1.5 | 0.9 | 1.0 |

*Source:* Commission (2003).

Over the year as whole, the main factor contributing to slow output growth was inadequate domestic demand. Weak private consumption appears to have been due to many factors, including a relatively high rate of inflation, lower wages increases and rising unemployment. In some Member States, the ratio of savings to income rose, reflecting increased uncertainty about the future. A negative wealth effect also operated through falling share prices, with stock markets in the euro area falling by more than those in the United States. In some Member States, however, this was offset by a continued rise in house prices although, in Germany, house prices fell. Fears about unemployment and some concern about pensions added to the anxiety of consumers. Over the year as a whole, private consumption grew at a rate of only 0.7 per cent on average.

With the demand for goods and services depressed, firms cut back their investment plans. Investment in equipment fell by 4.3 per cent in the euro area during the year, with Germany and Austria experiencing the biggest fall. Profit margins were squeezed by rising unit costs, as a slowing down in productivity growth was accompanied by steady rise in wages. A further squeeze on companies resulted from an increase in the costs of raising capital, despite the fact that interest rates were falling. Worries about potential accounting fraud in the wake of the Enron crisis, combined with a general uncertainty, resulted in capital markets building a risk premium into the cost of company borrowing. Negative stock accumulation also had a dampening effect on domestic demand, as firms responded to the uncertain climate by reducing their stock holdings.

### *Employment*

Faltering economic growth resulted in a decline in the rate of employment growth in the EU. Having grown at a rate of 1.2 per cent in the previous year, the rate of employment growth fell to 0.4 per cent. Indeed, by the third quarter of the year, employment growth had turned negative, for the first time since 1994. The contraction was entirely concentrated on the manufacturing and agricultural sectors, with employment in services continuing to expand. As a result, the average rate of unemployment went up from 7.3 per cent in the previous year (8 per cent in the euro area) to 7.6 per cent (8.3 per cent in the euro area). This was the first increase in the unemployment rate in the EU for five years. Nevertheless, the unemployment rate remained well below the levels recorded in the 1990s, although still higher than in other advanced industrialized countries.

Table 2 shows the unemployment rates for individual Member States for the period beginning 1964. Large differences continued to exist within the EU. At one end of the spectrum, Spain, Greece, Italy and Finland continued to experience rates of unemployment in excess of 9 per cent, although these were significantly lower than five years ago. At the other end of the spectrum, Luxembourg and the Netherlands enjoyed rates of unemployment below 3 per cent. Generally, unemployment levels were raised less in countries outside the euro area than in countries that were inside. The biggest increase in unemployment occurred in Portugal, where unemployment rose from 4.1 to 5.1 per cent. However, large increases also occurred in Spain, Austria and Belgium.

Although EU rates of unemployment remain above the levels recorded in the United States and other advanced industrialized countries, employment policies appear to have been successful in several Member States in raising employment levels (see IMF, 2002). Thus, from 1996 to 2000, employment in the EU grew at an average rate of 1.4 per cent a year, after falling 0.2 per cent a year between 1991–95. Although this was still lower than the rate of employment growth in the United States for the same period (2 per cent), it

Table 2: Percentage Share of the Civilian Labour Force Unemployed in EU Member States, 1964–2003

| | *1964 –90* | *1991 –5* | *1996 –2000* | *1998* | *1999* | *2000* | *2001* | *2002 Estimate* | *2003 Forecast* |
|---|---|---|---|---|---|---|---|---|---|
| Belgium | 5.7 | 8.3 | 8.7 | 9.3 | 8.6 | 6.9 | 6.7 | 7.3 | 7.8 |
| Denmark | 4.1 | 8.1 | 5.1 | 4.9 | 4.8 | 4.4 | 4.3 | 4.5 | 5.0 |
| Germany | 3.2 | 6.5 | 8.7 | 9.1 | 8.4 | 7.8 | 7.7 | 8.2 | 8.9 |
| Greece | 4.5 | 8.3 | 10.6 | 10.9 | 11.8 | 11.0 | 10.4 | 9.9 | 9.5 |
| Spain | 6.8 | 17.0 | 14.9 | 15.2 | 12.8 | 11.3 | 10.6 | 11.4 | 11.6 |
| France | 5.4 | 10.7 | 11.0 | 11.4 | 10.7 | 9.3 | 8.5 | 8.7 | 9.2 |
| Ireland | 9.7 | 14.5 | 7.8 | 7.5 | 5.6 | 4.3 | 3.9 | 4.4 | 5.6 |
| Italy | 6.7 | 10.0 | 11.3 | 11.7 | 11.3 | 10.4 | 9.4 | 9.0 | 9.1 |
| Luxembourg | 1.1 | 2.5 | 2.6 | 2.7 | 2.4 | 2.3 | 2.0 | 2.4 | 3.3 |
| Netherlands | 4.9 | 6.1 | 4.1 | 3.8 | 3.2 | 2.8 | 2.4 | 2.7 | 4.2 |
| Austria | 2.1 | 3.7 | 4.2 | 4.5 | 3.9 | 3.7 | 3.6 | 4.3 | 4.5 |
| Portugal | 5.2 | 5.7 | 5.6 | 5.1 | 4.5 | 4.1 | 4.1 | 5.1 | 6.5 |
| Finland | 3.9 | 13.3 | 11.7 | 11.4 | 10.2 | 9.8 | 9.1 | 9.1 | 9.4 |
| Sweden | 2.2 | 7.2 | 8.0 | 8.2 | 6.7 | 5.6 | 4.9 | 5.3 | 5.3 |
| UK | 5.4 | 9.3 | 6.5 | 6.2 | 5.9 | 5.4 | 5.0 | 5.1 | 5.1 |
| EU-15 | 5.1 | 9.3 | 9.2 | 9.4 | 8.7 | 7.8 | 7.3 | 7.6 | 8.0 |
| Euro area | 5.1 | 9.4 | 9.9 | 10.2 | 9.4 | 8.5 | 8.0 | 8.3 | 8.3 |

*Source:* Commission (2003).

was a marked improvement. Moreover, in recent years, employment growth has held up well in the EU, while stagnating in the US. Although cyclical factors have played their part, structural reforms have had a beneficial effect. These have included more flexible employment contracts, reductions in the tax burden on lower paid workers, changes in the tax–benefit systems and active labour policies to put the unemployed back to work. A moderate rate of wage increase in the EU as a whole has also contributed.

*Inflation*

In 2002, the Harmonized Index of Consumer Prices (HICP) rose by 2.1 per cent (2.2 per cent in the euro area), compared with 2.3 per cent (2.4 per cent in the euro area) in the previous year. Moreover, the rate of HICP inflation was increasing steadily during the year, peaking at 2.3 per cent in December. The main factors appear to have been cost induced. These included the rise in world oil prices caused by uncertainties in the Middle East, higher food prices brought about by colder weather, increased indirect taxes in some Member States, an increase in public sector tariff charges and some rounding up of retail prices resulting from the euro cash changeover.

A better indication of underlying inflation is given by the HICP excluding energy and unprocessed food – so-called 'core inflation'. Throughout most of 2002, this was above the HICP rate of inflation, with a sharp increase in service inflation being the main contributory factor. The Commission explains this in terms of an upward push of wages in the economy as a whole (Commission, 2003). Because productivity traditionally grows more slowly in the service sector, such wage increases push up unit costs by more in services than in other sectors of the economy. Moreover, because the service sector is more protected from international competition, it is easier for firms to pass on such cost increases in price.

Table 3 shows the rates of HICP inflation for the individual Member States for the period since 1961. Inflation differentials within the EU remain wide. Differences in inflation rates between members of the euro area matter more because they make the operation of a single monetary policy more difficult. At one extreme, inflation remained high in the fastest-growing Member States, namely, Ireland, the Netherlands, Greece, Spain and Portugal. At the other, very low rates of inflation were apparent in Germany, Belgium, Luxembourg, Austria, France and Finland. The gap between the highest and lowest inflation rate in the euro area (3.8 percentage points) was a little higher in 2002 than in the previous year (3.3 percentage points). Outside the euro area, inflation rates were, generally, lower than inside.

Table 3: Percentage Change in the Harmonized Index of Consumer Prices in Individual Member States, 1961–2003

| | *1961 –90* | *1991 –5* | *1996 –2000* | *1998* | *1999* | *2000* | *2001* | *2002 Estimate* | *2003 Forecast* |
|---|---|---|---|---|---|---|---|---|---|
| Belgium | 5.1 | 2.4 | 1.6 | 0.9 | 1.1 | 2.7 | 2.4 | 1.6 | 1.4 |
| Denmark | 7.2 | 2.0 | 2.0 | 1.3 | 2.1 | 2.7 | 2.3 | 2.4 | 2.4 |
| Germany | 3.5 | 3.1 | 1.1 | 0.6 | 0.6 | 1.5 | 2.1 | 1.3 | 1.3 |
| Greece | 11.6 | 13.9 | 4.6 | 4.5 | 2.1 | 2.9 | 3.7 | 3.9 | 3.8 |
| Spain | 10.1 | 5.2 | 2.6 | 1.8 | 2.2 | 3.5 | 2.8 | 3.6 | 3.2 |
| France | 6.7 | 2.2 | 1.3 | 0.7 | 0.6 | 1.8 | 1.8 | 1.9 | 1.9 |
| Ireland | 8.6 | 2.5 | 2.6 | 2.1 | 2.5 | 5.3 | 4.0 | 4.7 | 4.2 |
| Italy | 9.1 | 5.0 | 2.4 | 2.0 | 1.7 | 2.6 | 2.3 | 2.6 | 2.4 |
| Luxembourg | 4.6 | 2.8 | 1.7 | 1.0 | 1.0 | 3.8 | 2.4 | 2.1 | 2.1 |
| Netherlands | 4.7 | 2.9 | 1.9 | 1.8 | 2.0 | 2.3 | 5.1 | 3.9 | 2.7 |
| Austria | 4.5 | 3.2 | 1.2 | 0.8 | 0.5 | 2.0 | 2.3 | 1.7 | 1.8 |
| Portugal | 13.2 | 7.1 | 2.4 | 2.2 | 2.2 | 2.8 | 4.4 | 3.7 | 3.2 |
| Finland | 7.6 | 2.3 | 1.6 | 1.4 | 1.3 | 3.0 | 2.7 | 2.0 | 1.7 |
| Sweden | 6.9 | 4.2 | 1.1 | 1.0 | 0.6 | 1.3 | 2.7 | 2.0 | 2.5 |
| UK | 8.0 | 3.4 | 1.6 | 1.6 | 1.3 | 0.8 | 1.2 | 1.3 | 1.9 |
| EU-15 | 7.1 | 3.8 | 1.7 | 1.3 | 1.2 | 1.9 | 2.3 | 2.1 | 2.1 |
| Euro area | 6.9 | 3.9 | 1.7 | 1.2 | 1.1 | 2.1 | 2.4 | 2.2 | 2.1 |

*Source:* Commission (2003).

With the rate of inflation above the ECB's 2 per cent ceiling throughout the year and rising, the monetary authorities were constrained in their ability to cut interest rates. Accordingly, the 3.25 per cent rate set in November 2001, was left unchanged throughout the year until December, when the ECB announced a 0.5 per cent reduction. Official forecasts envisage the HICP inflation falling over the next two years as output growth slows (Commission, 2003). Despite the fact that the ECB's official lending rate was left unchanged, short-term interest rates in the money markets were on a downward descent for most of the second half of the year. On the other hand, the rise of the euro against the US dollar during the course of the year contributed towards to a slight tightening of monetary conditions in the euro area.

By the second half of the year, concern was being expressed about the risks of deflation. In part, this was prompted by a drop in Germany's inflation rate to 1 per cent in the third quarter of the year. It was argued that, with a price stability ceiling of 2 per cent for the euro area as a whole, and with inflation rates in excess of 3 per cent in the fast growing Member States, it becomes a necessity to keep inflation below 1 per cent in Germany. However, if Germany's inflation rate is forced below 1 per cent, *real* short-term interest rates in Germany must rise unless nominal rates are cut further. The effect of this must be to depress demand further in Germany. Yet, if Germany, which accounts for one-third of output in the euro area, is forced into recession, growth rates in the whole of the euro area are reduced (see Crooks and Major, 2002).

It has been suggested that the problem is made worse by the operation of what is known in the theoretical literature as the 'Balassa-Samuelson effect' (see Balassa, 1964 and Samuelson, 1964 for an explanation of the model). This is the process whereby inflation is pushed up in a monetary union, by sectoral inflation differentials or 'dual inflation' rates in traded and non-traded goods sectors. When less advanced countries join a monetary union with more advanced countries, productivity levels in the tradeable goods sector of the less advanced countries are pulled up towards those prevalent in the advanced countries. As a result, the wage rates of workers employed in these sectors of the economy rise and this puts pressure on wage rates in the non-tradeable sector where productivity is growing more slowly. As we have seen, upward cost pressures in the service sector have been one of the main causes of the stickiness of core inflation over the past 12 months. The result is an acceleration of inflation in these countries, such as has occurred in Ireland, Greece, Spain and Portugal in recent years (for empirical evidence of this, see Alberola and Tyrvaïnen, 1998). Higher inflation in these countries necessitates lower inflation in Germany in order to keep the average rate of inflation below the ECB ceiling of 2 per cent. The alternatives are to raise the ceiling or to convert the ceiling into a target rate.

### *Public Finances*

During 2002, fiscal policy played a broadly supportive role, despite the constraints imposed by the EU's Stability and Growth Pact. The average level of government borrowing rose from 0.9 per cent of GDP in 2001 to 1.9 per cent for the EU as a whole and from 1.6 per cent of GDP to 2.2 per cent for the euro area only. The main reason for this was the economic slowdown, which resulted in a lower level of tax revenues than had been anticipated, although expenditure levels rose also. For the euro area, the Commission calculated the cyclical component of the rise in government borrowing as 0.6 of a percentage point out of 0.8 (Commission, 2003). Thus, the rise in government borrowing largely reflected the workings of automatic stabilizers in the EU economy, rather than discretionary stimulation. As a result, the *cyclically-adjusted balance* moved from a deficit of 2.1 per cent in 2001 to a deficit of 2.2 per cent in 2002, a much smaller deterioration than for the unadjusted deficit. Furthermore, because of the fall in interest rates, government spending on debt interest fell as a proportion of GDP, making possible an improvement in the *primary balance*. Together, these factors meant that the *cyclically-adjusted primary balance,* which is the best measure of the true fiscal stance, moved from a surplus of 1.8 per cent of GDP in 2001 to one of 1.5 per cent in 2002.

Table 4 shows the unadjusted, level of net lending/borrowing for individual Member States for the period since 1970. The Stability and Growth Pact requires every member of the euro area to achieve a budgetary position close to balance or in surplus over the medium term, and to ensure that the budget deficit in any year should not exceed 3 per cent of GDP. In 2001, Portugal failed to achieve this and was expected, again, to run a deficit of over 3 per cent in 2002. Accordingly, in July, the Commission launched the 'excessive deficit' procedures against Portugal under the terms of the SGP and a programme for the correction of the deficit was agreed by the Council

Table 4: Net Lending (+) or Net Borrowing (–) by General Government as a Percentage of GDP, 1970–2003

| | *1970 –90* | *1991 –95* | *1996 –2000* | *1998* | *1999* | *2000* | *2001* | *2002 Estimate* | *2003 Forecast* |
|---|---|---|---|---|---|---|---|---|---|
| Belgium | –6.8 | –5.9 | –1.4 | –0.7 | –0.5 | 0.1 | 0.4 | 0.1 | –0.2 |
| Denmark | –0.5 | –2.4 | 1.3 | 1.1 | 3.3 | 2.6 | 3.1 | 2.0 | 1.8 |
| Germany | –1.9 | –3.1 | –1.7 | –2.2 | –1.5 | 1.1 | –2.8 | –3.6 | –3.4 |
| Greece | –5.7 | –11.5 | –3.5 | –2.5 | –1.8 | –1.9 | –1.4 | –1.2 | –1.1 |
| Spain | –2.4 | –5.6 | –2.6 | –3.0 | –1.2 | –0.8 | – 0.1 | –0.1 | –0.4 |
| France | –1.2 | –4.5 | –2.6 | –2.7 | –1.8 | –1.4 | –1.5 | –3.1 | –3.7 |
| Ireland | –7.7 | –2.1 | 2.0 | 2.3 | 2.3 | 4.3 | 1.1 | –0.1 | –0.6 |
| Italy | –9.1 | –9.1 | –3.1 | –3.1 | –1.7 | –0.6 | –2.6 | –2.3 | –2.3 |
| Luxembourg | | 1.8 | 3.6 | 3.0 | 3.5 | 6.1 | 6.4 | 2.6 | –0.2 |
| Netherlands | –3.2 | –3.5 | –0.2 | –0.8 | 0.7 | 2.2 | 0.1 | –1.1 | –1.6 |
| Austria | –1.8 | –3.8 | –2.4 | –2.5 | –2.3 | –1.5 | 0.3 | –0.6 | –1.1 |
| Portugal | –4.6 | –5.2 | –3.4 | –3.2 | –2.8 | –2.8 | –4.2 | –2.7 | –3.5 |
| Finland | 3.9 | –5.0 | 1.2 | 1.5 | 2.0 | 6.9 | 5.1 | 4.7 | 3.3 |
| Sweden | 0.6 | –7.4 | 0.5 | 2.3 | 1.5 | 3.4 | 4.5 | 1.3 | 0.8 |
| UK | –2.2 | –5.7 | –0.3 | 0.2 | 1.1 | 3.9 | 0.8 | –1.3 | –2.5 |
| EU-15 | –2.9 | –5.1 | –1.6 | –1.7 | –0.7 | 0.9 | – 0.9 | –1.9 | –2.3 |
| Euro area | –3.4 | –5.0 | –2.1 | –2.3 | –1.3 | 0.1 | –1.6 | –2.2 | –2.5 |

*Source*: Commission (2003).

of Ministers in November. In fact, Portugal was successful in reducing the deficit below 3 per cent although, in the absence of further action, it will be exceeded in 2003. However, two other countries – Germany and France – both exceeded the 3 per cent ceiling and are forecast to do so again in 2003 unless action is taken to reduce the deficit. The outturn for Germany was due largely to a slower rate of GDP growth than had originally been forecast, and Germany was advised in January of this year on action to correct its 'excessive deficit'. At the same time, the Council of Ministers issued France with an early warning.

The SGP has been criticized for providing an excessively harsh discipline on Member State economies at a time of economic slowdown, especially as those countries that have been badly hit lack the freedom to stimulate their economies through a lowering of interest rates. Although a 3 per cent ceiling allows sufficient room for countries starting from a position of budgetary balance to apply a fiscal stimulus to the economy, it is unduly tight for countries whose level of borrowing is already close to the 3 per cent limit. A further argument is that, because these countries cannot use fiscal policy to stimulate their economies, excessive pressure is applied on the ECB to cut interest rates below what may be the desirable level given medium-term inflationary trends. 'Too strict budget deficit rules, however, make it impossible for these countries to counter recessions. Finding themselves naked, they are likely to put pressure on the ECB to do what they cannot – enact looser monetary policies' (de Grauwe, 2002). Some critics question whether there is any need for strict rules on government borrowing in the euro area, seeing the rationale for the SGP as being essentially political.

## III. Economic Developments in the Member States inside the Euro Area

### *Germany*

In 2002, Germany, the EU's largest economy, was the worst performing Member State in terms of output and employment growth. For the fourth year running, it had the lowest growth rate of any Member State. In the final quarter of the year, GDP grew by a rate of only 0.2 per cent on the previous quarter. As result, unemployment rose from 7.7 to 8.1 per cent, with Germany being the only country to experience negative employment growth during the year. Closer analysis shows that the main reason for Germany's lacklustre performance was a combination of falling domestic demand and slower export growth. Private consumption fell by 0.6 per cent, as the number of unemployed grew and consumer confidence collapsed, while investment spending fell by 6.7 per cent. Although the weakness of the euro at the start of the year helped exports, export growth fell dramatically. Over the year as whole, export demand grew by only 2.8 per cent, compared with 5 per cent in 2001. With the level of government borrowing exceeding the 3 per cent ceiling under the SGP, there was no room for providing additional fiscal stimulus through tax cuts or increased government spending.

Some observers have argued that Germany's problems are structural rather than cyclical (see, e.g., Wolf, 2002). Relatively high unit labour costs due to a combination of high wages and low productivity are seen as contributing to a loss of competitiveness internationally. In order to effect devaluation in the *real* exchange rate, Germany must achieve a lower rate of inflation than the rest of the euro area. With inflation falling in the rest of the EU, this implies a rate of inflation approaching zero. The fall in the euro over the course of the year has helped, but has not been sufficient to close the gap.

The alternative is structural reform to raise productivity in German manufacturing and, thereby, reduce costs and the price level. The large element of non-wage costs in total labour costs is seen by some observers as a major factor contributing to declining competitiveness. This necessitates measures to reduce the extent to which employers contribute to healthcare, pensions and unemployment insurance. Measures to boost investment are also required if productivity levels are to be raised. Labour market reform to reduce barriers to the employment of workers, such as Germany's strict job protection laws, high levels of unemployment benefit and centralized wage bargaining, are seen by some observers to be necessary. The difficulty for Germany is how to bring about these changes while raising taxes or cutting public spending so as to reduce government borrowing below the 3 per cent ceiling prescribed by the SGP.

### *France*

In France, GDP grew at a rate of 1.2 per cent in 2002, compared with 1.8 per cent in the previous year. Output, however, was more resilient than in neighbouring Germany. A sharp drop in export growth in the second half of the year was a major factor contributing to weak final demand. However, both private consumption and investment remained depressed throughout the year, as consumer and business confidence remained at a low ebb. Only a strong increase in public consumption (government spending) provided support for aggregate demand, but at the expense of a rising fiscal deficit. Over the year as whole, the general government deficit was 3.1 per cent of GDP compared with 1.5 per cent in the previous year and is forecast to rise to 3.7 per cent in 2003. As result, France received a formal warning from the Council of Ministers in January of this year for exceeding the 3 per cent ceiling under the SGP and requiring it to take action to reduce the deficit for the current year.

As a result of sluggish output growth, employment grew by only 0.6 per cent during the year and the unemployment rate rose to 8.7 per cent. The difficulty for France, as for Germany, is to how to expand demand while reducing the level of government borrowing. A rise in the savings ratio of households from 15.9 per cent in 2001 to 17.1 per cent in 2002 suggests that the fall in consumption spending had much to do with declining confidence. The fact, however, that house prices have continued rising in France, while falling in Germany, meant that the wealth effect was more favourable in France.

### *Italy*

In 2002, Italy's GDP grew at a rate of only 0.4 per cent, one of the lowest growth rates in the EU and only a little faster than in Germany. Apart from a brief spurt in 2000, Italy has consistently recorded one of the lowest growth rates in the EU for more than a decade. Over the year as whole, export demand fell, as did private consumption and fixed investment. Some revival of domestic demand did take place in the second half of the year, as tax reductions gave a boost to spending on durable consumer goods and business investment. However, a large part of this extra demand leaked out of the economy in increased imports, while export demand fell over the year as whole. Despite slow output growth, employment increased by 1.1 per cent, only slightly down on the previous year. As a result, the unemployment rate fell to 9 per cent from 9.4 per cent in the previous year. Inflation, however, remained stubbornly high at 2.8 per cent for the year as whole.

Despite concerns that the size of the budget deficit could come close to the 3 per cent ceiling, the level of government borrowing for the year was only 2.3 per cent, compared with 2.6 per cent in the previous year. However, this was due largely to a series of one-off measures (sales of certain public assets and a tax amnesty on assets held abroad), rather than to any structural changes. As a result, the forecasts of the Commission show the deficit exceeding the ceiling in 2004 in the absence of any further changes. The SGP aside, Italy faces the dilemma that government borrowing needs to fall if government indebtedness (equal to 106.7 per cent of GDP in 2002) is to be reduced. A further concern is that, as Italy's population is ageing, pension liabilities in the future will be large.

### *Spain*

In Spain, GDP growth fell from 2.7 per cent in the previous year to 2 per cent, but its growth rate remained at the top end of the range for the euro area. A weaker increase in private consumption and fixed investment were the main causes of slackening growth. As a result, employment growth faltered and, after falling for several years, the unemployment rate rose to 11.4 per cent. Although this is lower than the levels that prevailed in the early 1990s, the unemployment rate remains the highest in the EU. Inflation also rose strongly from 2.8 to 3.6 per cent, well above the average for the euro area as a whole. Although unit labour costs grew only modestly during the year, a rise in indirect taxes and the effects of the changeover to the euro appear to have contributed to a faster rise in prices. A sharp rise in the prices of unprocessed food and energy added to the inflationary momentum in the second half of the year.

*Other Member States*

In *Austria*, GDP grew at a rate of 1 per cent, compared with 0.7 per cent in the previous year. Slow growth in private consumption and fixed investment contributed to a relatively disappointing recovery. Employment growth was negative and the unemployment rate rose to 4.3 per cent. The inflation rate also fell from 2.3 per cent in 2001 to 1.7 per cent.

For the second year running, *Belgium* experienced sluggish economic growth, with GDP rising by 0.7 per cent, slightly below the average for the EU as a whole. Export demand fell due to the drop in economic activity in the rest of the EU, while private domestic demand remained depressed. Employment growth turned negative and the unemployment rate rose to 7.3 per cent. General government borrowing remained relatively low at 0.1 per cent of GDP yet, with a ratio of government debt to GDP of 106.3 per cent, Belgium remains one of the most indebted countries in the euro area.

After a fall in GDP growth to only 0.6 per cent in 2001, *Finland* experienced a mild recovery in 2002, with GDP rising by 1.6 per cent. The main factors were a strong boost from government spending and a recovery of export demand, beginning in the second quarter of the year. Private consumption also grew more rapidly than in the previous year, helped by a rise in real disposable incomes as inflation fell to 2 per cent. The unemployment rate remained stable at 9.1 per cent. Finland continued to enjoy one of the strongest budgetary positions of any member of the euro area, with a budget surplus equivalent to 4.7 per cent of GDP.

In 2002, *Greece* was the second fastest growing economy in the euro area, with GDP growing by 4 per cent, compared with 4.1 per cent in the previous year. The main contribution to GDP growth came from private domestic demand, with consumption rising by 2.5 per cent and investment by 6.2 per cent. This was boosted by increased financial flows from EU structural funds and by investment in preparation for the 2004 Olympic Games. As a result, the unemployment rate, which is one of the highest in the EU, fell further from 10.4 per cent in 2001 to 9.9 per cent. A large element of this, however, appears to be structural unemployment, especially among young and female workers. Inflationary pressures remained relatively strong, with the HICP rising by 3.9 per cent, slightly faster than in the previous year.

*Ireland* continued to enjoy the status of being the EU's fastest growing economy, with GDP growing by 6 per cent during the year, compared to 5.7 per cent in 2001, although some deceleration is forecast for 2003. Strong export demand was a major contributory factor, while import growth remained relatively subdued. Private consumption grew less rapidly, as a result of continuing high inflation and reduced consumer confidence. Employment growth slackened during the year and the unemployment rate rose to 4.4 per cent. However, inflationary pressures remained strong, with the HICP increasing by 4.7 per cent, compared with 4 per cent in the previous year. Wage pressures continued to exert a strong upward push on labour costs, with compensation per employee rising by more than 9 per cent during the year. However, prices also rose as a result of an increase in indirect tax rates and of user charges.

Up until 2000, *Luxembourg* was one of the fastest growing economies in the euro area. In 2001, however, growth fell to 1 per cent and, last year, to only 0.4 per cent. An important factor was the adverse effects of developments in financial markets on the economy, given the country's strong specialization in financial services. However, private consumption also proved weak, as a result of low consumer confidence and increased household savings. Unemployment increased only moderately to 2.4 per cent, while the inflation rate fell to 2.1 per cent.

Like Luxembourg, the *Netherlands* experienced hardly any output growth during the year. After growing by only 1.3 per cent in 2001, GDP grew by only 0.3 per cent last year. With a heavy dependence on trade, the Netherlands was hit badly by the slowdown in the rest of the EU, with export demand falling by 1.3 per cent. Export demand was also adversely affected by declining international competitiveness, with unit labour costs rising sharply by 4.3 per cent. However, the slowdown was also made worse by weak domestic demand and large-scale destocking.

Having been a relatively fast growing economy in the second half of the 1990s, *Portugal* experienced a sharp slowing down of output growth in 2001. In 2002, output growth decelerated further to 0.5 per cent, which the Commission explained as a process of adjustment to past imbalances (Commission, 2003). In particular, in recent years, Portugal has been suffering from a relatively high external deficit and a large government budgetary deficit. A strong rise in private sector indebtedness has been identified as a further imbalance that has developed in recent years. As output growth has slowed, negative import growth has brought an improvement in Portugal's trade balance, while the government's budget deficit has been held below the 3 per cent ceiling under the SGP. The latter was achieved by stringent cutbacks introduced by the newly elected administration. As a result of the slowing down of the economy, inflation fell further from 4.4 per cent in 2001 to 3.7 per cent, despite a 2 percentage point rise in the VAT rate.

## IV. Economic Development in Member States Outside the Euro Area

### *United Kingdom*

Along with the other countries that were not part of the euro area, the UK was less adversely affected by the slowing down of economic activity in the EU. GDP grew by 1.8 per cent, compared with 2.1 per cent in the previous year. The main contribution came from a relatively robust level of private consumption, which increased by 3.8 per cent over the year as whole. Rising wage levels, combined with a low rate of inflation, saw incomes rise in real terms. At the same time, despite the adverse effects of falling share prices, household wealth was boosted by an increase in house prices of over 20 per cent over the year as whole. In contrast to other Member States, households further reduced the ratio of savings to income to only 5.1 per cent and increased their borrowing.

A gradual reduction in short-term interest rates and a significant loosening in the stance of fiscal policy also played a part. The government's budget balance swung from a surplus of 0.8 per cent of GDP in 2001 to a deficit of 0.7 per cent of GDP in 2002. Due to large increases in public spending, this is expected to increase further to 2.5 per cent of GDP in 2003. Investment spending, however, remained weak, declining by 3.2 per cent over the year as whole, with a bigger fall for equipment spending. A particular concern for the UK was the relatively slow rate of growth of labour productivity, as employers held on to their labour force in the face of slower growth in demand. Real GDP per worker grew by a relatively slow 1.1 per cent, although this was higher than the average for the rest of the EU. In terms of the other 'fundamentals', however, the UK performed well, with unemployment and inflation below the average level for other Member States.

### *Denmark*

Denmark was one of the most buoyant economies in the EU, with output growth of 1.8 per cent a year, higher than in the previous year. A major factor was strong export demand, due mainly to a favourable composition of goods, despite an appreciation of the krone of more than 7 per cent against the euro. However, private consumption and investment both held up strongly as well.

*Sweden*

Like Denmark, Sweden was also much less severely affected by the slowing down in output growth than the rest of the EU, with GDP growing by 1.9 per cent compared with 1.1 per cent in the previous year. In recent years, Sweden has been adversely affected by the global slump in the telecommunications sector, which has dampened growth in the manufacturing sector. Export growth remained weak, but was more than offset by a continuing fall in imports. Although private consumption was subdued, public consumption rose strongly and helped to strengthen final demand. Inflation fell from 2.7 per cent in 2001 to 2 per cent, the inflation rate ceiling operated by the *Riksbank*.

## Conclusion

2002 was a disappointing year for the EU economies and for the members of the euro area in particular. A recovery that began in the first quarter petered out. By the end of the year, there were signs that the euro area countries were slipping back into another period of slowdown. Of particular concern was the sluggish performance of the EU's largest economy, Germany, on which the euro area economy depends for any lasting recovery to take place. Compared with other regions of the world, but with the single exception of Japan, the performance of the economies of the euro area was dismal. Worse still, the Commission's most recent forecasts are predicting even slower growth in 2003.

Although the EU's problems have been, in part, of a global nature, the fact that the EU has performed so poorly in comparison with other regions of the world suggests that they cannot be entirely explained in these terms. There are some fundamental problems that need to be addressed on the policy side. Both fiscal and monetary policy appear to have played a much more important role in supporting the level of economic activity and promoting a recovery in other countries of the world (again, Japan remains an exception). In the EU, however, this has been more difficult to bring about because of the constraints imposed on policy-makers.

Some critics see the problems of the euro area as arising from the excessively rigid rules imposed on Member States by the Stability and Growth Pact. With the ECB constrained in operating monetary policy by the need to keep inflation below 2 per cent, it is argued that Member States must have greater freedom to combat downturns of the kind that have occurred in recent years by running budget deficits in excess of 3 per cent. Other critics question the necessity of having any limits on government borrowing, preferring instead rules covering only overall levels of government indebtedness relative to GDP. Others see the problems as lying in the inflation target set for the ECB, which imposes deflation on countries with rates of inflation below the area average.

Whatever the outcome of this debate, it is clear that, if the EU is to achieve its objective of becoming the most dynamic region of the world, it will need to reflect on the effectiveness of existing macroeconomic policy-making in the euro area. However, effective macroeconomic policies alone are not sufficient to ensure faster growth. Structural reforms to raise the underlying growth rate of the economy and raise international competitiveness have an important role to play, as the problem of the German economy demonstrates.

## References

Alberola, E. and Tyrvaïnen, T. (1998) 'Is their Scope for Inflation Differentials in EMU? An Empirical Evaluation of the Balassa-Samuelson Model in EMU Countries'. *Bank of Finland Discussion Paper* 15/98, Helsinki.

Balassa, B. (1964) The Purchasing Power Parity Doctrine: A Reappraisal, *Journal of Political Economy,* Vol. 72, pp. 584–96.

Commission of the European Communities (2002) 'Economic Forecasts Autumn 2002'. *European Economy* No. 5/2002, Brussels.

Commission of the European Communities (2003) 'Economic Forecasts Spring 2003, to be published as *European Economy* No. 2/2003, Brussels.

Crooks, E. and Major, T. (2002) 'How both Fiscal and Monetary Policy are Stifling the Eurozone'. *Financial Times*, 11 October.

Grauwe, Paul de (2002) 'Europe's Instability Pact'. *Financial Times*, 25 July.

International Monetary Fund (2002) *World Economic Outlook*, September (Washington DC: IMF).

International Monetary Fund (2003) *World Economic Outlook*, April (Washington DC: IMF).

Samuelson, P.A. (1 964) 'Theoretical Notes on Trade Problems'. *Review of Economics and Statistics,* Vol. 46, pp. 145–54.

Wolf, M. (2002) 'Berlin's Turn to Suffer in a Trap of its Own Invention'. *Financial Times*, 23 October.

JCMS 2003 Volume 41. Annual Review pp. 191–206

# Developments in the Economies of the Applicant Countries

DEBRA JOHNSON
University of Hull

## I. Overview

The international economic climate in 2002 was unpropitious. The US recovery was shaky, hit by the aftermath of the terrorist attacks in September 2001, high-profile corporate scandals and the continuing weakness of stock markets. The EU and Japan also proved vulnerable to these trends and the severe economic crisis in Argentina began to infect other Latin American countries. General business and investor confidence was not helped by the uncertainty created by the international crisis surrounding Iraq. As a consequence, economic forecasts were generally revised downwards. European Commission forecasts for EU-15 growth in 2002, for example, were lowered from 1.5 per cent to 1 per cent between autumn and spring (Commission, 2002a).

In view of this difficult external climate and the growing reliance of those countries seeking entry into the European Union on EU markets, a significant negative impact on the economies of those countries could have been anticipated. However, this has not happened. Although their economic growth has slowed slightly, the candidate countries have continued to progress and were among the world's most robust economies in 2002. With the exception of Poland, where growth was below 1 per cent in 2002, growth in all other candidate countries easily exceeded 2 per cent and approached 5 per cent in the Baltic states.

This resilience amidst widespread negative economic factors indicates that the commitment of the candidate countries to fundamental economic reform is beginning to bear fruit. This achievement is all the more notable given the substantial real currency appreciation experienced by many of them. Without the productivity improvements reaped by many of these countries as a result of their restructuring, this phenomenon could have dangerously reduced their competitiveness in a weak export market.

A major factor in this resilience was strong domestic demand, which rose 2.4 per cent in the ten countries due to accede in 2004 and 3.4 per cent across all 13 candidate countries. A combination of continuing strong investment; steady growth of private consumption, falling inflation, real wage increases and continuing capital inflows all played their part in buoying up domestic demand. Strong domestic demand also helped offset weakening exports: indeed the contribution of net exports to growth in the candidate countries was slightly negative in 2002. However, as a result of the structural shift in export offerings towards higher value-added, more advanced manufactured products brought about by the extensive inflows of foreign direct investment (FDI) of recent years, the slowdown in export sectors was less severe than it could have been.

Table 1: Real Growth in Gross Domestic Product (GDP), Annual % Change

| | *1997 –2001* | *2002 Estimate* | *2003 Forecast* | *2004 Forecast* | *Real GDP in 2001 (1989=100)* |
|---|---|---|---|---|---|
| Cyprus | 4.2 | 2.2 | 3.5 | 4.1 | n/a |
| Czech Republic | 1.0 | 2.2 | 3.2 | 3.8 | 106 |
| Estonia | 5.2 | 4.5 | 4.7 | 5.1 | 90 |
| Hungary | 4.5 | 3.4 | 4.5 | 4.9 | 112 |
| Latvia | 6.1 | 5.0 | 5.5 | 6.0 | 75 |
| Lithuania | 3.6 | 5.0 | 3.5 | 4.5 | 72 |
| Malta | 3.4 | 2.8 | 3.4 | 3.6 | n/a |
| Poland | 4.2 | 0.8 | 3.2 | 3.9 | 129 |
| Slovakia | 3.3 | 3.9 | 3.9 | 4.8 | 110 |
| Slovenia | 4.2 | 2.6 | 3.6 | 4.0 | 121 |
| AC-10 | n/a | 2.1 | 3.6 | 4.2 | n/a |
| Bulgaria | 2.0 | 4.0 | 5.0 | 5.5 | 80 |
| Romania | –1.0 | 4.2 | 4.6 | 4.7 | 84 |
| Turkey | 1.2 | 3.9 | 3.7 | 4.4 | n/a |
| CC-13 | | 2.9 | 3.8 | 4.4 | n/a |
| EU-15 | 2.6 | 1.0 | 2.0 | 2.6 | n/a |

*Source:* Commission (2002); EBRD (2002).
*Note:* AC-10 = countries scheduled for accession in 2004; CC-13 = candidate countries, i.e. the AC-10 plus Bulgaria, Romania and Turkey.

## II. Preparedness for EU Membership

With the exception of Romania, the initial and most traumatic stages of economic transition have been completed for the majority of central and east European countries. The policy emphasis has shifted towards fulfilling the *acquis* and bridging the gap with EU levels of development. However, catch-up is a distant goal: the GDP per head of the group of candidate countries is approximately 40 per cent of the EU average, ranging from 80 per cent in Cyprus and 70 per cent in Slovenia to around one-quarter in Romania and Turkey, by far the most populous applicant country.

The prospect of accession is having and will continue to have positive effects on the candidate economies. Structural reforms, the adoption of the *acquis* and improved governance structures are needed to boost economic efficiency and potential growth, and to enable the enterprises of the candidate countries to compete in the single European market. As a result of these measures, many candidate economies have benefited from increased domestic demand and foreign investment, which itself both requires confidence in the domestic business environment and is an important generator of further growth and transformation.

FDI has come to play an important role in central and eastern European countries by facilitating growth in higher value-added sectors, enhancing productivity and generally increasing competitiveness and capability – all essential for fulfilment of the Copenhagen criteria and smooth accession. At the beginning of transition, only Hungary, already familiar with the market system, had received FDI in any significant quantities. By the mid-1990s, FDI was distributed more evenly throughout the region and in 1996, for the first time, Poland pushed Hungary into second place as a destination for FDI in the region. Table 2 shows that in terms of FDI inflows per capita, the Czech Republic has become the preferred destination for foreign investors among the transition economies and that Bulgaria and Romania lag a long way behind. Accession itself is unlikely to boost FDI: much investment has already taken place in anticipation of accession and the greater accessibility to European markets it affords.

The transition process began with large productivity and product quality gaps between the transitional states and those of the EU. Enterprise restructuring has involved labour shedding and has refocused activity in more technologically advanced and higher value-added sectors. Although the investment gains of recent years entailed some job creation, this has been restrained by the much-needed increases in labour productivity brought about by investment. The EU maintains that, in most transition countries, the impact of job shedding will be exceeded by job creation in 2003–04, that unemployment

Table 2: Foreign Direct Investment (FDI) Inflows in the Transition Economies of Central and Eastern Europe (US$ m)

| | *1990* | *1993* | *1996* | *1999* | *2002 Projection* | *Cumulative FDI Inflows 1989–2002* | *Cumulative FDI Inflows per capita 1989–2001* |
|---|---|---|---|---|---|---|---|
| Bulgaria | 4 | 40 | 138 | 789 | 800 | 4,761 | 259 |
| Czech Rep. | n/a | 563 | 1,276 | 6234 | 8,000 | 34,960 | 2,615 |
| Estonia | n/a | 156 | 111 | 222 | 300 | 2,651 | 1,727 |
| Hungary | 311 | 2,328 | 2,279 | 1720 | 2,559 | 24,310 | 2,137 |
| Latvia | n/a | 50 | 379 | 331 | 250 | 2,920 | 1,138 |
| Lithuania | n/a | 30 | 152 | 478 | 395 | 3,221 | 813 |
| Poland | 0 | 580 | 2,741 | 6348 | 5,000 | 39,426 | 890 |
| Romania | –18 | 87 | 415 | 1025 | 1,200 | 9,128 | 356 |
| Slovakia | 24 | 107 | 199 | 701 | 4,000 | 9,629 | 1,042 |
| Slovenia | –2 | 111 | 188 | 144 | 553 | 2,400 | 934 |

*Source:* Derived from EBRD (2002).

peaked in 2002–03 and should decrease slightly thereafter in most candidate countries. However, in a number of countries, labour market rigidities could stifle job creation, although some governments are already taking steps to remedy this problem.

Real convergence of the acceding countries with the EU is important but they are also seeking nominal convergence to enable them to adopt the euro. Indeed, the majority of acceding candidates have expressed their intention to join the euro area as soon as possible after accession. In order to do so, they will have to comply with the Maastricht criteria and the terms of the Stability and Growth Pact (Table 3).

This poses big challenges for these countries at their current stage of transition. In relation to the fiscal criteria, for example, the budget deficits of the Baltic states, Slovenia and Cyprus already fall within the 3 per cent budget deficit and 60 per cent national debt limits. In order for the other countries to comply with these criteria, a period of fiscal retrenchment is needed. However, fiscal retrenchment could clash with expenditure demands to comply with other accession requirements or to ensure the ability of enterprises to compete in new markets. For example, a common problem throughout the candidate countries is inadequate infrastructure, in terms of both quality and quantity, a feature that reduces the attractiveness of locations for investors. In order to rectify this situation, which constrains growth and real convergence,

Table 3: Indicators of Real and Nominal Convergence

| | *Inflation (%)* | *Govt. Balance/ GDP* | *National Debt/ GDP* | *Unemployment (%)* | *Current Account/ GDP* | *GDP per Head (EU-15=100)* |
|---|---|---|---|---|---|---|
| Bulgaria | 6.0 | –0.6 | 57.3 | 18.5 | –5.8 | 31.4 |
| Cyprus | 3.0 | –2.6 | | 4.3 | –28.1 | 80.0 |
| Czech Republic | 2.0 | –6.4 | 23.3 | 8.8 | –5.5 | 59.8 |
| Estonia | 3.8 | 0.7 | 5.1 | 10.5 | –18.0 | 44.6 |
| Hungary | 5.2 | –6.9 | 53.3 | 5.8 | –5.7 | 51.6 |
| Latvia | 1.9 | –1.8 | 13.9 | 13.5 | –16.9 | 32.2 |
| Lithuania | 0.2 | –1.8 | 28.4 | 16.6 | –10.4 | 38.1 |
| Malta | 2.7 | –6.2 | | 6.9 | –13.4 | |
| Poland | 2.1 | –4.4 | 48.0 | 18.5 | –3.1 | 37.2 |
| Romania | 22.2 | –2.9 | 29.2 | 7.3 | –5.9 | 25.5 |
| Slovakia | 3.7 | –6.0 | 34.5 | 18.9 | –9.6 | 49.1 |
| Slovenia | 7.6 | –1.8 | 31.0 | 6.3 | –2.9 | 69.5 |
| Turkey | 45.4 | –15.1 | | 9.2 | –4.4 | 25.5 |

*Sources:* Commission (2002a, c); Deutsche Bank (2003); EBRD (2002).

major public investment is required. However, such investment would make attainment of the Maastricht criteria difficult even though, in these circumstances, it could be argued that upward pressure on the public deficit could denote real progress in transition and that future deficits may be lower as a result.

Despite the fact that the budget deficits of several candidate countries exceed the 3 per cent limit by some way, the overall record of the transition countries in controlling their deficits is good, given the scale of the transition undertaken. In general, they have been helped by their low level of pre-transition debts, strong growth since the mid-1990s and the inflow of privatization revenues. These positive factors will not continue: the large-scale privatizations of earlier years are coming to an end and the downturn in growth makes control of the deficit more difficult.

The transition countries have experienced appreciation of their real effective exchange rate: the phenomenon has been strongest in Lithuania and least notable in Hungary and Slovenia. In all cases however, the appreciation has been significant and poses questions for the Maastricht criteria relating to currency stability and inflation. This appreciation, which so far has not apparently damaged the export performance of the candidate countries, is partially explained by the so-called 'Balassa-Samuelson effect' whereby rapid productivity growth in the tradeable goods sectors boosts real wages in all sectors, including non-tradeable sectors, where productivity growth is lower. A rise in real wages in lower productivity sectors pushes up relative prices and maintains inflation above euro area levels. Given that internationally traded goods are sold at world market prices, the appreciation is an equilibrium condition that allows this to happen. Inflation is also determined by factors other than differential productivity, and the annual average inflation rate in the candidate countries has been falling, although much more needs to be done in Romania and Turkey.

In short, despite the above, early EMU membership is not out of reach in several cases. However, whether this is achieved will depend largely on resolution of the present international crisis which is creating economic uncertainty and holding back recovery in EU economies. So far, the candidate countries have coped by relying on domestic demand to ride out the economic storm. However, this will not be sustainable indefinitely, nor is it desirable because over-reliance on domestic demand will create its own imbalances.

## III. Economic Developments in Individual Applicant States

### *Poland*

As eastern Europe's biggest economy, Poland is under close scrutiny as accession approaches. Since the onset of transition, Poland has in many ways been the region's most successful economy: it returned to growth by 1992, the first eastern European country to do so, and has seen sustained growth ever since. By 2002, Poland's real GDP was 29 per cent greater than in 1989 – the greatest rebound among all candidate transition countries, half of which still register real GDP below 1989 levels.

However, since 2001 Polish economic growth has slowed significantly. Indeed, growth in 2002 was only 0.8 per cent, the lowest of all candidate countries. Declining domestic demand lay at the root of the problem. In particular, fixed investment fell by 9.8 per cent in 2001 and 6.5 per cent in 2002. This is a worrying trend given the contribution of investment to the reorientation of Polish exports towards higher valued-added, more capital and skill-intensive products which enabled Poland to increase significantly its penetration of EU markets. Although Poland has the region's largest stock of FDI, it lags behind other transition countries in terms of FDI per capita, an indication that foreign investors continue to find the Polish business environment difficult compared to its neighbours.

Polish problems have been intensified by a combination of over-expansionary fiscal policy and restrictive monetary policy, including high interest rates. These have subsequently been cut from the February 2001 peak of 19 per cent to 8 per cent in August 2002. The government deficit, reinforced by low growth, increased to 5 per cent of GDP from around 3 per cent in the mid-1990s. Measures taken in August 2002, including an amnesty on tax and social security arrears, state credit and tax deferral for small enterprises and additional state guarantees for enterprise debt, will intensify upward pressure on the budget deficit.

The economic slowdown also helped push unemployment to 18 per cent during 2002. However, not all Poland's employment problems are cyclical: some result from increases in the working age population, whereas others reflect labour market rigidities. In February 2002, limited measures were taken to increase labour market flexibility. Stronger growth, the lagged effect of labour market reforms and ongoing industrial restructuring could begin to reverse the rising unemployment trend in 2003.

Slower growth has helped control the macroeconomic imbalances arising from strong domestic demand. The current account deficit has fallen from its peak of 7.5 per cent of GDP to 3.8 per cent in 2000. Inflation has fallen to a post-1989 low of 2.1 per cent and is still falling – a factor that also helped reduce interest rates. Falling inflation has also been helped by currency appreciation. One of the encouraging features of the Polish economy is that, despite this appreciation and the slowdown in its major markets, Polish exports, although inevitably weakening somewhat, still grew by almost 4 per cent in real terms in 2002.

### *Hungary*

Hungary's head-start in structural reform created a dynamic export sector that produced robust growth by the mid-1990s. In 2000, policy objectives shifted to boost living standards through wage and pension increases, especially in the public sector, and greater public infrastructure investment. This policy shift helps explain why a small, open economy (Hungarian exports and imports account for over 120 per cent of GDP) was able to sustain economic growth of 3.4 per cent in 2002 despite serious weaknesses in the EU market, the destination for three-quarters of Hungarian exports, and sluggish growth in industrial production and private investment.

Strong domestic demand has been driven by both public and private consumption and has come at a price – namely a budget deficit in 2002 of 6.9 per cent of GDP (compared to 3 per cent in 2000) – and puts continuing falls in government debt in jeopardy. A second budget towards the end of 2002 sought sharp cuts in current expenditure and delayed transport infrastructure investment, essential for integration with Europe and for addressing the problems of lagging regions. The proposed spending cuts could prove difficult to carry through, but continuing fiscal expansion could undermine inflation targets. Real wage growth, which exceeded productivity growth in 2002, could also undermine these targets. Since the mid-1990s, Hungary's inflation has been among the highest in the region. In 2001, there were signs that inflationary expectations were being broken: average inflation for the year fell to 9.2 per cent, and by 2002 it had fallen to 5.2 per cent, helped by currency appreciation, lower oil and food prices, falling producer prices and general economic slowdown.

One driver behind private sector wage growth is labour shortages. Budapest, for example, operates at almost full employment. Indeed, unemployment throughout Hungary has been on a downward trend for some time, falling from over 12 per cent in the mid-1990s to under 6 per cent in 2002. Hungarian labour markets are generally regarded as flexible, and current policy is directed towards increasing incentives for participation in the workforce.

Employment has also shifted towards higher value-added technology, knowledge-intensive and service sectors, a development fostered by Hungary's policy of active investment promotion, relatively skilled workforce, liberal foreign trade regime, competitive labour costs and generally welcoming business environment. Until 1996, Hungary attracted the largest FDI inflows among the transition economies: it still maintains the region's second highest level of FDI per capita behind the Czech Republic.

So far, Hungary's economy has absorbed recent economic problems well. Despite a real appreciation of the forint of about 15 per cent and global economic downturn, Hungary's growth for 2002 was only slightly below earlier forecasts. Challenges from continuing global economic uncertainty and the fiscal and inflationary pressures building up within the Hungarian economy will further test the robustness of Hungary's economic restructuring.

*Czech Republic*

Czech growth in 2002 slowed to 2.2 per cent from the 3 per cent plus of the previous two years. Three factors played a key role in this growth deceleration: the floods of August 2002, the appreciation of the Czech crown and sluggish growth in the Czech Republic's main trading partner, namely the EU and Germany in particular.

The floods devastated large swathes of central Europe, but the Czech Republic was hardest hit. The direct clean-up costs could be as high as €3 billion and other related losses arose from interruptions to industrial and agricultural production and lower tourist numbers. Although the Czech government has played down the impact of the floods, the European Bank for Reconstruction and Development (EBRD) has estimated that they could have damaged the Czech Republic's growth by as much as 0.5 per cent in 2002.

Buoyant domestic demand, in particular private consumption, cushioned the impact of these negative effects. Household expenditure benefited from low inflation, real wage increases and low interest rates. Productivity growth is in line with real wage increases and inflation (helped by the stronger currency, moderate growth and lower food and commodity prices) continues to decelerate. Prices for 2002 as a whole were only 2 per cent above those of 2001 and inflation was as low as 0.6 per cent by the end of the year. Against this background, private consumption is expected to remain a significant factor in growth into 2003.

Public consumption was also an important factor sustaining growth in 2002. Indeed, despite the GDP growth of recent years, budget deficits have crept upwards from an average of 3.8 per cent during 1997–2001 to over 6 per cent in 2002. Some of this increase is attributable to the cost of the floods' clear-up, but much of it arises from high social transfers and the large amounts going towards much-needed infrastructure investment. As yet, no significant measures have been taken to address the imbalance in public finances, making any major decline in the budget deficit unlikely in the next couple of years. Indeed, a priority of the government that came into office in July 2002 was to maintain the relatively generous levels of welfare provision.

Furthermore, the slow but steady rise in unemployment, which increased from below 3 per cent in 1995 to almost 10 per cent in 2002, will not help the government's budget problems. The jobless increase reflects the combined effect of enterprise restructuring and associated job shedding, and the rigidities in the labour markets that have inhibited job creation. Aggregate unemployment figures also hide big regional employment differences and mask an emerging shortage of appropriately skilled workers. The government has acknowledged the problem of labour market inflexibility and has pledged reform in this area.

### *Smaller Acceding Countries*

Since the 1998 crisis, *Slovakia*'s GDP growth has increased steadily every year to reach 3.9 per cent in 2002. Initially driven by the export sector, growth has been maintained by strong domestic demand since 2001. Private consumption was fostered in 2001 by direct tax cuts and in 2002 by high real wage growth. Further direct tax cuts and slight increases in employment continue to stimulate private consumption. An expansionary fiscal policy also contributed to growth in 2002.

Despite its recent success, Slovakia's economy must negotiate major dangers. First, unemployment, driven by enterprise restructuring and generous welfare provision, reached 19 per cent in 2002. Second, Slovakia is confronted by uncomfortably high current account and fiscal deficits, the former driven by strong domestic demand and the weak external environment, and the latter by higher spending on social welfare and the continuing use of subsidies to cover the losses of some public enterprises. As a consequence, the budget deficit reached 6 per cent of GDP in 2002. Third, although Slovakia's inflation fell from 12 per cent in 2000 to under 4 per cent in 2002, indirect tax increases and increases in administered prices could lead to renewed inflationary pressure.

*Slovenia*'s economic transition began from a relatively high level of economic development and, by 2001, its GDP per head had reached 69 per cent of the EU average. Since 1997, GDP growth has been in the 4–5 per cent per annum range, although it slowed somewhat in 2001 and 2002, falling to 3 per cent and 2.6 per cent respectively. For some years after 1997, growth was driven by domestic consumption and investment but, by 2001, net exports had become the main growth factor. In 2002 despite the weakening of the EU market, Slovenia's main customer, exports remained central to GDP growth as a result of strong export performance to Russia, the former Yugoslavia and CEFTA. However, by 2002 domestic demand was also beginning to revive as a result of an investment recovery following the 2 per cent fall in 2001.

Slovenia's main policy concern is its stubbornly high inflation rate which, buoyed by increases in indirect excise taxes, administered price rises, public sector wage pressures and high growth in money aggregates, has remained in the 7–8 per cent range for a number of years. The beginning of a process of de-indexation and a tighter monetary policy will help, but may not be enough to reduce inflation significantly.

*Estonia*'s GDP growth in 2002 was 4.5 per cent and was supported by strong domestic demand, namely borrowing and investment, themselves buoyed by stable inflation and low interest rates. This level of growth also helped unemployment fall from 12.6 per cent in 2001 to 10.5 per cent in 2002. However, despite the small size of the economy, large regional disparities in income and employment persist. Indeed, per capita incomes in parts of the northeast and the south are less than 40 per cent of those in the north. Unemployment is forecast to fall gradually, but this process could be hampered by skills shortages.

Estonia maintained a small budget surplus in 2002. Greater demands on the expenditure side are expected as a result of Nato and EU membership, but should not cause too much concern. The most worrying source of economic imbalance is a current account deficit that reached 11.4 per cent of GDP in 2002. This resulted from strong domestic demand and a weak external environment. The growth forecast for 2003 is more balanced, with an anticipated moderation in domestic demand being offset by a larger contribution from the external sector.

From 1996 to 2001, *Latvia*'s GDP growth was twice that of the EU and 1.5 times that of the average of all the candidate countries. Investment, which averaged 19 per cent per annum during this period, was central to this strong performance. Hit by problems in its main export markets, growth decelerated markedly during the first half of 2002 from the 7.7 per cent of 2001. However, by the second half of the year, export growth accelerated and by December GDP growth was back to the previous year's levels, resulting in GDP growth for 2002 of over 5 per cent. Continuing buoyant growth is needed to tackle unemployment: total unemployment in 2002 was 13.5 per cent, but was as high as 20 per cent in the east and as low as 4 per cent in Riga.

As in the other Baltic states, domestic demand, particularly private consumption, was the major component of growth in 2002. This was helped by an inflation rate of only 1.9 per cent and significant wage increases that led to a rise in real income of 5.2 per cent. Given the continuing productivity gains, such high real income growth is unproblematic. Latvia has also managed to keep its public finances in good order. Its national debt is about 14 per cent of GDP and its 2002 budget deficit was below 3 per cent of GDP. Continuing growth should help the government increase its revenue. Domestic demand is forecast to remain strong, and has the potential to create serious imbalances in external accounts. However, although the current account deficit is over 8 per cent of GDP, it has so far been covered by FDI inflows.

*Lithuania*'s domestic demand in 2001 was weak, and its 5.9 per cent GDP growth was based on stock-building. However, helped by lower interest rates and high wages, domestic demand recovered strongly in 2002 and was the main factor behind GDP growth of over 5 per cent: private consumption grew 6 per cent in 2002, up from 2 per cent in 2001, and investment increased by 15 per cent. Strong domestic demand plus weak external demand resulted in a widening of the current account deficit to 6 per cent of GDP in 2002. Lithuania, however, has had more success in reducing its fiscal deficit from 8.5 per cent of GDP in 1999 to 1.8 per cent in 2002. This has been achieved by wage cuts, postponing the introduction of some measures and lower investment.

Growth has not yet contributed much to Lithuania's most intractable problem – continuing unemployment of 17 per cent. In 2002, a new labour code aimed at increasing labour market flexibility whilst protecting employee rights was introduced, and should contribute to job creation. High unemployment levels have helped keep real wage increases moderate, a key factor in keeping Lithuania's inflation rate around zero, along with a strong currency and high productivity growth. Resurgent domestic demand and a number of indirect tax increases that are in the pipeline will put some, albeit not worrying, upward pressure on prices.

*Malta* is an open economy in which trade accounts for over 85 per cent of GDP. Its two most important sectors are electronics and tourism, both of which were threatened in 2001, the former by global problems in the telecommunications sector and the latter by the aftermath of the terrorist attacks in the US. The result was a drop in GDP of 0.8 per cent in 2001 after several years of robust growth. However, growth resumed in 2002 and reached 4.1 per cent by the third quarter. Growth in domestic demand, namely private and public consumption rather than investment (which fell by almost 14 per cent in early 2002), began the recovery. However, domestic demand growth quickly tailed off and the external sector took over as the engine of growth later in the year. Electronics exports were central to recovery and more than offset the continuing decline in tourism arrivals.

Malta's most serious economic imbalance relates to government finances. Although falling from almost 11 per cent of GDP in 1998, the government deficit remains over 6 per cent. However, the government has adopted an expansionary fiscal stance and the potential for further major deficit falls is limited unless the 2002 recovery proves to be strong and well grounded, an assessment which it is too early to make given the uncertainty in the external environment.

In 2002, *Cyprus* experienced a fall in real GDP growth to 2.2 per cent following annual average growth of 4.2 per cent during the previous five years. Increasing economic uncertainty and slow wage growth damaged business and consumer confidence, leading to a deceleration in private consumption growth to 3 per cent in 2002 from 5 per cent the previous year. The terrorist attacks in the US hit the tourism industry particularly hard, and visitor numbers fell by 14 per cent in 2002. Given that tourism traditionally offsets the trade deficit, the downturn in tourism, despite declining imports induced by lower domestic demand, helped push the current account deficit to 6 per cent of GDP. Although there was a moderate increase in joblessness in 2002 as a result of these problems, the labour market remains at near full employment. As a result of indirect tax increases, inflation increased from 2 per cent in 2001 to 3 per cent in 2002, but is anticipated to fall back again to 2 per cent by 2004.

Despite the recent growth slowdown, the overall outlook for Cyprus is positive. Indeed, GDP per capita is already 80 per cent of the EU average, significantly higher than in other acceding countries. Government policy is directed towards preparation for EU accession: the associated liberalization, infrastructure projects and technological upgrading that are underway should boost investment and growth in years to come. Inflation and public finances are reasonably healthy and meet the Maastricht criteria. The big question mark in the short to medium term relates to the outcome of the crisis over Iraq: given its location at the eastern end of the Mediterranean, Cyprus is highly vulnerable to disruptions to its most important economic sector – tourism.

### *Candidates for Post-2004 Accession*

*Bulgaria* has recovered well from its 1996–97 crisis and since 1998 has experienced average annual growth of 4 per cent, a level that was also achieved in 2002. However, Bulgaria's average per capita income is only 28 per cent of the EU average, and the country will have to register growth above the EU average for decades to bridge this gap.

Domestic demand has been the most important factor behind real GDP growth. Investment growth has been particularly strong, increasing by 20 per cent in real terms in 2001 and 8 per cent in 2002. In order for competitive transformation and catch-up to take place, this investment surge must be sustained: at present, investment comprises only 18 per cent of GDP and FDI stock per capita is significantly below that of other candidate countries. Private consumption growth has been helped by tax cuts and moderate rises in real income. Despite the recovery, unemployment remains stubbornly high, peaking at 20 per cent in 2001, and falling back in 2002 to 18.5 per cent as a result of restructuring and skills mismatches.

Since the crisis, a policy consensus has emerged around tight fiscal policy (the budget deficit was 0.6 per cent in 2002) and market-based economic reforms, facilitating a return to macroeconomic stability and growth. Inflation performance is the most obvious example of this success. As recently as 1997, the annual increase in consumer prices was over 1000 per cent. By 2002, inflation had fallen to 6 per cent.

The future looks more positive for *Romania* than for some time. Romania only embarked upon serious economic transformation several years after other transition countries in the region. Initially progress was hampered by government ambivalence towards sustained reform, resulting in stop–go economic performance, slack fiscal policy, high inflation and external imbalances. Consequently, between 1997–99, real GDP contracted by 11 per cent and investment by almost 9 per cent.

However, recovery is underway. Growth rebounded to 5.3 per cent in 2001 as a result of buoyant private consumption, stock-building and an acceleration of investment growth. Strong export growth was offset by even stronger import growth, resulting in a negative contribution from the external sector. Growth in 2002 was slightly down at 4.2 per cent: domestic demand continued to grow albeit more slowly (private consumption growth slowed, but investment growth remained strong at 7 per cent) and export growth, despite the unfavourable external environment, strengthened whilst import growth declined.

One of Romania's most prominent economic problems has been persistent and high inflation. Helped by falling food prices, a tight fiscal policy and slower currency depreciation, inflation fell to 22 per cent in 2002. Although high by regional standards and way above EU levels, 22 per cent inflation represents a significant improvement over the 34.5 per cent of 2001, itself a marked improvement over earlier years. In the short term, Romania will encounter renewed inflationary pressures: the 2002 harvest was disappointing, and the government has agreed a 50 per cent increase in the minimum wage from 2003. This in turn could encourage a renewed surge in imports.

One indicator that will get worse before it gets better is unemployment which increased to 7.3 per cent in 2002 from 6.6 per cent a year earlier. Unemployment has remained relatively low because of the limited enterprise restructuring that has so far taken place in Romania. Despite the positive employment effects that will eventually come from economic growth, they will be offset for some time by the impact of economic reform.

*Turkey* experienced a banking and financial crisis in 2001 that resulted in negative GDP growth of 7.4 per cent, Turkey's deepest recession for decades. The crisis saw several banks brought close to bankruptcy and necessitated a major financial rescue package and tighter banking surveillance and regulation. The result was a major drain on the public purse and the abandonment in February 2001 of a three-year stabilization programme after 14 months. This led to a two-thirds depreciation of the Turkish lira against both the dollar and the euro, a sharp increase in inflation and interest rates, erosion of household incomes and an investment collapse. By May 2001, a new programme was in place and the first substantial disbursement of IMF funding occurred on the back of it in February 2002.

The new programme attempts to address the economy's fundamental weaknesses by emphasizing public sector reform, construction of a sound banking sector and liberalization to facilitate market led growth. Financial market conditions, including some rallying of the currency, began to normalize towards the end of 2001. In mid-2002, political uncertainty and tensions arising from the Prime Minister's ill health resulted in higher interest rates and further currency depreciation. In November 2002, the election of a government committed to continuation of the reform programme resolved this uncertainty.

Despite this turmoil, Turkey's economy registered growth of 4 per cent in 2002 and a significant decline in inflationary pressure. The main factors in recovery were stock-building and exports. Domestic demand remained weak in the face of the slow growth of disposable income and because of the need for fiscal discipline. Investment, hit by real interest rates and confidence problems, had plummeted by over 30 per cent in 2001, but grew by 2 per cent in 2002.

During the crisis, the need to bail out the banks drove the budget deficit from 6 per cent of GDP in 2000 to over 28 per cent of GDP in 2001 according to the EU, causing high interest rates and crowding out private investment. The need to rein back the debt burden and reduce the pressure on interest rates necessitates tight fiscal policy. The recovery in 2002 helped improve public finances. However, the public deficit remains at 15 per cent of GDP and is not helped by the parlous financial state of state-owned enterprises, particularly in the energy sector.

Control of inflation and reduction of interest rates are also major challenges. Although falling, the inflation rate remained as high as 45 per cent for 2002. Hitherto, backward indexation of wage agreements, a practice that has recently ceased, had resulted in persistently high inflationary expectations. Weak domestic demand and a tight public sector wage policy also contributed to disinflation and a deterioration in labour markets. The outlook for unemployment, which at 9.2 per cent in 2002 was at its highest level for two decades, is poor given the focus on restructuring of state-owned enterprises in the government's economic programme, and projected increases in the labour force of working age.

## Conclusion

In general, the economic performance of the candidate countries was impressive in 2002, given the unpromising external environment. Although there are clear significant variations, the countries in question do share some common features and problems. For example, they tend to be small, highly open economies with a level of interdependence with EU markets that has increased significantly in recent years. Many of them require major improvements in quantity and quality of infrastructure to enable them to take further advantage of their integration with the European Union and to help them address their wide internal regional disparities.

The EU forecasts for the candidate countries are sanguine about the outlook for the next couple of years. This optimism is based on an assumption of an improvement in the international economic environment, including significantly stronger performance within the EU itself. This will, in turn, boost the export performance of the candidate countries. Given the current international uncertainty, this optimism may well be misplaced.

## References

Commission of the European Communities (2002a) 'Economic Forecasts: Autumn 2002'. *European Economy,* No. 5/2002.

Commission of the European Communities (2002b) 'Towards the Enlarged Union: Strategy Paper and Report of the European Commission on the Progress towards Accession by each of the Candidate Countries'. *COM* (2002) 700 and *SEC* (2002) 1400-12.

Commission of the European Communities (2002c) 'Forecasts: Autumn 2002 for Candidate Countries'. *European Economy Enlargement Papers,* No. 12.

Deutsche Bank (2003) *EU Enlargement Monitor: Central and Eastern Europe.* January 2003 (Frankfurt-am-Main: Deutsche Bank).

European Bank for Reconstruction and Development (2002) *Transition Report 2002: Agriculture and Rural Transition* (London: EBRD).

JCMS 2003 Volume 41. Annual Review pp. 207–11

# Chronology: The European Union in 2002

LEE MILES
University of Hull

## At a Glance

Presidencies of the EU Council: Spain (1 January–30 June) and Denmark (1 July–31 December).

Launch of the euro notes and coins and the phasing out of national currencies in the 12 Member States participating in the euro area.

Completion of the membership negotiations with ten candidate countries opening the way for full accessions on 1 May 2004.

The ratification of the 2000 Nice Treaty finished after its approval by Irish voters in a (second) public referendum.

*January*

1 Spain assumes the Presidency of the EU Council until 30 June. Introduction of euro notes and coins.

16 Commission reviews progress in implementing the Lisbon strategy (*COM* (2002) 14).

*February*

13 Commission communication to Council on preparations for meeting of the Euro-Mediterranean Foreign Ministers' Conference, Valencia, 22–23 April (*SEC* (2002) 159 final).

28 The Convention on the Future of Europe holds its inaugural session.

28 EU Council adopts a Comprehensive Action Plan to Combat Illegal Immigration and Trafficking in Human Beings (Council Document 6621/1/02).

28 Formal Establishment of Eurojust following a Council Decision (*OJ* 2002 C 58).

*March*

15–16 European Council summit in Barcelona. Agreements at summit on the liberalization of the energy sector and review of the 'Lisbon process'.

*April*

11 Commission presents a communication in which it updates for the third time the target actions provided for under the internal market strategy defined in 1999 (*COM* (2002) 760).

22–23 Fifth Euro–Mediterranean Foreign Ministers' Conference in Valencia.

25 European Parliament endorses Commission communication of May 2001 on the Union's role in promoting and consolidating democracy and human rights (*Bulletin* 4-2002, point 1.2.5).

*May*

4 European Commission presents Communication on 'Towards an Integrated Management of External Borders' (*COM* (2002) 233).

12 Commission sets out its 'Project for the European Union' in a communication adopted in 22 May outlining three fundamental tasks for the European Union of consolidating its model of economic and social development, building up an area of freedom, security and justice and exercising responsibility as a world power (*COM* (2002) 247).

28 Commission in a communication presents its action programme to reform the common fisheries policy (CFP) (*COM* (2002) 181).

28 Commission presents new eEurope 2005 action plan with the aim of stimulating services, applications and content in the new 'knowledge society'.

*June*

13 Framework introducing the European arrest warrant adopted by Council (*OJ* 2002 L 164 and *OJ* L 2002 L 190).

19 Commission reviews the first three years of the euro in a communication (*COM* (2002) 332).

21–22 European Council summit in Seville. Agreements on the CFSP incorporating the fight against terrorism. Immigration also a central issue with measures to combat illegal immigration and towards co-ordinated, integrated management of external borders.

21 Council formally adopts the 2002 Broad Economic Policy Guidelines for the Member States and the Community.

27 European Parliament and Council adopt the sixth multi-annual European Community framework programme for research, technological development and demonstration activities (with a budget of €16.27 billion).

*July*

1 Denmark assumes the EU Council Presidency, lasting until 31 December 2002.

10 Commission propose a review of the CAP in line with *Agenda 2002* and the general framework laid down by the Berlin European Council in 1999 (*COM* (2002) 394).

17 Commission takes stock of European employment strategy (*COM* (2002) 416).

22 Decision No. 1600/2002/EC of the European Parliament and Council approve sixth environmental action programme (*COM* (2001) 31 final).

23 The Treaty of Paris establishing the European Coal and Steel Community (ECSC) expires as stipulated by the 1997 Amsterdam Treaty.

26 Final ordinary session of the ECSC Consultative Committee adopts a resolution on the legacy of the ECSC (*OJ* C 176, 24.7.2002).

*August*

25 World Summit on Sustainable Development opens in Johannesburg.

28 Ministerial Conference on the Northern Dimension and the Arctic Window held in Greenland.

*September*

3 Commission advocates streamlining of the annual economic and employment policy co-ordination cycles in order to enhance the efficiency of policy co-ordination and improve coherence (*COM* (2002) 487).

12 Deliberating phase of the work of the Convention on the Future of Europe begins.

*October*

9 European Commission presents regular 'progress reports' and a 'strategy paper' for enlargement ('Towards the Enlarged Union') on the 13 candidate countries, concluding that ten states would be ready to join in 2004 (*COM* (2002) 700 final).

19 Ireland holds its second referendum on the Nice Treaty. The Irish voters approve the Treaty with a majority of 63 per cent for (and 37 per cent against).

21 Council adopts the fourth report of the European Union on human rights in the world (*Bulletin* 10- 20002, point 1.2.1).

23 European Parliament passes resolution calling for the Convention on the Future of Europe to adopt the Charter of Fundamental Rights.

24–25 European Council summit in Brussels. Member States agree the EU financial package to be offered to the candidate countries for negotiation.

28 Præsidium presents preliminary draft Constitutional Treaty to the plenary session of the Convention on the Future of Europe (CONV 369/02).

*November*

11 EU–Russia Summit in Brussels.

11 Final agreement between Russia and the EU on a facilitated transit document for travel to and from Kaliningrad.

13 Commission adopts its draft joint employment report for 2002 (*COM* (2002) 621).

19 EU Civilian Crisis Management Capability Conference at ministerial level.

27 Commission presents a communication on strengthening the co-ordination of budgetary policies with a view to improving the implementation of the Stability and Growth Pact and the way in which Member States' budgetary policies are conducted (*COM* (2002) 668).

*December*

4 Ceremonial meeting of the European Court of Justice (ECJ) to mark its 50th anniversary.

5 Commission supplements 'Project for the European Union' with further initiative in a communication entitled 'For the European Union – peace, freedom and solidarity' (*COM* (2002) 728).

11 Commission publishes report on European governance, drawing lessons from public consultation on the White Paper and taking stock of the 16 months of progress since the White Paper was published (*COM* (2002) 705).

12–13 European Council summit in Copenhagen. The Union closes accession negotiations with ten candidate countries, agrees 'road maps' with Bulgaria and Romania, and new concessions to Turkey.

16 Council adopts Regulation (EC) No. 1/2003 on the implementation of articles 81 and 82 of the EC Treaty which marks one of the most fundamental overhauls of the anti-trust rules of EC competition policy.

23 Commission presents fifth report on the functioning of the Community product and capital markets.

# Index

*Note*: Italicized page references indicate information contained in tables.